Day One & Beyond

Practical Matters for New Middle-Level Teachers

Rick Wormeli

Stenhouse Publishers
Portland, Maine

**National Middle
School Association**
Westerville, Ohio

Stenhouse Publishers
477 Congress Street
Portland, ME 04101
www.stenhouse.com

National Middle School Association
4151 Executive Parkway, Suite 300
Westerville, OH 43081
www.nmsa.org

This book includes material that has been adapted from articles and columns first published in the *Crucial Link*. The author and the publisher are grateful to the editor for her permission.

Library of Congress Cataloging-in-Publication Data
Wormeli, Rick.
     Day one and beyond : practical matters for new middle-level teachers / Rick Wormeli.
     p. cm.
     Includes bibliographical references and index.
     ISBN 1-57110-355-4 (alk. paper)
     1. First-year teachers—United States—Handbooks, manuals, etc. 2. Middle school teachers—United States—Handbooks, manuals, etc. I. Title.
LB2844.1.N4 W67 2003
373'.11—dc21   2002042777

Cover photograph of middle school students hiking Old Rag Mountain in Shenandoah National Park, Virginia. Photography taken by the author.

Manufactured in the United States of America on acid-free paper
09 08   9 8 7 6

This book is dedicated to those talented and compassionate individuals who've decided to serve the world by becoming middle school teachers, and to the veteran teachers who take them under their wing, eager to share the excitement.

Contents

v

Acknowledgments

I wish to extend sincere thanks to Philippa Stratton and the editors at Stenhouse Publishers for their thoughtful mentoring in this second adventure in professional writing. In addition, I'm indebted to those readers of my first book, *Meet Me in the Middle*, who took the time to send me their responses to the book and its ideas. Our dialogue has been among the most professional and inspiring experiences I've ever had. I also wish to thank the visionary leaders of Fairfax County Public Schools in northern Virginia who demonstrate courage and integrity every day. They equip teachers for exemplary practice, and they inspire dedication to every child, not just those easiest to teach.

I am also grateful for the wise and generous contributions to *Day One and Beyond* from the following individuals: Joanne Payling, Roxanne (Rock) Rose, Magorie Shepherd, Alexis Ducat, Beth Huddleston, Laurie Wasserman, Eric Stewart and family, Sal Treppedi, Mark Lewis, Caroline Cullen, Chad Cooper, Mendy Gannon, Carolyn Beitzel, Will Karras and family, Deb Bambino, Brenda Dyck, Michael Quackenbush and family, Anne Jolly, Beverly Maddox, Imogene Forte, Nancy Long, Bill Ivey, Marsha Ratzel, KSWteach, M.S., and Nick DeRobertis and family.

As always, my wife, Kelly, and my children, Ryan and Lynn, have continued to share their love, laughter, and insights throughout the writing process. They keep me grounded and soaring. They are amazing people, and I'm lucky to be in their company.

vii

You Mean I Get to Do This Every Day?

I don't expect to be the most fantastic teacher on this earth, although I would love to be. I also don't expect to be the worst, and if I thought I was, I'd quit in a heartbeat. First and foremost, I will make every effort to connect with each of my students. Without a relationship and a trust developed, how can anyone be open to learning, and how can I effectively teach? I will do my best, and hope that my students learn. I will strive to be a lifelong learner so I can improve my teaching abilities, and I hope I can inculcate that love of learning in my students.

—*Joanne Payling, eighth-grade language arts teacher, Pleasanton Middle School*

As many novice skydivers take their first jump, they shout at the top of their lungs:

"YAHOO!!!"
"COWABUNGA!!!"
"REMEMBER THE ALAMO!!!"
"I LOVE YOU, MOM!!!"
"LIVE FREE OR DIE!!!"
"I'M A BIRD, A PLANE. NO, I'M SUPERMAN!!!"
"WHAT'S THIS CORD FOR???"

The jump is the culmination of a whole day of training. Arriving at the jump center (usually a small airport) early in the morning, they spend the day learning how to fall safely, how to steer, communicate, land, and handle emergencies and themselves on the first jump. They listen to every word of their jump masters, worried that they might miss something crucial to a successful jump. They watch the packing of their parachutes with unblinking eyes. "Can I do this outlandish thing?" they ask themselves. "Am I up to it?" Their hearts pound, their minds and bodies gear up for the thrill.

When their feet touch Earth after the jump, they leap in triumph. Their senses flood open—colors are more vivid, sounds more intense, textures more invigorating. The air is rich with possibilities, and no problem is too large. They grin in quiet reverie, sensing that this experience is somehow sacred.

For the new middle school teacher facing his first class of students, the experience is similar. Well, at least most of it. We learn from mentors how to fall safely, how to steer, communicate, land, and handle emergencies and ourselves in our first year. The sacred thing hits us later on in the year.

There is nothing like teaching this age group. It's different from elementary, high school, or university teaching. Next to ages zero to two, young adolescents are in the fastest metamorphosis of their lives—physically, emotionally, intellectually, and socially. This makes for a wondrous and challenging journey, and as a new middle school teacher, you are on the front edge of all the fun. Better take a picture of yourself right now—you'll never be the same again.

Every day will affirm the grand potential of humanity, although some days you'll have to look harder for it. Trust those of us who've come before you: it's there. And as you find it, spread the good word about today's talented young adolescents, who will be tomorrow's wise leaders. You'll encounter individuals who are at their most unlovable stages of development but are full of hope for themselves and the world around them. Some students will ply you with questions about unified field theories, nuance in literature, and mathematical progressions one day, and the next day they'll be wondering which cartoon character can beat up Superman and how to pop a growing zit without anyone noticing. Students who beg for a debate on the merits of various political systems one minute will seriously ponder the effects of igniting a cigarette lighter near their inseam the next time they pass gas. In no other job do we get to laugh as much or so often humble ourselves in the presence of greatness.

Day One and Beyond: Practical Matters for New Middle-Level Teachers is a guide for the first few years of your journey as a middle school teacher. While teaching strategies appear in almost every chapter, its focus is on everything surrounding instruction, not instruction itself. It's the book I wanted to have at my fingertips but never found when I first started in this profession. I had books on differentiated instruction, our subject's content, teaming, cooperative learning, constructivism, educational psychology, and reading in the content areas, but I needed a book that answered those rising primal voices regarding basic classroom survival: How do I set up my grade book? How do I do a seating chart? How do I discipline students who misbehave? How do I get students' attention? What do I do if I have to share a classroom with another teacher? What do I say on Back-to-School Night? How do I grade homework? Can I be my students' trusted friend and a respected authority at the same time? What do I do on the first day of school? What if I don't get along with my colleagues? Is my bladder strong enough?

Day One and Beyond does not contain all the wisdom there is to know about any of these topics or maintain that these are the only topics a new teacher needs to understand. I started out naively thinking I could create a book that included everything a middle school teacher would need to know for the first year. The earliest drafts, however, convinced me that such an undertaking might be possible on a compilation of 1,000 CD-ROMs needing upgrades every few months, but was more than I could tackle and further proof of what an incredibly complex job middle school teaching is, requiring the very best minds to perform it. Amidst the pile of endless practical tips and strategies whittled from multiple revisions stands this collection of salient practices for classroom management and development of the new teacher's professional self. It will get new teachers through their first years with great success. Readers are invited to check out the lengthy list of recommended resources in Appendix B, however, for additional approaches to achieving effective middle school practice.

When I went through the National Board Certification process, I discovered that writing about what happens in the classroom was more meaningful than I thought it would be. It gave me perspective, and it ignited the reflective side of me. I was amazed by the insights and by the quality of my decisions as a result of writing each evening. It was also cathartic, allowing me to vent, dream, and renew. The National Board Certification process gave me the structure and inclination to write. When it was over, I missed the analytical intimacy with classroom practice the writing provided. I had grown more through the process than I could have alone. It became acceptable to take risks, make mistakes, and turn around and do something positive with anything that initially failed. The growth I experienced was addictive, and I wanted to explore more. At the same time, I could see my students' work improving as I made better decisions.

After achieving National Board Certification, I wrote my first article, which became a regular column, for the *Crucial Link*, a professional education magazine in Virginia. Between the NBC process and writing for the magazine, I could now speak about what I do with confidence and coherence. In the column, I explored areas I wanted to learn about and ones about which I had something to say. That was probably my greatest discovery—that I had something to say and that others would find it worth listening to. Prior to all this, my response to writing for publication was, "I'm just a teacher. What could I possibly know that others don't already know? Who would listen to me?" The NBC process changed that, especially when school board members started calling me and asking my advice on decisions. It was a new world. I encourage all first-year teachers to start writing reflectively about what they do in the classroom, even if it's just for your own use and not for publication. Your teaching skills and effectiveness will grow much faster.

For readers at the university level, it is my hope that this book will accomplish four goals:

First, that readers will become ambassadors for good middle school practice and for middle-level teaching as an exciting, meaningful, and intellectually rigorous career. This is the time—ages ten to fourteen—to inculcate humans with the values and skills for handling life in adulthood. We create a very real future by what we do with these students today. Since every day is so fresh, given our students' ceaseless transitioning and completely honest reactions to their environment and others, we must stay awake as classroom leaders, sometimes flowing with the river around the bend to see new vistas and sometimes channeling the river's flow ourselves. I've worked with both high school and primary/elementary schools: neither one shows as much evidence of students on the front line of humanity as is found in a middle school.

Second, I hope this book becomes a launching point for each chapter's topic. By no means is any chapter a comprehensive review of all there is to know on a topic. Rather, it's a balance between what the editor and I thought would make for proper length and compelling reading. Our intent is for readers to want to pursue the topics with other authors and to reflect on these ideas in their own practice.

Third, I encourage everyone to read a chapter while teaching or after teaching for a bit, then write a response using evidence that agrees or disagrees with the book's premises. In writing, you will generate your own teacher's voice, not just a writer's voice. You will find the vocabulary and constructs to communicate clearly about what you do in the classroom—the signs of a professional and the basis of a cogent teaching practice. If reading and reflecting on material from *Day One and Beyond* leads one person to take up pen or keyboard to analyze her practice and thereby improve it, then the book has served its purpose.

Finally, I hope readers who are just starting out in the teaching world will see that teaching middle school is doable. I hope they find *Day One and Beyond* accessible and can see themselves doing the practices described in the book, or practices inspired by the book. Teaching is hard work, but it's not insurmountable, not even close. We can do it, and we can do it well. In a time of a teacher drought with little hope for more teachers on the horizon, I hope *Day One and Beyond* entices new teachers to stick with it.

I encourage all new middle-level teachers to allow yourselves to be 200 percent better at teaching during your second year of service instead of battering yourselves during your first year for every mistake you've made. Teaching middle school is difficult, and doing it well is a challenge. There are CEOs of major corporations, military leaders, professors at prestigious universities, and folks who rival Mother Teresa for patience and virtue who would shudder at the thought of working daily with young adolescents and teaching them all there is to teach. Being an expert in subject content, young adolescent development, people skills, and the myriad instructional strategies necessary for middle-level success is enough to qualify you for membership in MENSA, if not become its president.

Because that first year is a time of such growth, give yourself this latitude: Tell yourself each morning that you will make at least twelve big mistakes during the day. When you make them, feel bad for a moment, then move on—you're still within budget. Mistakes one through twelve are normal for any progressing teacher; the teacher gods allow them. If you keep it to twelve or less each day, then it was a good day. If you have more than twelve, you can go home and wallow in guilt for a few hours, but then restart the count when you wake up the next morning. This may be a childish conceit, but it allows us to face the world with dignity and accept the fact that we are always growing. After twenty years, I still allow ten whopping mistakes per day in my daily regimen.

Four quick survival tips: First, start right now—in preservice or in the first few years—by establishing a folder or box in which to collect all the positive comments you receive from students, administrators, parents, and others. These might be thank-you notes, printed e-mail messages, pictures, positive evaluations, or thoughtful reflections. This treasure chest will be an emotional boost to you on those days when you feel nothing's going right and you doubt your ability to make a difference. Taking twenty minutes to read about these past successes will give you the wind you need to fill your sails and take on the world. Get the container for these positives today.

Second, introduce yourself to the custodial staff and the front office staff and maintain a good friendship with them. They are the magic secret behind many great teachers. They will affect your ability to be the teacher you want to be more than any other people on the staff, including the principal. They make powerful allies, so start off right by connecting with them.

Third, save your lesson plans from student teaching and your first year. Don't reinvent the wheel each year. If you get the chance, record ideas for improving them after you've used them, but file them carefully for use next year. You'll breathe easier.

Fourth, get several boxes of thank-you cards and start using them your first month. A personally written message of gratitude goes a long way to connecting with others and establishing yourself as a considerate and respectful colleague. Your inquiries and appeals for assistance will resonate a little further with the rest of the faculty, and you'll find parents and community members willing to work with you more readily. Besides, it's just a classy thing to do.

Let me add my voice to those expressing gratitude to you for choosing the teaching profession as the way to make your contribution to the world. Those of us who've been in the field for a while are looking to your fresh ideas, energy, and perspectives to inspire our efforts. You will build upon the foundations we've laid, but you'll turn those bulwarks into cathedrals. You will surpass what we've built, which is the way it should be if we're doing things correctly. There is no other profession, outside of parenting and science, with the potential for such a positive impact on humanity. This is especially true in the middle school, where specific events in students' lives will directly impact how they handle life as adults. As President John F. Kennedy said in his 1963 address to the United Nations,

> Never before has man had such capacity to control his own destiny, to end thirst and hunger, to conquer poverty and disease, to banish illiteracy and massive human misery. We have the power to make this the best generation of mankind in the history of the world—or make it the last. (Kennedy 1963)

The same is true of us, today's middle school teachers. We have the power to shape all that is to come. That's an amazing opportunity. Let's take the noble calling and teach well.

Don't pull the cord just yet; ride the exciting air currents instead. Check out the rivers below, and enjoy the first thrills of the ride. COWABUNGA AND WELCOME!

The Unique Nature of Middle School Teaching

When teaching young adolescents, we can't fall back on "Kids will be kids" or "Let them solve it on their own." Our students need us to be with them every step of the way.

—Roxann Rose, Woodring College of Education, Western Washington University

Some of you may have picked up this book by accident. Let's make sure you really are interested in being a middle school teacher. Veteran middle school teacher Marjorie Shepherd from Crozet, Virginia, borrowed a tag line from comedian Jeff Foxworthy to write her version of "You Might Be a Redneck." Here's her version:

You Might Be a Middle School Teacher
If you have no qualms about telling adolescents to pull up their pants, spit out their gum, and get their hair out of their faces, even if these adolescents are not in your normal jurisdiction—in grocery lines, at fast-food restaurants, at family reunions, or at your spouse's boss's house—you might be a middle school teacher.

If you can detect gum chewing at fifty paces, by one movement of the jaw, you are a middle school teacher.

If you have become adept enough at reading between the lines of "Principal Compliments," to know, for example, that: "You're so

Flexible" means "I want you to teach yet another class outside of your endorsement area"; "You've got great ideas" means "I want you to join another committee"; "You're so creative" means "I've scheduled you for yearbook in the fall"; and "You're so patient" means "Wait 'til you see this new kid I just placed in your fourth-period class"; then you might be a practiced middle school teacher.

If your peripheral vision range is now up to 240 degrees, you just might be a middle school teacher.

If you can stroll down an aisle of adolescents checking homework, and snarf a note from one, a skateboard catalog from another, and a Gameboy from a third without so much as disturbing the modulation of your voice as you explain the causes of the Civil War or the formula for the calculation of the volume of a cone, you might be a middle school teacher.

If you have successfully eliminated from your vocabulary all words and phrases which could be construed as having anything to do with pubescent body parts or things those parts could do with each other—such as nut, ball, melon, jug, crack, hard, soft, limp, rubber, bone, French, stick, stroke, whack, poke, bang, feel, lick, insert, suck, or blow—then you most definitely are a middle school teacher.

And if, although people tell you, repeatedly, that you must be a saint, or that you must have such patience when they hear what you do for a living, and you are fully aware that you are where you are because really, you never actually left young adolescence in the first place, then you are definitely a middle school teacher.

The Transitional Nature of Adolescence

Still here? Okay, then you must really want to be a middle school teacher. Let's take a look at what makes teaching middle school truly unique.

Philosopher and physician Deepak Chopra reminds us that the cells of our human skin completely recycle every month, the liver every six weeks, and the brain changes carbon, nitrogen, and oxygen every twelve months. Since our tissues are literally being replaced constantly with new tissues, we are all more like a river moving through life than like something frozen in time and space. Chopra adds that even though our physical selves "flow" in this manner, the essence of who we are stays the same. For example, even though the molecular components of the brain change, our memories stay with us, somehow being transferred to the new molecules coming online to replace the departing molecules.

The transitional nature of young adolescents is a perfect manifestation of this idea of humans as rivers. They are constantly flowing and changing. Students are in a state of flux, beyond elementary school practices, not quite ready for high school practices. They are unique in their transitional nature. What works one week won't work the next, but it will work again a month from now—the river carves its way through the land. What works for one teacher doesn't work for another. What students learn one week may be distorted by the next week, given new experiences—they are that malleable. Membership in formal and informal groupings at this age is dynamic, not static, and it can be based on interests, readiness, and/or personality. As their teachers, we can choose to ride the river with our students—enjoying the rapids as much as the still waters that run deep— or we can create a log jam and get nothing but swirling eddies that take us nowhere. The best middle school teachers are well provisioned and optimistic, for they know that the river always leads somewhere.

Young adolescents' brains are at a critical point of development. Research in the last few years has found that the brain continues to grow at a phenomenally fast rate through age fifteen. We used to think that brains were hardwired by age twelve and there wasn't much we could do to change that wiring. Now we understand how malleable our students' brains truly are. They are at their last point of successful intervention (if things aren't wired in a healthy way), and they are at their most receptive point for intellectual and moral reasoning. In humans, the prefrontal cortex is the last to develop. It often doesn't achieve maturity until age eighteen or beyond. The prefrontal cortex is responsible for moral and abstract reasoning, planning, understanding consequences, and being aware of the effects of one's words and actions on others. Some teachers would use this knowledge as an excuse to stop trying to teach these things—after all, they reason, if their brains are simply not developed enough to learn these things, why spend so much time banging our heads against the wall trying to teach them?

This reasoning is faulty. The brain is similar to a large sponge or amoeba. It's constantly absorbing information and responding to experiences and environments, stimulating dendrite development in some areas, retarding growth in others. It requires an interaction-rich learning environment for every area it develops. If an area is not stimulated regularly, the brain prunes the "dead wood," increasing efficiency in other areas. If a student spends hours playing video games, for instance, the skills associated with playing such games develop and become permanent, while other areas are deemed less important and allowed to wither. The brain is adapting itself for survival. Personally, I'd like the hardwiring focus to be on the dendrites responsible for writing, reading, art, music, physical sports, reasoning, caring, and mathematics. We can let the video-game dendrites fade to oblivion.

With this in mind, we middle school teachers need to provide even more experiences involving moral and abstract reasoning, planning, awareness of consequences, and the effects of one's word and actions on others, not fewer. We can be tenacious and provide these experiences as professional middle-level educators, instead of succumbing to cynicism with declarations like "What kind of a future are we going to have with kids like we have today? What a mess!" We don't have to take our students' transgressions from proper standards of conduct personally. It's in their nature to do these things. We can be the mature adult in the room, the one with understanding and a big-picture perspective, and we can respond with courage and grace, staying with our students every step of the way.

In order to be developmentally responsive to today's young adolescents, a number of groups have done research to see which practices work best. The research and practices were compiled in a landmark report, *Turning Points 2000* (Davis and Jackson 2000). I highly recommend the publication. One of the most significant factors the report cites is the implementation of the middle school concept instead of the junior high school concept.

Junior high schools are just that—junior versions of high school. High school departmentalization and protocols go against what we know to be sound instructional practice with students ages ten to fourteen. More specifically, junior high schools have less-positive teacher-student relationships, less-useful assessments, and fewer opportunities for student decision making, choice, and self-management. They have more competitive and controlled environments and more whole-class practices that don't meet individual needs. Most junior highs make social and ability comparisons that do nothing to advance the student. In short, they are developmentally inappropriate.

In the brief stage of young adolescence, our students undergo rapid physical growth, changes in moral reasoning, and the onset of abstract thinking, and are introduced to a range of social pressures, including sex, drugs, and violence. Simultaneously, they're creating a personal identity, acquiring social skills, gaining autonomy, developing character, and setting values. Young adolescents crave

1. positive social interaction with adults and peers;
2. structure and clear limits;
3. physical activity;
4. creative expression;
5. competence and achievement;

6. meaningful participation in families, school, and communities;
7. opportunities for self-definition.

Notice I used the word *crave*. It's not just lucky or nice if they experience these things; they're vital. When we crave something, little else will satisfy us, and if we don't get it, we don't function well. If we don't meet these needs in our classrooms, we often find students alienated from school, lacking self-esteem and belonging, and choosing destructive methods of coping with life's struggles, including delinquency and drugs. Students might sit politely if these components of instruction aren't being provided, but nothing is moving to their long-term memory, which is the goal of learning, and eventually, there will be behavior problems.

Is there any one of these seven cravings that we can't satisfy in our subject area? Of course not. Can we have structures and clear limits in a free-flowing art activity? Yes. If we don't, the lesson will bomb. Can we have physical activity in our grammar lesson? You bet. Can we have creative expression and opportunities for self-definition in our unit on coefficients and polynomials? Yes. Just because we can't think of how to do this doesn't mean it can't be done. When we're stuck for ideas, that's when we turn to colleagues, print or multimedia sources, or even to our students to get ideas. We should never limit our instructional practice and our students' learning to our own creativity.

Of the seven cravings, it is a sense of competence and achievement that students most need in order to learn the content and skills we teach. They might not say, "Mr. Smith, I'm craving competence and not currently experiencing any. Can you provide some?" In truth, they need to experience competence with the material we're teaching every single day or we'll lose them.

Components of a Successful Middle School

To deal with all of these student needs, the middle school approach has developed seven important components that distinguish middle schools from junior high schools:

Advisory programs Advisory programs consist of small groups of students (fewer than twenty) assigned to a teacher, administrator, or other staff member for a regularly scheduled meeting to discuss topics of concern to students. The purpose of these programs is to develop close, trusting relationships between students and adults. Through advisory, students feel they belong and have an advocate in that adult. One of the greatest reasons young adolescents don't drop out of school, become depressed, or become involved with gangs and violent behavior is that they develop a trusting relationship with at least one adult in the school. Meetings could be set up on a daily or biweekly basis or, as an alternative, consider four to six full-day Advisory Days during the year along with quarterly interviews.

Interdisciplinary teaming A second component of successful middle schools involves a core team of two to five teachers from multiple disciplines assigned to the same group of students. Because these teachers share the same students and have a common planning period, they are able to respond more quickly to the needs of individual students through collaboration, meeting jointly with parents, and designing thematic units that transfer ideas across disciplines to increase their relevance.

Varied and developmentally appropriate instruction Varied and appropriate instruction includes rigorous curriculum with an updated core of knowledge; integrated experiences that address students' own questions and focus on real-life issues relevant to students; active engagement in problem solving; differentiating instruction; collaboration; caring for others; democratic values and moral sensitivity; student-centered classrooms; constructivism; hands-on activities even in subjects that are primarily abstract; and the use of block-length classes, flexible scheduling, and cross-age tutoring. Teachers assess learning authentically, frequently, and in such a manner as to diagnose and teach, not just to evaluate or to document deficiencies. The increased desire for autonomy and resolving identity issues can be addressed through learning strategies involving choice, a curriculum based on social and individual interests, exploratory programs, and the prevalence of a safe environment for experimentation. Noncompetitive intramurals, flexible classroom structures, and hands-on activities incorporate the need for physical activity and movement. Service projects and project-based learning strategies capitalize on young adolescents' creative expression and need for meaningful participation and experimentation with identity within a community, including the need for ethnic expressions of identity.

Exploratory programs Exploratory programs capitalize on the innate curiosity of young adolescents, exposing them to a wide range of academic, vocational, and recreational subjects for career options, community service, and enrichment. Middle school students need freedom and support to make choices. They are at a stage of learning where exploration has its greatest impact. The chances of discovering lifelong talents, interests, and goals are heavily influenced in this transitional time of their lives. Exploratory topics can include foreign languages, intramural sports, health, clubs, student government, home economics, technological arts, independent study projects, music, art, speech, drama, careers, consumer education, creative writing, and several other special areas.

Shared vision among faculty Members of exemplary middle school faculties are committed to young adolescents, not just their subject area. In fact, they see themselves as teachers of young adolescents first, their subject areas second. These teachers also go out of their way to maintain family and community partnerships, which can often fall off after elementary school. These teachers have very high expectations for all students, not just those who show promise early on. The faculty is well trained in how to teach young adolescents. Their schools have clear, positive, well-understood missions, as this example from Rachel Carson Middle School in Herndon, Virginia, shows:

> Within a safe and nurturing community, the students, staff, and parents of Rachel Carson Middle School seek to foster personal and academic excellence, treat one another with dignity, respect our environment, embrace diversity, and develop character which merits trust and honor. We encourage positive risk taking and perseverance in pursuit of our goals.

Healthy transition experiences From elementary levels to middle school, and from middle school to high school, transition experiences begin in the middle of the year prior to transition and continue for a year following transition. They include more than one experience, and they address all aspects of student life in the new grade levels: social, physical, emotional, and intellectual. These experiences are conducted by educators trained in the nature of young adolescence and familiar with young adolescents themselves. An element of this transition effort is the clear and frequent communication between teachers and staff of elementary, middle, and high schools.

Healthy parental involvement The school reaches out to parents with information and an invitation to develop and maintain the parent-teacher team, and thereby assist parents in the challenge of raising healthy young adolescents. This might include parents working in classrooms, individual parent conferences with teams, parents serving on committees, parent seminars on timely topics once a quarter, parent newsletters, parent volunteer programs, and coaching parents on how to help their children study at home. It also means providing easily accessed channels by which parent concerns are communicated and given serious consideration by teachers and staff. Teachers and administration see parents as critical elements to instructional success of students.

The Role of the Teacher in the Classroom

The first thing I learned is that we're in the classroom for the students; the students are not there for us. Whatever we ask students to do during the course of the day should make it easier for them to learn, regardless of the impact on us. We are there to do whatever it takes for students to be successful, and sometimes that means being flexible and swallowing our own preferences. For example, do they absolutely have to do assignments on wide-ruled paper? What about the kid who prefers college-ruled paper because it helps him keep his written words and ideas from sprawling? Some students require multiple folders, one for each class, and some prefer one massive notebook with sections for each class. Let's help students see the pros and cons of each approach and then help them decide which one works best for them. Our goal is not student compliance; it's masterful learning in whatever way works best. Sure, we can force them to try new skills and concepts, but we can also be flexible if the goal of learning is achieved.

Good middle school teachers remain virtuous. We never forget we are modeling citizenship every single moment of every single day. We decide what kind of world we want twenty years from now and we model it under the close scrutiny of tomorrow's impressionable leaders. Students remember every word we say. What we say and do better be worth remembering.

A big part of the unique nature of teaching middle school is the humanity we teach every day, and that humanity includes healthy doses of humor. I have yet to see a successful middle school classroom that was devoid of humor. Laughing at ourselves and at life are survival skills all students at this age develop and use. Allowing humor in the classroom, even pursuing it on occasion, is just as vital to teacher and student success as are those carefully designed lesson projects and assessments. Go out of your way to explore humor's possibilities and be open to its occurrence.

Finally, middle school teaching is unique in its demand for unconventional thinking. We have to be willing to break the rules, to transcend convention, in order to teach young adolescents. We can teach paragraph writing by asking students to pull apart well-done paragraphs and to create the outlines or webs from which they came. Students learn the power of verbs in a sentence by trying to converse without them for more than a few minutes. Young adolescents learn about the effects of metabolism and exercise by making a video about those connections for third graders. They can see themselves as scientists when they correspond directly with scientific researchers in the field. They understand the power of mathematics when building bridges that must support particular weights and studying fractal designs in science and art classes. We can open their eyes to the power of words by asking them to describe something in five or more sentences without using adjectives. Civic issues are made vivid in mock trials, Socratic Seminars, debates, and simulations. Students find new motivation for writing in math, science, and history when those writings are put on display in local medical offices, a Pizza Hut, and the town hall. There is much to learn about the effects of line, space, and shading in artwork by studying the shafts of sunlight coming through the windows in the gymnasium, or about algebra while standing in a parking lot filled with cars. We can ask questions to which we don't know the answer, and when students ask us why they have to learn something in the curriculum, we can admit that we don't know if we don't know, and ask them to find out for us. Taking advice from George Bernard Shaw, we can see things as they are and ask, "Why?" and we can dream things as they never were and ask, "Why not?"

Don't forget some of the physical basics for yourself. Remember to wash your hands several times a day. Young adolescents as a group tend to get sick more often than other age groups—they're under stress and their immune systems are suppressed. First-year teachers get almost every flu or cold that runs through the student population if they don't keep up with their own personal hygiene, and washing hands is one of the smartest and easiest things we can do. If you have a sink in or near your room, it's not too much to wash after every class.

Get sleep, even if it means putting off other things. Sleep is restorative, and it keeps your brain and immune systems operating at peak. Our whole attitude toward students, curriculum, and teaching can change, depending on the previous night's amount of sleep.

Eat sensibly. You'll be expending an incredible amount of energy each day. Go ahead and eat four small meals a day instead of three, if that works for you. Snack often on fruits, vegetables, and a few healthful carbohydrates. Avoid junk food, if possible. Drink more water than you think you need, even when you're not thirsty. Institutions of learning are known for creating cotton mouth in teachers and for poor air circulation. You'll avoid headaches and fatigue if you've refueled yourself with healthful foods. You'll have the energy to teach well.

Learn cardio-pulmonary resuscitation (CPR) for children, infants, and adults. This isn't just for working with young adolescents; it's smart for teachers of all levels.

Stay sharp verbally. Read and talk with colleagues and individuals in and outside of education as much as you can. In his book, *Qualities of*

Effective Teachers, James H. Stronge cites considerable evidence that correlates a teacher's verbal ability to his students' achievement: "Effective teachers with higher verbal abilities can better convey ideas to students and communicate with them in a clear and compelling manner" (2002, 4). So learn new vocabulary for its own sake; read those novels, education books, and journals; and participate in discussions, both professional and social, if you want to develop the skills to talk and write with young adolescents. If you want to keep up with the latest in educational jargon and what it all means, I highly recommend the Association for Supervision and Curriculum Development's (ASCD) online resource, "A Lexicon of Learning: What Educators Mean When They Say . . ." It's comprehensive and well maintained. The URL is http://www.ascd.org/educationnews/ lexicon/lexiconoflearning.html.

Over the next ten months, write your own version of what makes middle school teaching interesting. Some of what you write may be similar to what is here, but if your young adolescent students are anything like mine, you're bound to learn more about teaching from them than from a book. What you experience with your students will be as dynamic as weather patterns on distant planets. That's the engaging part for us, though: how do we teach specific and plentiful content to young adolescents, given all their variables and needs? It's a challenge worthy of Sherlock Holmes, made meaningful by your students' faces, lit with understanding. Yes, the river leads somewhere, and you're a part of it.

What to Do on the First Day and in the First Week

On the first day? Make sure every student feels like he or she belongs.

—*Roxann Rose*

In the first class on the first day I ever taught, I learned one of the biggest lessons of my middle school teaching career: the students are out for the teacher's success just as much their own. On that Tuesday after Labor Day, I called roll.

"Brown, William?"

"Here."

"Cavelletti, Antonio?"

"That's, 'Tony.' And, here."

I crossed out "Antonio" in the attendance book and wrote "Tony."

"Thank you, Tony. I made the correction."

Then I came to the third name. The last name was D-U-C-H. The first name seemed Cambodian or Vietnamese, so I didn't think that the name was pronounced "Dutch."

"Okay, this next person's last name is pronounced 'Duck,' I believe," I started with the class, then paused. I stared at the first name. No, it couldn't be. I looked again. The first name was spelled "P-H-U-C." If I said that phonetically, I would be calling the name of "Fuck Duck" (phonetically) in the middle of a group of thirty young adolescents. I naively plowed ahead.

"Phuh [using the short 'u' sound] . . . Phuh . . . Phuh," I started again. The room was getting warmer. My cheeks burned. Great, I'm making a fool of myself on the very first day, I thought. I can't do this.

Suddenly, the class called in unison, "It's 'Foo,' Mr. Wormeli, 'Foo.' The 'c' is silent."

I exhaled in relief, smiling sheepishly. "Thank you," I mouthed. The students grinned back at me. "Foo Duck?" I called phonetically (pleadingly, too).

"Here," Phuc said, and we continued with the roll call. We were going to be okay.

The biggest fears I had before that first day of school were how to plan out the year, whether or not the students would like and respect me, whether or not I knew enough about my subjects to teach them, and most important, what I was going to do with that first day and week of school. Once I was up and running, I thought I could handle it. "Just get me started," I pleaded with the teacher gods.

It turns out I was barely ahead of the students in terms of learning the material that first year, and the planning for the rest of the year went well thanks to the patience of my colleagues, who tolerated twenty questions a day from me for that first quarter. My students seemed to respect me and, I hoped, enjoy my company, but I found out later that respecting me and enjoying my company weren't the main goals of good teachers. It was the list I maintained of what I would do differently next year that kept me sane and hopeful that I'd make it as a teacher in the middle school world. The following year, I made those changes, especially in how we began the year, and it has made a tremendous difference every year since.

Mixing Academics with Get-to-Know-You

A sad thing happens to novels when readers have to stop after every chapter and write a summary or analyze literary devices: the story is killed; it's no longer engaging. One of the worst things you can say to a language arts or English teacher is that a child learned to hate the subject as a result of his class. It's the same with teachers of other courses.

As teachers, we are "selling" our subjects to our students as worthy of their pursuit. We are convincing them that they can be competent regarding our subjects and even find meaning in them. At the same time, students enter classrooms in September with the inclination to do well, to think in a scholarly manner, and to produce great thoughts and works. Really, they do. They are a grade higher, they reason, more advanced. Things will be challenging, and this is a fresh start. As their teachers, we need to ride this momentum wave as far as we can. The expectancy and ability are there; all we have to do is get out of the way.

With each period of nothing but endless forms, get-to-know-you activities, and reviewing classroom protocols, we kill that excitement. Students grow increasingly disillusioned. We miss a golden opportunity for them to dive into the subject material with neurons firing on all thrusters. It's probably the most significant time of the year to hardwire students' minds to embrace our subjects; we don't want to lose it. Yet we still have to get to know the students, ask them to fill out those school forms, and teach them classroom protocols, such as where to turn in papers and where to go during a fire drill. So how do we do all of this and keep the fires burning for our subjects at the same time?

Through balance. Each day, make sure students learn something brand-new in your subject area, not just something they are reviewing from last year. Add to this one or two new forms to complete, one get-to-know-you activity, or one or two new classroom protocols and you'll have a pretty good period. Give academic homework on the first day of school. It sets a tone of serious study and responsibility. They may never admit it publicly (though many have privately), but after two months off from anything cerebral, students welcome the mental engagement. They're doing something purposeful. Teach from the very first day.

To figure out what to offer them academically and administratively in that first week and month, go back to your planning for the year. Give yourself three to four weeks to teach all the classroom procedures, do the get-to-know-you activities, and fill out the forms. Don't cram it into the first week or two. You'll never have time to grab the students with your subject. Just make sure you complete the forms that let students get their lockers first!

Each day for the first two weeks, I do about 50 percent academics and 50 percent administrivia. This works pretty well. By the way, don't forget your teammates if you're on a team. One person doesn't have to do all the forms. Spread out the responsibilities for completing forms across all subjects on the team so one subject isn't always associated with paperwork. It's wise, however, to have one teacher who collects all the forms from students. At a meeting later, all teachers on the team can help process them.

Getting to Know Students as Individuals and as Learners

If we want to be successful, we have to know our students as individuals and as learners. Often these overlap, but they are not the same dimension. Choose a balance of activities that elicits both types of information. Let's take a look at three effective get-to-know-you activities appropriate for any subject:

"The Best Way for You to Learn" Cards

When students enter my room on the first day of school, they find an index card on their desks. Students are asked to describe on the cards how they best learn. The prompt can be something like, "What will it take for you to learn well in this subject?" or "In what ways do you best learn?" or "Give me advice on how to be the best teacher you've ever had in this subject." It's amazing how insightful students are each year. I get comments like, "Give me a lot of examples. I don't get ideas without examples"; "If you write it on the board, can I get a copy?"; "I need to see it, don't just tell me it"; and "Speak slowly, I get confused with a lot of noise and speed." Many young adolescents are beginning to know and advocate for themselves as learners. What they offer in these cards is invaluable. To get the full picture, I send parents a card and similar prompt to complete on that first night, referring to their child's learning. Between the two cards, I have enough information to make some early decisions about lesson design, grouping, and interacting with students. I reference them all year, and I sometimes ask students to complete them again in February to see if things have changed over the course of the first few months.

Interest Surveys

Interest surveys are one- to two-page polls that ask a variety of questions and give students an opportunity to express sides to them that don't otherwise get revealed. The prompts or questions must not be invasive, of course, and students always have a right to pass if they don't feel comfortable. Information that might be requested includes

a favorite book from childhood
the farthest point you've traveled away from home
a recent movie you enjoyed and what you liked about it
your favorite place to be and why
your favorite food
your favorite kind of music
your favorite sport
organizations/teams/clubs to which you belong
someone you admire and why
two common activities you do after getting home from school
a responsibility you have

a wish you have for someone else
what you want to do for a career
something about which you daydream
something about which you are curious
the title of a book about your life
some advice you would give yourself if you could go back two years ago
a description of yourself as a friend
a description of your best friend

Learner Profiles

Learner profiles include any information about a student that affects his learning: six schools in as many years; divorce; ADHD; Fetal Alcohol Syndrome; learning disabilities. They also refer to those surveys/assessments/instruments that students complete in which they demonstrate their proclivities/strengths/preferences for how they best learn. There are many instruments available to middle school teachers, some costing money and some not. Ask around, as there are probably some in your building already. Many publications about multiple intelligences and learning styles have instruments free for your use. If you're using an Internet search engine, I highly recommend the Dunn and Dunn Learning Style Inventory, Anthony Gregorc Scales, and Myers-Briggs Personality Type indicators. There are also many good Web sites and publications with multiple intelligence surveys. Students can often do the assessment as well as its analysis with direction from you, so don't worry about analyzing the results of 150 student assessments. You just have to read the results and incorporate the information into your planning. No small job, I know.

Other Ideas for the First Day and the First Week

Problem-Solving Tasks

Some of you may be familiar with ropes initiatives courses. These are Project Adventure and similar courses in which students have to climb a twelve-foot wall, make it through eight swinging tires, pass each other through openings in a pretend spider's web, and cross an "electric" fence. Bringing some of those ideas into the classroom or onto school grounds to see how students solve problems individually and as a group sheds light on who they are as students. For example, in the human knot activity, six to eight students stand in a circle shoulder-to-shoulder, facing the middle of the circle. They extend their hands into the center space, taking someone else's hand as long as it's not the hand of the person on either side of them or both hands of the same person. They then unravel themselves without letting go of their grasps of one another's hands. To do it, there's a lot of stepping over and under, squeezing inside and outside, and most important, a lot of talk—students directing and listening to one another. It's easy to see how students deal with physical contact, problem solving, leading, following, thinking critically, and speaking so that their ideas will be heard. In the debriefing that follows, we focus on what helped and what hindered the group, the roles that everyone played, and what we learned about ourselves.

We can mix some of these activities with content as well. For example, when we ask students to line up in ascending order according to birthdays, they do it easily, even when we ask them to do it without talking. Add another twist—blindfolds on everyone as well as the silence—and it becomes more challenging. We can use this activity for content study as well. How about lining up in ascending order in terms of numerical value? Students are placed in groups of twelve, holding cards of various value and forms—percents, decimals, and fractions—then asked to line up from smallest to greatest. How about lining up in order of steps in the ecological succession of a deciduous forest? How about in a pattern of category, example, category, example, such as, "noun, giraffe, verb, is, demonstrative pronoun, this, personal pronoun, you"? Or in order of conjugation of an irregular verb in Spanish? How about in order of taxonomy?

Kingdom	*Animalia*
Phylum	*Chordata*
Class	*Mammalia*
Order	*Primates*
Family	*Hominidae*
Genus	*Homo*
Species	*Sapiens*

Now do it silently . . . now do it blindfolded. Just because we teachers can't imagine how it can be done doesn't mean the kids won't do it beautifully. They will outdo us, which is exactly the way it's supposed to be if things are going well.

In the course of these experiences, we see sides to our students that the regular classroom interaction prevents us from seeing. They're worth doing.

In-Class Field Trip

Take students on a tour of the classroom. If there's enough space, get them out of their seats and have them follow you around as you point out different features of the room—the portfolio area, computer stations, the in-class library (a must for all subjects, not just English class), sink areas, supply areas, walls for student work, the homework assignment posting area (use an old Boogie Board from the beach; it will hold tacks well without leaving little holes behind after removing postings), paper-turn-in areas, plants and animals, photos of your family, instructional bulletin boards, sign-in sheets for tardy students, extra handouts trays, and anything else that is unique to your class.

Textbook Scavenger Hunt

If the textbook for your course is going to be referenced often, take students on a scavenger hunt through the book in the first week of school. This familiarizes them with how the book is set up. That familiarity increases the likelihood that students will use the textbook as the frequent resource it was meant to be, and it makes students more autonomous.

To prepare a scavenger hunt on the textbook, review the textbook yourself and identify how it's structured and which areas you'll want students to reference throughout the year. Don't worry that you don't know which areas these are right now. Take your best guess for what you know for sure, and ask colleagues for their opinion. Depending on your subject, these textbook elements might include

units	glossaries
chapters	indices
subtopics	tables of contents
sidebars	"words to know" sections
"questions to ponder" sections	scope and sequence of the textbook
chapter summaries	major themes of the textbook
time lines	enrichment sections
background of the author/editor	where major topics are located
copyright date	autobiographies of experts in
explanation versus application pages	your subject area

Once you're familiar with the textbook, create prompts for these elements that require students to search for them. For example:

- What are the five basic themes of our textbook? (hint: they are color-coded in the table of contents)
- Though they are written out of order here, you'll find the following components in all chapters: Applications, Chapter Review, Samples,

Extensions, Practice, Introduction, Words to Know, Background, How Does It Fit with What We Know? Place them in proper order according to how our textbook sequences them in each chapter.

- Who invented the periodic table of elements?
- Does pressure go up or down as air speed increases?
- In what section would we find information about where to place a comma in a divided quote?
- In what section would we find the definition of *coefficient*?
- Has this book been updated in the last ten years?
- In what section of each chapter would we find creative ideas for projects about the chapter's topic?
- If we wanted to test our knowledge about a chapter's topic, in what section would we find a test to do that?

Don't make the textbook survey more than one or two pages. I recommend that you ask students to work individually on this so they get the knowledge firsthand. If you decide to ask students to work in pairs or table groups, make it necessary for everyone in the group to agree on the answers, forcing them to check up on one another.

Tour the School

In the first few days, make sure you or a teammate takes students new to the school on a tour of the building. This not only relieves anxiety but creates autonomy and opens students' minds to other possibilities. For example, students who've never considered the art elective (or "encore" class as some schools call electives), walk by the kiln and see ceramic sculptures firing. They file that vividly in their memories for next year's electives. Students struggling with a project later in the year might remember the tour they took with you through the multimedia lab and ask to work there after school. "Those drama students look like they are having fun," a student remarks while on the tour, and the seed is planted for a new interest. Another benefit of a school tour: you will have a whole class of knowledgeable messengers to run errands to other parts of the building for you.

Walk the Fire Drill Route

In every period, walk the students out of the classroom according to the fire drill route posted in the room or your teacher's manual. Do this after sitting for a while and it will be well received—it'll also get oxygen to the brain. Make sure to review proper conduct for fire drills such as no talking

or running, moving quickly, facing away from the building, and responding clearly when roll is called outside the building.

What to Do When the Teacher's Not Available

Oscar Wilde reminded us that the goal of every teacher is to put himself
out of a job. He's right; we want students to learn all we have to teach them
and move on to bigger and better things. We do that with our curriculum,
and we do that with classroom management.

Spend ample time in the first week or month teaching students what to
do if they have a problem with something and the teacher is working with
someone else and not available for assistance. As you teach these options,
post them at the front of the room as an easy reference for everyone. Cover
all the bases. What students should do if

- Their pencil breaks.
- Someone is bothering them.
- They need more paper or other supplies.
- They can't find the directions.
- They need to use the bathroom.
- They are tardy to class.
- They can't find the page in the book.
- They need someone to look over their work.
- They finish early.
- They don't finish in time.
- They need their portfolio.
- They have a problem with the computer.
- They don't feel good.
- They don't understand the problem.
- A visitor comes to the classroom door.
- They become upset about something.
- They want to get a drink.
- An animal gets out of its cage.
- It starts snowing outside (and "Will we get out early?" becomes the
  all-consuming topic of the day).
- Other situations that students brainstorm.

Remember, you don't have to have answers for all of these scenarios.
Put them out there for students to consider. They'll come up with great
responses. Be prepared to help them sift through the not-so-helpful ones,
however.

Introduce Yourself

I usually wait until the second or third week to introduce myself so that students are clearly the focus of the class, but it's important that we do this early in the year rather than remain mysterious to them. Young adolescents need role models who are moral, competent, and engaged citizens with personal interests. Find ways to tell students about your family, hobbies, interests, career plans, and hopes. Give them a three-dimensional picture of who you are as a person. Love the Washington Redskins? Let them see the strength of your devotion to the team. Work on Saturdays at the homeless shelter? Coach baseball or swimming? Going camping this fall? Love Milky Way bars, dolphins, or the state university? Let them see these sides of you. I can't emphasize this enough—students succeed with adults who are not coy or secretive about who they are. Young adolescents respond well to adults with whom they feel some connection, and whom they find vivid.

This doesn't mean you need to talk about yourself every day or spend a whole period presenting your family album. It means putting up family pictures on your desk or a nearby wall, mentioning items of personal interest in the news, telling a few appropriate stories from your past if they fit with the lesson, displaying Gary Larson posters if you're into his humor, joking about a weakness for chocolate chip cookies when students want a good grade on a project, and posting your graduation certificates (after all, this is your professional office, so post those certificates just as we'd see in a doctor's or lawyer's office). Students will take these aspects of you to heart. They'll be a way to connect with you throughout the year. Better yet, you've given them a personalized vision of how to grow and become a successful adult. They'll see their lives as a journey, not an instant arrival and you as someone in a position of respect who has a well-rounded life with varied interests. They need a clear image in order to achieve it. For some, you are the only image they have of what's it's like to be a healthy, involved adult. That vision will transcend everything else you teach.

Heading Their Papers, Setting Up the Notebook

In the first few days, explain to students how to head their papers with name, date, subject, and page number on the top, right side, left side, or center of the paper. Whatever you choose, try to be consistent across the team or school. It's frustrating when teachers force students to jump through seven different and arbitrary hoops, heading their papers a different way for every teacher they have. Get rid of this stress by using the same format as your teammates.

Students also need direction on how to set up their notebooks, but don't proscribe too much; students need some individuation. Give them the section titles for their notebook tabs, for example, but let them choose the sequence in which they're placed, if possible.

Daily Poem(s)

No matter what you teach, try to share a new poem daily. Poetry is not for the elite only; it is for every person. It gives dimension to learning and living, and it's something on which our minds can snack all day. A poem that is initially opaque to us can snap our heads back with stunning clarity, given an experience later in the day. It doesn't matter if we are poetry-phobic or can't think of one poem that we understand, let alone share. Remember that you are not alone on your faculty. Seek assistance from an English, language arts, or reading specialist in your building, or from your school's media specialist (a.k.a. librarian). A daily poem sets a thoughtful tone for the room in math, history, science, music, technology, Spanish, French, Latin, art, and drama classes, not just English classes. If you make a habit of it, you'll have that tone, and you'll find students looking forward to it, even to the point of bringing in poems for you to share. Some of these will be original poems by those students, some written by others, but all about something important to students. An added dividend: some students may start writing poetry about your subject's content as a way to learn it.

Explain the Schedule

Just like many of us adults, young adolescents want to see the big picture, and they require constant reminders of the details to achieve it. Go out of your way during the first few days to explain the general class schedule—opening activities, objectives explained, learning experiences, summarization—as well as the daily schedule—times for class periods and passing times between classes. If you have a block schedule, go over its unique meeting times in every period, especially if it's a flexible, rotating block. It's not reasonable to expect young adolescents to have heard the schedule first period and remember it the entire day, especially during the first week of school.

Teach Study Skills

Begin teaching students how to take notes, use graphic organizers, and review new knowledge in the very first week. Again, it sets a tone for serious study, but it also gives them the tools they need to learn for themselves.

Remember that middle school is the first experience young adolescents have with reading for information, managing complex information, and expressing that information in a scholarly manner. Our students don't come into middle schools knowing how to study material successfully. We have to teach this over the two to three years we have with them. Create success a month from now by teaching study skills today.

Great study skills to teach early in the year and then reinforce each week of the year include at least five different ways to take notes, how to determine what is important in a reading passage and how to summarize it, how to learn new vocabulary, how to prepare for a test, how to manage your study time effectively, and how to know when you don't know (how to monitor your comprehension of something). Several books listed in Appendix B provide excellent strategies to teach these skills. Among them are *Words, Words, Words* (Allen 1999), *Learning to Learn* (Frender 1990), *Write Source 2000* (Great Source Reading Group 2000), and *I Read It, but I Don't Get It* (Tovani 2001).

Remember, you can teach content and study skills at the same time. For instance, if you are teaching two-column note taking, you can do it with the material you want students to master, such as President Wilson's Fourteen-Points speech.

Major Ideas	**Details**
Reasons President Wilson	1.
Designed the Plan for Peace	2.
	3.
Three Immediate Effects	1.
on U.S. Allies	2.
	3.
Three Structures/Protocols	1.
Created by the Plans	2.
	3.

Reveal Pet Peeves

Don't ask me why, but it really drives me nuts when my students spell *a lot* as one word, *alot*. I go out of my way to teach them the proper way to use these words, but some students continue to make the mistake. It's a small thing, but it gets under my skin: it's a pet peeve. I felt the same way in math about not lining up columns when students did long division, or bringing down the variable on the left side of equations when solving for the variable in algebra problems.

Letting students know your pet peeves right away does two things: First, it serves notice in a due-process manner about items for which they will be held accountable, formally or informally, in our classes. Second, it makes students aware of negative behaviors and helps them learn the proper ways to do things.

You can do this in ways that are not harsh. I often dress up as a character that becomes increasingly distressed with each occurrence of my pet peeves in a particular discipline. The character is known as Peeved and Ugly, and the costume includes a black graduation robe, a long gray wig, and green makeup with smudges of charcoal on my face. I "uglify" the character completely: I dip my hands in Elmer's glue and let it dry before wrinkling it to look like acid burned my skin, and I create sores all over my face using blobs of Vaseline covered with tissue paper blended into the green makeup. The hideous countenance and nasty demeanor make me peeved and ugly to students, especially when I get close to their faces and cackle my pet peeves. I overdramatize my dismay, the students laugh, and the message hits home.

Communicate Grading, Homework, and Classroom Policies

On the first day of school, send students home with a quick reference sheet on your classroom policies regarding grading, homework, and other management aspects. This proactive step prevents numerous misunderstandings and bad feelings down the road. It's particularly effective if your practices are consistent with other members of your team, but that's not absolutely necessary.

How you choose to communicate these policies is up to you. You may want students to read each section of the sheet privately while in class and respond to prompts you've given, or you may want them to review the information in class in small groups, listing questions that arise. You can then respond to these group questions with the whole class. It could also become a homework assignment for them to go home and explain the policies to their parents, with Mom or Dad signing off at the bottom when they've read and understood the policies. That signature is important for your protection, too. If there's ever a complaint that students or parents did not know your policy regarding something on the quick reference sheet, the signature is proof that they did.

Figure 2.1 is a sample quick reference I've been using for the past few years. The teaching philosophy that it promotes may or may not be what you prefer, but it is important to have your particular information all in one place for easy parent and student reference throughout the year.

Figure 2.1 Sample Quick Reference on Classroom Policies for Parents and Students

Parents' Quick Reference

English 7 Policies and Practices   **Crusaders Team, Mr. Wormeli**

Grading Scale:

A	= 4.0–3.7	C+	= 2.6–2.2	D	= 1.1–1.0
B+	= 3.6–3.2	C	= 2.1–1.7	F	= 0.9 and lower
B	= 3.1–2.7	D+	= 1.6–1.2		

If a particular assessment is more clearly expressed by percentages or points, it will be done that way for your child, but the score will be converted to the 4.0-scale equivalent before being recorded in the gradebook. Tests, writings, and projects are weighted more heavily than quizzes and homework. Assignments that are given checks or zeroes count no more than 10% of your child's overall academic grade. Checks and zeroes describe the extent of your child's practice with the content and skills, not mastery thereof. Be assured, however, that a check means your child has a good grasp of the content or skill intended; otherwise, a check minus or a zero will be recorded.

Personal growth as well as mastery of English skills and knowledge are more important than grades. Please help your child keep perspective on his or her achievement. While we focus on academics, we will also build stable and compassionate individuals. In this class, our school's Mission Statement is fully recognized:

> Within a safe and nurturing community, the students, staff, and parents of Rachel Carson Middle School seek to foster personal and academic excellence, treat one another with dignity, respect our environment, embrace diversity, and develop character which merits trust and honor. We encourage positive risk taking and perseverance in pursuit of our goals.

Redoing Assessments (including tests, quizzes, projects, writings, and assignments):
At teacher discretion, any assessment may be redone if the student did not completely master the intended content or skills, and the student has demonstrated sincere effort to prepare for the assessment the first time it was given. Rigorous relearning or review in preparation for a second attempt will qualify a student to redo an assessment. Redoing assessments is a privilege, not something to be taken for granted. Students must redo assessments within one week of their return; otherwise the original grade stands. The higher grade between the original attempt and the second attempt will be recorded, not an average of the two grades. Occasionally, assessments cannot be redone, but instead students may correct their mistakes and receive half credit for each item they correct. Students must redo assessments on their own time, not during direct teaching time in our class. In order to redo any test, major project, major writing, or quiz, students must first submit the original work signed by a parent and requesting the retest or redo opportunity.

Makeup Work:
Students are expected to contact their homework partners (study buddies) to determine missing work when absent, or they may access our class's homework Web site on Schoolnotes.com described below. They may also stay after school to record missing assignments, get explanations, and work on makeup assignments. They are allowed the same number of days they were gone to make up the work, unless a note is received from parents requesting more time. If you have access to e-mail, don't forget to use it to get caught up quickly. School: 555-3600. Mr. Wormeli's e-mail: rwormeli@erols.com.

Homework:
There is a list of all homework assignments made for each period posted on the homework board (a surfboard) in our room. Students should be encouraged to review that list regularly. If you or your child would like to see the homework for the day (posted after school), please access Schoolnotes.com on the Web and enter our school's zip code: 20171. Once there, find my name, click on it, and the day's homework will be listed. You can go directly to the homework listing for our class using http://schoolnotes.com/20171/wormeli99.html.

Figure 2.1 *(continued)*

No homework is ever assigned on weekends or holidays in our English class. Those times are reserved for students to be with their families, relax, get exercise, and come back ready to learn on the next school day. At their discretion, students may choose to work over weekends and holidays on long-term projects, rough drafts, or their student choice books. If a student is working beyond his or her normal bedtime on homework, please tell him or her to stop and go to bed. Sleep and health will do more for a student's education than finishing assignments when the student is tired. In these situations, parents need to send in a note asking for a brief extension of completion time in order for students to receive full credit. Please be aware of the student's need to manage his or her life such that homework is a priority—sports, music, church, Scouts, visits from relatives, time with friends and family events are just some of the things that can make a student too tired to do homework each night. Creating balance is a vital skill to learn while in middle school.

Student Papers:
Papers with no names are put into a "No Name, No Credit" tray. A student may check the tray and upon finding his or her work, write his or her name on it and resubmit it. The tray is emptied into the trash every few weeks. Once assignments are evaluated by Mr. Wormeli, they are placed in a tray called "Papers to Be Returned to Students." If a student hasn't had a paper returned in a while, he or she should check there.

Writing Portfolios:
A Writing Portfolio contains the final versions of student writings, and reflections on those writings and the student's progress and goals this year. It is the most valid statement of the students as writers and thinkers. Students will place all graded writings in these portfolios after they are reviewed by Mr. Wormeli. These collected works are kept on bookshelves in our classroom. Please feel free to stop by and view your child's portfolio at any point in the year, or send in a note and we'll send it home for your review. We will send it home for official parent review at the end of each semester.

Visiting:
You are encouraged to visit our English classroom any day you wish. If you want to see your child's class, be sure to ask him or her when his or her English class meets. The front office folks are very careful to prevent interruptions to our class, so they will want to confirm your visit with me before letting you proceed to room C107. Please be sure to call ahead to make sure they know you are coming. They'll check with me if I haven't already told them about your visit, and they'll provide you with a visitor's badge.

Contacting Teachers:
Our school number is 555-3600. I can be contacted through e-mail as well at rwormeli@ erols.com. This is my home e-mail address and I check it each evening between 9:00 and midnight. The school's address is Rachel Carson Middle School, 13618 McLearen Road, Herndon, Virginia 20171.

Extra Supplies?
Keep your eyes and ears open for extra paper, pens, pencils, markers, erasers, tape, scissors, hole punches, and staplers! We maintain an in-class supply center, which frequently needs replenishing. We're also looking for puzzles! We're looking for problem-solving puzzles (written or using manipulatives or physical objects) on which students can work if they finish assignments early or for use during our "Puzzle Day" activity period. Put your name on the puzzle if you want it returned to your family.

Want to Volunteer?
Send in a note stating your name, your child's name, your phone number, and your interest in volunteering. Indicate whether you can do work only in your home, or if you're available to help at school. We'll contact you with a list of possibilities given your availability and get you started right away.

The first moments in the first class we teach each year are exhilarating. We're on the edge, capable of toppling or soaring in a heartbeat. And though middle schoolers will never admit it, they are eager to explore our subjects and be successful students. We can use that knowledge to craft experiences that stimulate students while completing the required first-week administrivia. That balance in the first week of school between advanced study in our subject areas and establishing classroom protocols is key.

After twenty years of first days each September, it never fails to amaze me how fast the time goes. Suddenly it's a week later and we wonder why we were ever worried about filling the time and engaging students. For many of us, there's solace in the fact that we teach the same subject more than one period a day. We can fix all the mistakes we make in the first period when we do it again in subsequent periods. The opportunity to start fresh with the wisdom of our previous experience is something we extend to our students and ourselves at the same time every first week of the school year.

3

Discipline

I went through every method of classroom management—Lee Canter, marbles in the jar, lights off, peace signs, cooperative learning for points—eventually, I discovered the best classroom management was to have really engaging lessons and be totally honest with the kids . . . I walked in with expectations for them and we spoke about their expectations from the teacher. In one class, I had a piano and I hit a chord. Eventually, I just asked the kids what worked best for them. I love those teachers who stand in front of the room and say, "I'll wait." I keep thinking if I am the kid talking to my neighbor, that teacher will just be waiting.

—Alexis, middle school teacher

Effective teachers work with students as opposed to doing things to or for them.

—James H. Stronge, Qualities of Effective Teachers

Okay, okay, you say. You've heard all about constructivism, differentiated learning, technology, subject integration, brain research, homework policies, teaming, and everything else about middle school teaching. All that pales, you say, when it comes to disciplining students. How is it done? How do we herd cats? The best advice is to look at discipline as a teaching tool.

Some folks imagine the middle school disciplinarian as a stern-faced, red-cheeked, ruler-in-fist, never-give-an-inch stereotype who lurks in hallways and classrooms, watching for students to step out of line, even by a millimeter, so that she can pounce and punish. Nothing could be further from the truth—or less effective.

The most effective disciplinarians are those who understand the nature of the young adolescent and who employ what works, not what's punitive or vengeful. Accomplished middle school teachers see management issues as opportunities instead of annoying intrusions. They realize the full scope of who they're teaching: humans in a highly susceptible stage of transition. These humans need formal instruction not just in how to factor polynomials but also in how to live up to society's expectations for civilized behavior. To focus only on our subject is a cop-out. It's not what we're about as middle-level teachers.

Let's set up discipline from the beginning as a dimension of instruction and assessment, not something outside of normal class operations. It's embedded in all we do: in our planning (proactive discipline), in how we connect with students (interactive discipline), and in how we react to poor decisions by students (reactive discipline). Most discipline or classroom management issues boil down to disconnections between teacher practices and student needs. For example, if we teach primarily by talking while students listen, we'll not meet the needs of the students who are visual learners. They may or may not sit politely and listen for a few moments, but either way, we'll lose them quickly. When students' minds wander, they elevate other ideas to prominence, ideas such as poking each other with pencils, tapping their desks, writing notes, wondering who likes whom, and whether or not they can get the dried mucus out of their nose without anyone noticing.

A teacher may push ahead with something cognitive without addressing students' basic survival needs, which further dilutes student credence and engagement in the lesson. For example, if a student is feeling emotionally threatened by an impending test or an intimidating classmate, or worries about a family member, she is not going to stay on task, mentally or physically. If students are paying attention to their growling stomachs, the temperature of the room, or their joints that are sore from stress on the bone growth plates, they are not going to listen to our fascinating lessons on subordinating conjunctions. We have to understand and respond to where students are physically and emotionally before we can do anything cognitively. The brain is a survival organ. It will avoid stress at all points of interaction. Anything we can do to lower that stress will result in improved attention spans and decreased discipline problems. If we teach with developmentally responsive methods, discipline gets much easier.

A student who is constantly moving or interrupting may settle down during a lesson if we give him an M. C. Escher tessellation pattern to color, a koosh ball to squeeze, or an active role in the learning. We can head off potential problems by providing students with something that redirects conflict or excess energy. Some activities such as the tessellation coloring provide intellectual "white noise" so students can concentrate while other activities, such as copresenting material with the teacher, give them purpose in the lesson. Both work to stem discipline problems.

Many discipline issues begin with denial. Students don't accept responsibility for their behavior: "Why are you getting on my case about this? I wasn't doing anything. Matt was goofing off and you didn't say anything to him!" Anything we can do to help them accept their behavior is worth pursuing. One method for helping students accept the reality of their actions comes from Dr. Tom Gatewood at Virginia Tech in Virginia. When a student denies the reality of his actions, Gatewood recommends that we repeatedly ask the student what he was doing in the situation about which we're concerned. After each response from the student, we ask him what he was doing until he finally reveals his role in the situation. It's like a scientist focusing on pure observation, saving interpretations of results for the conclusion portion of the lab write-up. That's a difficult skill for youth to learn, but it's important. Gatewood reminds us not to be emotionally distorting with voice inflections or accusatory tones. Stay calm and be persistent. The following dialogue illustrates this technique.

Teacher: What did you do?
Student: Nothing.
Teacher: What did you do?
Student: I said, "Nothing." Can't you hear? Man, you are always crackin' on me.
Teacher: Tell me what your role was.
Student: What do you mean?
Teacher: What did you do to cause me to pull you out here in the hallway?
Student: I wasn't doing anything. Why aren't you talking to Brian? He was messing around, too!
Teacher: What did you do?
Student: We were just messing with the sharpener.
Teacher: What did you do specifically?
Student: We weren't hurting anybody . . .
Teacher: What did you do?
Student: All I did was give Brian the tampon that Maria dropped out of her backpack.
Teacher: Was that all you did? Think of every step you took.

Student: Well, I laughed when Brian tried to sharpen the tampon in the pencil sharpener.

Teacher: It broke, too.

Student: Yeah.

Teacher: So you're saying that you picked up somebody else's private property, gave it to a classmate whom you knew would put it in the sharpener and damage it, and you found the action funny, indicated by your laughter?

Student: Well, yeah, I guess so.

I've done this successfully with a number of young adolescents. Once we get to that level of what each person's role was, I follow it up with, "What was the effect on your learning?" "What was the effect on your classmates' learning?" and "What will you do to rebuild our trust in you?" These questions focus the student on the reasons why we gather in our classrooms.

I-messages are another way to help students accept responsibility for their actions. I-messages communicate our points without the student's becoming defensive. If he isn't defensive, he's more inclined to listen to the message and give it serious thought. In an I-message, the teacher claims to have a problem with something that the student is doing, and he enlists the student's help in the resolution of the conflict: "T. J., I am frustrated when you talk aloud during my lessons. Students are distracted and few people learn. Can you help me figure out a way to let you know when it's okay to talk and when it's not okay to talk in class?" I-messages come at the problem from a different angle. Because it is someone else's problem, the student isn't threatened by the accusation. His defensive walls are lowered, and he hears the message.

Sometimes persistent repetition or I-messages don't work. A good alternative to get students to accept responsibility for their actions is videotaping. Videotape doesn't lie (at least the technology to which most teachers have access doesn't allow for modifications of video images and sounds). We can be like former New York sportscaster Warner Wolfe and say to students who are not accepting responsibility, "Let's go to the videotape!" I use this approach with my chronic disrupters. The camera is placed at an angle that picks up the student about whom I have a concern. Later in the day or after school, the student sits with me to watch the tape. In the first run-through, I usually post a piece of posterboard with a small window in it on the television screen. The posterboard frame allows only the image of the student to be seen as the tape plays. Again, I ask the student to describe what he was doing and the effect of his actions on his learning. Then I rerun the tape, but I post a piece of posterboard frame with a slightly larger window showing the student and the classmates immediately around him. I ask the student to describe the effect of his behavior on the learning of those classmates. Finally, the posterboard is removed and the student is asked to describe the effect of his behavior on the teacher and the class as a whole. This experience is particularly effective when Mom or Dad sits with us while conducting the interview and analysis.

So far we've looked at samples of discipline that include a proactive approach such as teaching in a developmentally responsive manner, and a reactive approach such as getting students to accept the reality of their behavior after they've become a problem. Let's also take a look at interactive discipline.

We use interactive discipline to connect with students. The interaction can be in physical, oral, or in written forms. Interactive discipline is also found in the proactive and reactive discipline strategies. A tenacious discussion with a student who finally admits his responsibility is one such example. As we interact, we guide.

Interactions are functions of our relationships, so effective interactive discipline strategies are best found in the steps we take to cultivate respectful relationships with students. While Chapter 12 has multiple suggestions for creating and maintaining those relationships, be aware of the interactive nature of discipline in the further discussions of proactive and reactive discipline below. You'll see the chance to guide students toward healthy behavior decisions with the types of questions you ask, the assignments you give, group tasks, curriculum alignment (does it match students' needs?), your application of consequences for particular actions, your reestablishment of a positive relationship with a student following an altercation, and how you negotiate behavior plans. In each interaction, you have the opportunity to discipline—to teach—students. Every word and action you use is an opportunity for student maturation.

Proactive Discipline

Effective middle school teachers who have good classroom discipline are usually folks who've done a lot of planning and can apply it flexibly. They put most of their energy into proactive and interactive discipline.

The first step is to align instruction and assessment with young adolescent minds. For example, 80 percent of young adolescents are concrete thinkers, so we have to find ways to turn our symbolic or abstract concepts into physical manifestations in order for them to be perceived correctly. If we don't, discipline erodes. Our lesson on the differences between an indirect and direct democracy can use labeled Tinkertoys to show paths of communication and representation; our lesson on the basic elements of an essay can have students building layered sandwiches representing those elements.

Since the prefrontal cortex of the young adolescent brain is the last portion of the brain to develop, and since that section of the brain is where we process moral and abstract reasoning, planning, and awareness of the consequences of our actions, it doesn't make sense to require great leaps of growth in these areas for all students in every lesson. The steps we take with students in these areas will be smaller, yet intense. In a teacher-advisory lesson on cheating, for instance, we might limit our focus to how and why students cheat on homework assignments, not all the ways and reasons students cheat in school. In another lesson, we might make sure to create a personal connection for students to new material prior to learning it, so that the new concepts will have meaning, something that the brain will regard, not disregard. Research tells us that the brain pays attention to what is familiar, so creating prior knowledge is key. Using such developmentally responsive methods engages students.

Being proactive doesn't just involve instruction and assessment. We also prevent discipline issues with the physical classroom. We have seating charts that reflect thoughtful placement of students according to where they'll best learn: Are they seated close to or far from the window/friend/door/chalkboard/supplies? We've noted the potential traffic bottlenecks as students move around the room and we've removed those obstacles. We've lowered the blinds so there's no glare on the television screen when we show a video. We write large and vivid words on the chalk/wipe/smartboard so that students can see. We've designed an adaptable rotation chart for students to work on the one computer in the classroom so we're not constantly negotiating who's next in line. We've made sure students keep their desk areas clean so there are no issues for the next class when they arrive. We've counted supplies so there are plenty for each period. Students can access everything they need, from extra copies of handouts to their personal portfolios, without teacher assistance. Taking care of these possible threats to momentum and discipline ahead of time makes a big difference.

Establishing classroom rules for behavior is another proactive strategy. For each period at the beginning and midpoint of the year, ask, "What will it take for us to work together successfully?" Brainstorm possible conduct statements like "Be polite. Wait until others are finished speaking before taking your turn" with students, then post them. Keep the list to five or fewer rules. My classroom has two posted expectations: "respect others and property; take responsibility for your actions." Every classroom infraction we can think of fits under one of these two so they work for us. National

Board Certified teacher Beth Huddleston has specific rules in mind as she negotiates with each year's students:

> I find that brainstorming with the kids allows them to assume ownership in the process. I like for my students to have their materials ready for class, to raise their hands for sharing or questioning, to respect the property of others, and to respect the learning atmosphere of others. These rules require discussion and clarification. By the time students reach middle school, they really are aware of what these mean to them, but they often verbalize them differently from the way an elementary child would. Some of my students asked me to add the following visual to our rules poster:

RESPECT

―――――――

ALL

(Meaning "Respect Above All")

Many teachers also post a sequence of consequences for students who break the agreed-upon rules. This due-process approach seems fair to students. It helps them accept consequences when they cross the line.

Creating a positive emotional climate is another powerful discipline strategy. When a student feels known and respected by the adult in charge, he's less likely to counter the adult's authority. We earn "respect points" every time we affirm students' efforts, give students respect, elevate them rather than ourselves, and sincerely reach out to them when they are troubled. Students with whom we've had a positive history say things to other students like, "Don't act up with Mr. Wormeli, he's cool. We don't do that crap in here." This means showing our human sides once in a while, like letting ourselves tear up at something awful in the news, laughing at our mistakes, expressing honest joy at student achievement, and modeling dignified interactions with others. There's no room here for sarcasm or putdowns from the students or the teacher. (For other relationship-building ideas, see Chapter 12.)

Laurie, an eight-year teaching veteran, agrees that the best discipline comes from careful proactive attention to relationships. On a recent posting on the middleweb.com listserver she writes,

> I have found that when the kids think of each other as people, then they are easier and more forgiving of each other. It helps us to know each other, call each other by name, and build bridges before we really need them. In years where I haven't worked on this intensely the first two to three weeks (thinking I really need to

jump into curriculum more quickly), I regret all the time I devoted to discipline. So it's the whole penny saved, penny earned theorem. Class-building time invested, discipline time reduced later on.

Sometimes we ask students to adopt new behaviors, such as those needed for a debate, Socratic Seminar, or when being a proper audience for a guest speaker. In these situations, a T-chart is particularly helpful. A T-chart is simply a large *T* drawn on the chalkboard with an ear at the top of the left column and an eye drawn at the top of the right column. Under the ear, we ask the class to list those things we would hear from a group that was working well together. Under the eye, students list what someone would see happening in a group that was working well.

[Picture of an ear]	[Picture of an eye]
Different people contributing ideas, not just one person	People taking turns to speak
Conversational voices, not too loud or soft	Body language that expresses interest in what other people say
People using each other's names	Everyone participating, no one sitting by themselves
People working off of each other's ideas	Students have supplies/notes needed to do the task
When people argue, it's about ideas, not people	Students on the task

The important thing with the T-chart isn't to list the criteria for success. It's the analysis of behavior against the standards (the descriptions in each column) that takes place afterward. In a whole-class debriefing, check off those things that students did well, and circle any areas that need improvement. Elevate the circled areas to primary goals for the next day.

When introducing any new behavior we want students to adopt, it's best to conduct the first experiences in short bursts, five to seven minutes at the most, then discuss with the class how they did. Add a few minutes' time to subsequent experiences, building up to twenty to thirty minutes. You should also adjust the membership of the groups. For example, when teaching students how to work in a group, ask them to work in pairs first. Assign the partners at this point. Have them follow a structured interview format where they ask each other scripted questions. Later, have them select questions from a list, charting the conversation's course for themselves.

Students can participate in assessing the new behavior. Have partners record each other's responses in quick-note form to be turned in to you when the group is done meeting. Spend significant time strolling from group to group, recording evidence of success and nonsuccess on a notepad—no names are required for these observations unless you want to follow up with particular students. When the group session is done, you can read these observations aloud as feedback for what went well and what still needs development. This kind of immediate and specific feedback makes a big impact on students' learning the behavior.

When students can do the partnered discussions successfully, combine partner teams into groups of four, again with structured interactions at first, graduating to free exchanges of ideas later. If appropriate, work groups up to seven or eight for some projects, but in general, keep four to six students in a group. And carry around that notepad to record observations. I use a yellow sticky pad so that if I want to keep observations about a student's interactions, I can peel off the sheet and stick it quickly in the file I have on that student in my desk drawer. Later, I can record those observations on a formal record sheet stapled inside the folder. I can also peel off these sheets and stick them quickly in my lesson plan book for quick reference that evening when planning the next day's lessons.

Reactive Discipline

Even the best planning by the most experienced teacher doesn't prevent all discipline problems. Stuff happens. With luck, we have our wits about us, and we deal with it in an appropriate manner. That doesn't always happen, but we get better at it with each incident.

In every discipline situation, think first about the physical safety of the students and yourself. I once had a student pick up his desk with seemingly no provocation and hold it above his head, ready to heave it at a classmate. I took three big steps from where I was in the room and stood in front of the targeted classmate, telling that student to move to the back of the room. Once he was out of harm's path, I said to the angry student, "I understand that you are way beyond mad, but if you heave that desk, [the classmate] wins. Give me the desk."

The student took a step back and argued that he was tired of being made fun of. "That's a good point," I noted, "but you have to ask yourself whether or not you are prepared for all the consequences of throwing that desk, or if you just want the teasing to stop. If you want to stop the teasing and get on with your life, then you'll put the desk down." Of course, while I was talking, I was moving forward. By the time I had finished that last line, I would've been able to successfully grab the desk should he decide to throw it. Most students who act out this much do so out of fear, and their own feelings of being out of control make them even more frightened. "Put the desk down, and we will talk and hear your message. Fail to put it down, and you've lost our respect for your arguments." The student lowered the desk and I called the office to ask for a counselor to come to my room. It helped, of course, that I am six feet three inches tall and weigh over two hundred pounds, but I've seen teachers who barely crest five feet do the same thing.

Even middle school students who don't have severe emotional struggles occasionally lose it in the classroom or hallway. Normal young adolescents can weep when it's not warranted, become irritable over small things, talk or laugh at inappropriate moments, not pay attention to lessons when they're vital, destroy or vandalize school, classmates', or teachers' property—all within moments in the middle of our routine lesson on tropical biomes. If we have an atmosphere in which individuals and their quirks are embraced, such behaviors do not become major discipline issues. We hold them accountable for unacceptable behaviors, but we understand that they are a natural part of growing up. Calmly responding to them is a normal and important part of the middle school teacher's instruction.

A few suggestions after you've ensured the safety of everyone involved: Always have an out, a way for the student to save face. For instance, have a place he can go to gather himself when he's lost control. This might be some soft furniture in the room, the nearby bathroom to wash his face, or to a counselor's office. It also means using the ten-minute rule: If you've had a negative interaction with a student, then within ten minutes, ask a question for which he knows the answer, find a way to affirm his gifts or talents, or enable him to contribute positively to the class. You're rebuilding the bridge. Another way out is a confidential folder to you. I've posted one for years on the wall near my desk. When students are concerned about something, they can drop a note in that folder that I guarantee to read by the end of the day. Students can vent, share private issues, or even pass along advice to me via that folder. Over my career, it's been an invaluable source of insight about my students and my teaching.

Another successful idea is to move through that list of posted consequences. For instance, with the first infraction, ask the student to state the classroom rule he's breaking and give him a verbal warning. A teacher's concerned stare goes a long way as well. With the second infraction of the same rule (or chronic interruptions of whatever size and shape), a private conference is warranted—one out of earshot so as not to be humiliating, only instructional. Along with asking the student what it will take to get him to desist, this is a good time to remind him of the consequences of a third discipline issue—administrative referral, phone call to Mom or Dad, removal from the room, service to the school, after-school detention, and/or restitution of some sort. If things escalate to the third offense, then it's time to take serious action. Is it always wise to wait until the student has made the mistake three times before taking serious action? Of course not. If the mistake in conduct is severe enough, you may want to take action the first time he does it. You can also take such action for the first infraction on a particular day if it has been a small but chronic misconduct prior to today.

No matter how big the consequence for the misbehavior, ask your administrator if you can deliver the consequence. National Middle School Association Assistant Director Jack Berckemeyer, a former teacher, balks at the idea of administrative referrals. Instead, he asks teachers to take on the mantle of ultimate disciplinarian, even if it calls for in- or out-of-school suspension. If a principal or an assistant principal administers the consequences, then the classroom teacher's authority is made inert, he says. The teacher can't do anything, only the administrator can. When the teacher is the one with the final decision power, students take his words seriously, even in the first infraction. This may not be possible in every school, of course; protocols and administrators vary. It's worth exploring, however.

Once a student has crossed the line to that severe level, it's important that he have a road map to get him back on track. I've used a behavior management form for a number of years when this happens. After that third offense or after that serious first offense, students must complete the form (Figure 3.1).

Humor is never out of reach for a good middle school disciplinarian. Laughter diffuses the situation and helps students gain perspective. Laurie, a veteran middle school teacher, offers this advice:

> I'm not sure if I'm the only one who does this, but I actually warn the kids if they don't stop certain behaviors, I will SING to them!! Once they hear my absolutely horrible voice (my chorus teacher even told me in junior high to mouth the words rather than sing!), they stop immediately. I find the oldies work best, especially Monkees songs.

Document, Document, Document

Every veteran teacher will attest to the need to record all discipline incidents that result in more than that second warning. Make it brief but detailed—date, time, teacher, student(s), and a description of what happened. A number of teachers maintain an incident book in which they log infractions if their electronic grade book doesn't allow for such commen-

Figure 3.1 Behavior Plan

Behavior Plan

Name: _____ Date: _____

Period: _____ Teacher: _____

A. Describe what you did that resulted in the teacher's request for you to complete this form:

B. How did this incident make you feel?

How do you think others felt?

C. Which class expectation or rule did this action break?

D. What will you do to make sure such behavior doesn't occur again? (More than one idea, please.)

E. What will you do to regain our trust in you? (Check as many as you think are necessary to rebuild our trust and for you to learn from your mistake.)

___ verbal apology to injured person	___ letter written to parents
___ phone call to parents from you	___ phone call to parents from teacher
___ service to the classroom (cleaning, organizing, etc.)	___ service to the school (picking up trash, cleaning)
___ after-school detention	___ before-school detention
___ letter of apology	___ parental accompaniment to class
___ removal from enjoyable class activity (field trip, play)	___ expulsion
	___ sitting alone for a while
___ removal from cafeteria for lunch period (s)	___ discussion with principal
	___ pay for the damages with own money
___ in-school suspension (Crisis Center)	___ Other:

Student Signature: _____

Teacher Approval: _____

Additional Comments:

Date of our next meeting to discuss the success of this agreement: _____

tary, or if they don't have the technology to do so (Figure 3.2). Such documentation serves not only you, but the student as well.

Sometimes we can't see the forest for the trees. We get so caught up in the day-to-day management of 150 students and our own lives that we fail to see patterns of chronic discipline issues. We need the objective view of that incident book or another person telling us there's a problem with the

Figure 3.2 Discipline Log

Discipline Log

Student:

Parents' Names:

Phone Number(s):

E-mail Addresses:

Date	Issue or Incident	Response

student's behavior. With such perspective, we can take action. Without it, we flounder, putting out fires but never solving the problem. Maintaining accurate documentation is justified for instructional/managerial decisions alone.

Just as convincing, however, is documenting infractions for the sake of explaining one's actions to parents and administration. Explaining our discipline decisions is a natural part of a teacher's job. We don't need to feel like we're on trial when asked to share our thinking; we teach in a community, not a vacuum. Though it's impossible to escape the feeling of being under scrutiny ourselves, every member of a child's team needs to understand the child's progression or regression and our responses to it. Sure, such discussions might reveal mistakes we made while disciplining, but we get better only by examining our mistakes with others. It's a collegial thing. Disciplining with the hope that no one will find out is the worst way to go. Make decisions with the full expectation that everyone will know what you've done. Clear and consistent documentation enables team members— parents, colleagues, specialists, and administration—to reflect accurately and make appropriate recommendations.

This documentation also protects you. If a discipline case ever goes to the school board or local court system, and chances are you'll have more than one of these in the course of a career, you'll fare well as a professional and student advocate if you've documented all incidents, as well as your ongoing communications with both parents and administration. It's due process for the student, and it leads to sound decisions concerning his welfare. Unfortunately, there have been times when I have done a less-than-admirable job at documenting a student's misbehavior. When the student's behavior escalated to the point where it warranted an expulsion hearing and the subsequent appeal by the family, my incomplete documentation significantly compromised the school system's case, but even worse, it did not enable the court officers to make the decisions they needed to make—the student didn't get the help he needed. Learn from my mistakes: establish a routine and an inclination to document serious and/or chronic discipline issues from the start.

Additional Discipline Principles We Can't Forget

In middle school, it is never effective or morally acceptable to use physical punishment when disciplining a child. This means it is not effective or acceptable to hit or spank students or make them hold rocks out at arm's length for an hour. Some physical education teachers have students do extra sit-ups or push-ups or run around the track. Some teachers and administrators have students do physical service for the school such as cleaning up graffiti, picking up trash, or painting walls. To a certain extent, these are relatively harmless in most situations and they can be effective. Don't overdo it, however.

Avoid making threats or stating consequences that you are not prepared to enact. You'll undermine your own authority. Avoid these situations by clearly describing for yourself and students the well-considered consequences of poor behavior before misbehavior occurs.

Avoid all insults or put-downs. This is a hurtful response and it doesn't teach the student anything except that it's acceptable to hurl insults in the adult world. It makes you look weak, too, for adults are supposed to be more mature than that.

Get rid of the "I'm punishing the whole class because of the actions of these few students" attitude. It doesn't work and it breeds resentment. Class meetings work. Sometimes the group reflection and response to a discipline issue yields the wisest course of action.

Do *not* assign writing as a punishment. Writing "I will not throw erasers in the room" five hundred times does not change a student's behavior or his inclination to throw erasers in the future. Our discipline is about teaching and transforming, not just reacting. Don't assign writing tasks such as copying pages from the dictionary. They don't work, and they build resentment toward writing. Remember, English/language arts teachers are trying to convince those same students that writing is interesting and worth doing. As a math teacher, I would never want someone to assign math as punishment, or as a science teacher, a tedious lab experiment as punishment. It's the same for writing. The one kind of writing that *is* justified and seems to help with discipline, however, are reflective essays on the student's own behavior and the effect of his behavior on learning and on others. This may be done in the form of a letter of apology to the offended parties as well.

The Latin root of *discipline* and *disciple* means *student*. To be a student is to be disciplined—not necessarily in the militaristic style, but rather by adopting the demeanor and practices of one who studies well. If we accept this definition, then, it means teaching students not only what to learn, but how to learn it, and how to mature with that learning. It's not an add-on to the curriculum, it *is* the curriculum. Robert Frost said that education is the ability to listen to almost anything without losing your temper or your self-confidence. According to Helen Keller, the highest result of education is tolerance. Note the discipline angle of both of these—how learning transcends content and skills. We won't be successful teachers if we see discipline as an imposition, something we have to step aside and handle before we continue on the road to scholarly endeavor. It is as integral to our middle school classrooms as listening, thinking, and students' writing their names at the top of their papers. It's not herding untamed cats; it's riding currents with amazing fish.

47

4

The Physical Classroom

At the beginning of the school year, I take photos of all my students and place them in a photo album. I may now start putting them on the computer as well. This helps in several ways: It makes a substitute's job much easier. If someone acts out, they check the photos and they immediately know the name of the person. Cuts down discipline a bit. Seating charts are easier. I can do them by photo instead of names alone. We had a problem with students sneaking into classes where they did not belong, mine in particular during my first year. That stopped that nonsense. The problem is, what do you do about kids who enter your class late? I purchased a Polaroid and snapped instant pictures of them. [Author's note: Digital cameras work well, too.]

—Sal Treppiedi, Harrison Middle School, Albuquerque, New Mexico

Here's the test of a true teacher: The floor is dirt, and the walls keep out the sun and wind, but that's all. The door is thatch. Students sit on benches or on the floor. The community is impoverished, and the water is not safe to drink. Students' abilities range from one to four years below grade level. Half the class doesn't speak your language, and this is only the second year of formal schooling for some of them, even though they're twelve. "The water is wide," teacher and novelist Pat Conroy says.

And through it all, your lessons are effective and your students learn.

As outstanding middle school teachers, we can start with nothing and create something wonderfully effective. Our true colors shine in adversity, our professionalism apparent in our flexibility and self-sufficient pedagogy. We don't need a basal textbook series or workbooks to teach reading well.

We don't need a history textbook to teach history, a math book to teach math, or a microscope to teach microbiology. We don't need calculators, student desks, paper, pencils, computers, overheads, or novels in order for students to learn amazing concepts and skills. It boils down to what can we do with a group of students and the content we have to teach. We can't accept book and tool poverty as justification for not teaching well. It may take more planning, professional reading, and collaborating with others, but we will rise above our conditions.

If you're a science teacher, can you teach ionic and covalent bonds in an empty room with thirty students? If you're an English teacher, can you teach figurative language in poetry while sitting with your students in an empty baseball field? If you're an art teacher, can you teach the effective use of line and shading in artwork while holding class in the school's gymnasium? Sure you can. You can do these things because you don't let the physical environment limit your teaching methods. You turn the environment into the teaching tool you need it to be.

If we accept this premise, then everything we get beyond a basic room with seats, desks, and a chalkboard is icing on the cake. All extras over and above these basics should advance us beyond what we could achieve in a poor, third-world classroom in the middle of a desert. We can start with an empty room and build.

To determine an instructional tool's usefulness, imagine your classroom without it. If it advances student learning, keep it. If it doesn't, toss it. Classrooms tend to get cluttered even in the first few months, and with that clutter comes intellectual laziness. We take some things for granted and don't check for the real learning that so often comes to light when teaching and learning are cut to their basics, such as we might find in those empty rooms and on those baseball fields.

So, a barren wasteland is the rich soil of teaching inspiration, right? No. Just the opposite; we want to be stimulating and we want the tools that help us teach more effectively than we could otherwise. Modern conveniences and tools must be given serious consideration, however. We have to make sure that everything we design and provide in our classrooms is purposeful and advances our mission. We don't use procedures and tools because they are what others use. We use them because they work for us as we teach young adolescents. Sure, much of what we incorporate will stem from the wisdom of those more experienced, but we need to monitor our effectiveness with each suggested element. It's a waste to put energy into something that doesn't work. We can design something better.

Each of the following sections offers the best advice on successful classroom tools, procedures, and components culled from twenty years of teaching middle-level students. Take the portions that work for you and try them. After a few months, reread the sections for new ideas sparked by your new perspective.

The Teacher's Desk

There's something amiss when a middle school teacher's desk is consistently cleared of work and materials, or when we see a teacher always sitting at his desk while students learn. Teacher's desks can be facades behind which we can hide and find distraction. They can also be large black holes into which go our urgent notes from parents, missing phone numbers, referral forms, altered schedules, student projects, grade sheets, blueberry muffin crumbs, and the locker key, never to be found until retirement. They are also amazing intersections of students' efforts, our responses to those efforts, the professional duties that come with the job, and our personal idiosyncrasies. They are our office and a statement of our affairs at any given moment. Here's an idea to make your teacher's desk support your classroom mission: Get rid of it. Remove it from the room.

Okay, that might be a little rough. After all, you've looked forward to having a big teacher's desk in a classroom all of your own for years. It's a sign that you're the big cheese and doing the teaching in the room, right? It's easy to think this way—I thought this way in my first years as well. Down the road, however, we realize that teaching is about learning and students, not control or having a desk. The teacher is a major learner in the room. And students are teachers.

In order to save classroom space and shift my teaching emphasis to the students, I've moved my teacher's desk to a teacher workroom across the hall, making it similar to an office. That's where I go during my planning periods to get some of the professional paperwork done. Most of the paperwork we do, however, involves working with students and their efforts, designing lesson plans with materials spread out in front of us, composing notes, assessing curriculum, and grading stacks of papers. These activities are done more easily at a large worktable we put somewhere in the classroom, not at a small teacher's desk. An added benefit: If the worktable is used every period, we keep it clean instead of stacking things ceiling-high and leaving them for days. Without the teacher's desk in the classroom, we have more space for a learning center, another computer, an in-class library, a paper return area, a puzzle area, or for spreading student desks farther apart to limit distractions.

For many of you, removing the teacher's desk is impractical—you need it and all its supplies nearby, and there isn't a place outside of the classroom to have a pseudo office, even if you wanted to move the desk. That's fine;

use what works for you and your style. Whatever you do, try not to place your desk in the center at the front of the classroom. This sends a clear message that the learning experiences in that room center on you, not the students. A wiser idea if you want the desk up front is to place it diagonally across one corner so that it faces out toward the class but is not the center of attention. It's also effective to place your teacher desk halfway down one side wall or in the back of the room. You can keep an eye on things from all these positions and still maintain an area that is markedly yours.

In and around your desk, you'll want to have many supplies to make teaching, learning, and surviving easier. Make sure to stock your desk and surrounding shelves with the following items:

Clerical items—pencils, colored pencils, marking pens, overhead pens, felt markers, chalk, masking tape, Scotch tape, sticky tack, staplers (notice the plural; staplers break easily and there are never enough), staples, staple remover, scissors, Liquid Paper, glue sticks, rulers, hole punches (single and triple), calculator, large erasers, paper clips, pushpins or tacks, rubber bands, Post-it notes, safety pins, stamps, extra file folders, and your own pencil sharpener.

Professional items—handbooks; duty rosters; curriculum guides; grade book; plan book; all official school forms (such as referral forms, equipment requisitions, facility maintenance slips, and field-trip forms); professional articles of interest; office memos; blank thank-you cards; contact numbers for parent volunteers as well as curriculum coordinators, services, and resource centers in your school district; and a map of the school district (vital if you want to get to inservice training on time).

Survival items—Chapstick; tissues; aspirin; cough drops or throat lozenges; stomach medicines (check your school's policy on medicines in the classroom—they may be prohibited); crackers, fruit, vegetables, and water; map of the school; X-acto knife; screwdriver; hammer; first-aid kit; needle and thread; glue gun; phone numbers for favorite substitute teachers; late bus schedules; codes and procedures for accessing the TV/VCR, e-mail programs, the Internet, and photocopying machine; a calendar for the year.

Nice to have items—camera; book you're currently reading; address book; magnetic strips; lunch menus from local restaurants; roster of who's willing to play tennis, basketball, or go walking or running with you after school.

LABEL EVERYTHING with your name. I didn't label things in my first few years and consequently lost most of them. Folks don't really mean to take things and never return them; the items just get lost in life's daily shuffle. I felt like I had a pay raise the first year I labeled all my classroom supplies with my name—very little was lost and my wallet didn't suffer.

I highly recommend two quick tips for not losing pencils and pens in your room: First, have your own pencils made. I use Atlas Pen and Pencil Corporation (1-800-327-3232, www.atlaspen.com). On each pencil it reads, "Official Wormeli Brain Translator." Second, if students need to borrow a pencil, ask them to drop a quarter in a jar you keep for such purposes before taking a pencil. To protect your wallet, try to get these extra pencils from your school. When the amount of money in the jar hits twenty dollars or so, buy something for the room that everyone can use. You can also do the old standby: Have students give you something of theirs such as a shoe when they borrow a pencil or pen. They'll remember to return the item in order to get their shoe back.

Mark Lewis, an outstanding middle school teacher from Arizona, has further advice about the teacher's desk:

Middle schoolers are interested in everything you might have on your desk, especially pictures or interesting objects, but you must be firm or other items could disappear right before your eyes. I bought a daily joke calendar this year, and was forced to move it by the pencil sharpener due to the crowds it would cause to surround my desk daily. The next rule for a teacher's desk is the Rule of Piles. Teachers love piles and would feel empty and lost without them, but these piles must be organized. Never stack multiple assignments onto the same pile, even perpendicularly. Clip class sets together, and do it immediately or Susie's paper from third hour will find its way into seventh hour. Also move the piles along. The longer they sit, the more they will multiply (sort of like rabbits).

Attempt to put similar piles in the same area of your desk each time. For example, if you like to put office paperwork in one particular area, then put it there every time. It might sound militaristic, but you will not lose that important memo from your principal that you were supposed to read, sign, and pass on. Lastly, take a look at your desk at the end of the day. Before you leave for home, organize and clean it. Put away items you are finished with, throw away anything you can, arrange your piles neatly, and put whatever you plan on beginning the next day with in a prominent location. In the chaotic world of education, use your desk as a calm spot in the storm.

The Paper Shuffle

Have a clearly marked place in the room for students to turn in their work. There are a number of options for creating places where students can turn in papers:

- a set of tubs or trays, one for each period, desk cluster, row, or subject
- a set of magnetized or wall-mounted file folder trays, one for each period, desk cluster, row, or subject
- one main basket, tub, or tray into which everything goes
- folders, one for every assignment or one for every period, desk cluster, row, or subject

The way you prefer to grade will affect how you ask students to submit their work. You may want to grade all 150 projects so your mind is focused on the same things as you grade; or you may want to grade all the papers for each period you teach or all the work for one student, grading many different assignments. Grading by period seems to be the most efficient method. Breaking the larger task into five or six smaller groupings such as class periods gives a sense of accomplishment, and your mind is not dulled by huge quantities of repeated information. Don't forget to consider asking students to alphabetize a set of assignments for you. It will make record keeping easier.

Students will occasionally (and chronically, depending on the person) submit papers on which they've forgotten to record their names. Please don't throw these in the trash can as a way to teach students a lesson in responsibility. It won't work, and you'll be creating larger problems—resentment and an irretrievable assignment. Young adolescents are not capable of remembering to write their names on their assignments 100 percent of the time. Even my most conscientious students over the years have made this mistake. It's not reasonable to provide a harsh response to students when they forget. We can be developmentally appropriate and hold them accountable in other ways. First, if we recognize the writing, write the student's name on it and return it to him. Let him record his name and resubmit the assignment. It was a simple mistake; we can afford to be forgiving. If we don't recognize the writing, place the unnamed assignment in a tub or tray labeled "No Name, No Credit." Invite students to inspect the contents of the tub or tray once a week or when others have their papers returned but they don't. If students find their work, have them put their names on the assignment and resubmit it for credit. If you wish, take some points off, but not so much that it would significantly change the indicator of mastery you put on it.

A great way to maintain sanity with the paper shuffle in middle schools is to ask students to maintain a student assignment notebook or something similar. It'll help them complete, find, and submit papers on time, preventing frantic paper chases down the road. Though there are plenty of inexpensive versions for mass purchase, students can make their own assignment notebooks. Just make sure there is a page for each day of the school year, and on each page there is space for writing down assignments for each subject, as well as places to record additional reminders, a place for parents to sign, and a place for teachers to initial that the information is correct. It is particularly helpful, too, if there is a section somewhere in the notebook for recording phone numbers and e-mail addresses of classmates who can be contacted for homework assignments when students are sick, as well as a grade sheet on which students can record grades as papers are returned and thereby keep a running tab on how they're doing.

Make sure to have a final tub, basket, tray, or folder to store extra copies of handouts. Inevitably, students will lose original copies of what we've given them, or they'll be absent and not receive the handout. An "extras" tray provides a place where they can go to get back up to speed without bothering you or their classmates.

A caution about technology: Many teachers are exploring electronically submitted assignments and portfolios. I'm one of them. It's the way to go in the years ahead, but we aren't there yet in terms of security, technology, and equal access to technology. Experiment with your students, if possible, but be wise and back up every electronic submission with a hard copy, just in case. Until we can guarantee that diskettes and CDs won't be broken or lost, servers won't be down, and everyone has equal access and expertise with the technology, we can't require across-the-board use. Another benefit of hard copies: successful editing. It's been proven repeatedly in editors' offices and English classrooms across the nation that our minds catch mistakes on hard copy more often than on a computer screen where we're dealing with the oscillating pixels of the electronic image. Have students proofread by reading the hard-copy version of their work aloud.

Have a designated student of the week return papers or, if privacy is a concern, return papers yourself while students are working on something else. Be efficient with time. Just a reminder: There is a direct correlation between how long papers take to be graded and returned to students and the extent of complexity and depth students apply to the assignment. If students know they're going to get feedback quickly, they'll put more of themselves into it. If they don't get feedback for a couple of weeks, their motivation fades.

When it comes to your own administrative paperwork, deal with everything within twenty-four hours. If you get a request to complete a teacher narrative form for an upcoming IEP meeting, sit down and do it right away. Need to complete a form requesting buses for your field trip in four months? Get the forms and complete them right now while you're caught up in the trip's planning. You can put off your own paperwork only if you're stuck between a rock and a hard place. This means completing administrative paperwork even when you don't want to do it, tired or not. Believe this repentant paperwork procrastinator: it's worth doing it now. Don't wait until the pile of uncompleted paperwork has hit critical mass; do it as it comes across your desk or into your teacher box. You'll have a life if you do.

Seating Arrangements

Remember, do whatever it takes to maximize learning, not just what looks good. There are many successful seating configurations: ziggurat, senate, modified U.N., three hockey sticks, turtles, clusters, United Nations, 2-3-2, modified herringbone, and vertical Rorschach are shown in Figure 4.1.

Chapter 6 gives many reasons for changing students' seats as often as every two weeks, if possible. It's a smart move; learning is contextual and we want students to explore content in a variety of contexts. Some advice, however: Throughout the year, arrange students in a boy-girl-boy-girl pattern as much as possible. Mixing girls and boys tends to calm things down in a middle school classroom. Please do not arrange students alphabetically unless there is no other way to do it. Students are arranged alphabetically in many areas of their lives; they don't need it in your class as well. They end up with the same seatmates most of the time, year after year, and the student with the surname "Zyrckle" is always last. Take it from someone who is near the end of the alphabet: alphabetical sequences are not fun.

When sitting down to do your seating charts, place your anchors and your management issues first. The anchors are your consistently well-behaved and success-oriented students who serve as great models for struggling students. Your management issues are students with the most behavior concerns; they're just starting out on the road to maturity. In the first week of school, of course, you'll have no idea who these people are, but you'll get a sense of things within the first few weeks. Once these folks are spread throughout the room, either to ensure stability or in an effort to stay focused, insert the names of other students in and around them in ways that will lead to the greatest learning success. Your seating arrangement of anchors and management issues will change during the year. Be open to it. Every student deserves a chance to become an anchor, and every student should be allowed to misstep with his or her behavior and still be accepted

Figure 4.1 Basic Seating Arrangements

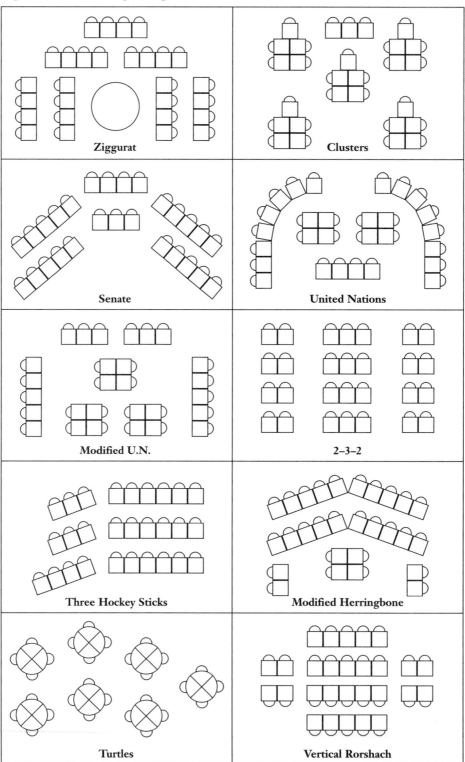

as a highly competent, worthy child in the room. Treat poor behavior as a temporary condition, not the foundation for all that is to come. Middle school is where they should be making and learning from mistakes and still be accepted.

Choose seating arrangements that minimize back rows. If no student is more than two or three desks away from you when you teach, they stay focused—you're practically in their face. If you have a back row that is across the room from where you teach, you're inviting students to be off task. Their sight lines to you are interrupted repeatedly. Distance from authority dilutes students' sense of urgency. Proximity is important to management.

Roxann Rose, a former classroom teacher and now a professor at Woodring College of Education at Western Washington University in Washington State, prefers tables to individual desks: "Tables aren't as territorial. It's not like someone's sitting at your desk when others sit at the same table. It's just a table, undecorated with your stuff. Tables free up floor space with less furniture, which eases movement around the room."

Beth Huddleston, a National Board Certified teacher in Virginia, likes arrangements that get students talking:

> As a language arts teacher, I like to have a setup that encourages discussion and peer editing, while allowing me to make eye contact with every child. For this reason, I do not like traditional rows. For my purposes, I use a U-shape of desks, or I have the desks arranged like the spokes in half of a wheel. Diagonal rows all angle in to the front of the room where I move to use the overhead, the chalkboard, or the NET TV.

Getting Their Attention

[*Begin with bass rhythm that starts slow, then quickens with each new line; a movie announcer's deep voice*]

Ann: Coming soon to a classroom near you . . . [*glimpse of a teacher explaining the next concept*] . . . a new level of cognition . . . [*picture of students raising hands and participating*] . . . a place of extended contemplation . . . [*image of students grimacing with effort, sweat rolling down their faces; music soars to sweeping crescendo*] . . . and untold glory! [*images of students with arms raised, jumping in triumph*] Join us for . . . [*pause, then music hits climactic theme*] . . . mean, median, and mode! [*music soars, walls of the classroom swivel and fold away to reveal interactive exhibits to which students run in academic frenzy*]

This is one way to get students' attention. Of course, cracking a full-length leather whip over their heads will have the same effect.

A number of years ago, I heard a respected workshop leader say that teachers who don't have a well-defined signal for getting students' attention lose three weeks of instructional time during the course of the year. What a waste! Establish a clear and easily used signal for getting students' attention in the first week, then use it judiciously throughout the year. Stopping every few minutes for a new instruction or a reminder is going to kill the signal's effectiveness. For example, if you have multiple groups and each one has a different task, don't spend time describing each group's task while the whole class sits and waits. Create task cards for each group and get them moving. Make sure that your announcements will positively affect most students' success when they hear and respond to them. If announcements are applicable to only one or two students, speak with them privately.

There are many attention-getting signals you can use. Choose one you find comfortable and effective, realizing you may have to experiment a little at the beginning of your first year. This is okay—students are flexible. The following are some you could use:

- Raise or make some other movement with your arms.
- Ring a bell or triangle.
- Play a note on an instrument (traditional or nontraditional instrument).
- Shake a rain stick.
- Stand or sit in a particular place in the room.
- Bang a drum.
- Knock on the table or chalkboard.
- Squeeze a squeaky toy or something that makes a unique noise.
- Say a particular word or phrase.
- Play a piece of music or sound effect.
- Turn the lights on and off (a bit overused by the time students are in middle school).
- Say something quietly that everyone who can hear your voice must do at that moment (like touch your nose, flap an elbow, or lift a pencil) while looking around the room to see who the last person is to catch on to the command.
- Ask students to suggest a signal.

This may sound too childish, but praising students who are doing what you want others to do works well in middle school. Try phrases like, "Thanks, Mark, for taking the time to clean up so well," "Thanks to Table E for stopping what they are doing and looking up here," and "Way to go, Jennifer and Mandi. You were the first to look this way when I needed to get your attention. That really helps." Even though they don't verbalize it, students want to be liked by you, and there's an ingrained desire to do anything that results in positive affirmation from you—even for hard-to-reach students. We can do this in "cool" wordings so that it doesn't come across as too syrupy.

Additional ideas for getting students' attention include

- using students' names
- standing or sitting nearby
- redirecting students' questions to one another (or asking them to agree or disagree with one another)
- startling students with a loud noise
- prealerting students to upcoming challenges
- doing a task in unison
- using incomplete sentences
- changing your voice or inflections
- playing devil's advocate
- challenging students
- making students assistants
- using props
- connecting to students' imagination
- being enthusiastic
- using humor
- using drama
- asking another student to agree or disagree with a student's statement

Some of these come from Jon Saphier and Robert Gower's (1987) excellent book, *The Skillful Teacher*. The book transformed much of my practice. I highly recommend it.

Bulletin Boards

The Disney Company has two requirements for all rides at its amusement parks: they must be a good show and tell a good story. People will come if you have both. It's the same for our classroom walls.

The "good show" part refers to the attractiveness of the bulletin board. Is our bulletin board enticing? Do folks want to be near it? Does the bulletin board draw their eyes? Does it create curiosity? Those of you blessed with a gene for graphic art design will find this sort of thing easy to achieve. The rest of us mild-mannered, Clark-Kent, stick-figure artists have to work at it.

A few suggestions: Have more than one color as your background. I often run out of fadeless or mural paper and have left only scraps. Arranging these in a patchwork mosaic, cutting edges so there are soft curves or harsh, jagged edges, makes for a great background. So does a whole background of wrapping paper—as long as it's not too "busy." Consider going 3-D with your bulletin boards—have objects, labels, or important concepts jut out from the bulletin board. Velcro works well for this. You can also hang items from the ceiling just in front of the board, or build minishelves into the bulletin board to hold display items.

Attach small tape or CD players to bulletin boards to offer an auditory component to the visual experience. I've used recordings of famous speeches, sections of text, poetry, radio dramas, definitions, debates, music, stories, and "What to Notice" scripts over the years.

The "good story" aspect is expressed in many different ways. This is your bulletin board's content. One of the most compelling elements for young adolescents is seeing their own names, their classmates' names, or their own culture on the bulletin board. If possible, create interest by using the students' names, their work, and/or their community in whatever's being presented—you'll get crowds. For example, when presenting grammatical concepts, use sample sentences about students or the local sports team. When presenting the proper diet and exercise program for good health, display the typical daily menu of one of your students (with permission, of course) along with his or her picture and magazine cutouts of sample foods from the menu. When presenting math concepts, incorporate elements from a currently hot movie: "Check Out the *Endeavour*'s Trajectory and Rate of Descent in Ben Affleck's *Armageddon III*." When presenting something about the Great Depression, grab students' attention with phrases from television commercials or cultural icons: "Wuzzup?! I'll tell you wuzzup: Fear and Financial Ruin!" or "Scrounging for ketchup and handouts at McDonald's?"

The best bulletin boards cause observers to think about the topics presented: "How did Pythagoras get his hypotenuse?" "What would happen if you traveled back in time and caused the death of your grandfather before he ever met your grandmother?" "Is that any way to treat a maggot?" "Do warriors cry?" (This was a topic question for our study of the novel *Warriors Don't Cry* by Melba Pattillo Beals.) According to Socrates, we have to create a sense of wonder before any thinking occurs. We can create wonder and offer substance with bulletin boards.

Beth Huddleston offers advice for new middle school teachers:

Instructional bulletin boards should emphasize only one to three points. Color, simplicity, and something that connects to the world of the middle schooler are also important for getting their attention. I have used pictures of students in our classroom or a three-dimensional of Harry Potter on a broom. I find that students love to create the bulletin boards themselves. They also like to see their work displayed. Two rules for myself: (1) When students are creating a board, let them present a plan first and offer guidance in a positive way; (2) Always receive permission from a student to display her or his work or picture. Self-concept is a major point with this age.

As much fun and substance as these bulletin boards might offer, it's important to take them down and replace them with fresh ones periodically. Bulletin boards that are up for more than a month lose their impact—they blend into the general clutter of a room and no one references them. Their staleness permeates the room, too, making everything a bit less compelling, even your dynamic instruction. Don't waste something so powerful; keep those boards changing. If you're too busy to design and change them, ask your students to take responsibility for them. What they do to create an interesting and accurate bulletin board on a given topic will teach them more about that topic than a lot of other activities would. An added benefit—they have ownership. They'll give the bulletin board more attention while it's on display.

One last idea: Bulletin boards don't have to be on your classroom walls. How about on your ceiling? I'm serious—we're talking total immersion into our subjects. When students get bored, lean back, and look away from you and to the ceiling, they'll find themselves surrounded by the concepts. How about having them taped out on the classroom floor? How about bulletin boards in hallways, in the library, and in the cafeteria? We're limited only by our imaginations.

Plants

Note your reaction when you walk into a room with plenty of living greenery, and contrast it to your reaction when you walk into a room with none of it. Living plants take the edge off the institutional nature of a classroom. We feel a bit more at peace, perhaps even more contemplative, not to mention well ventilated with all the oxygen around us.

A teacher who is disciplined and nurturing enough to have plants in the room tends to be that way when working with others. As unscientific as the claim may be, I'll stick by it: Teachers with a lot of plants in the room tend to be nice people who don't see serving others as a sacrifice, but more as a calling. It doesn't bother them to get dirty, to always water something, and to consider individual needs. They tend to be good problem solvers, too. This doesn't mean the reverse is true—no plants, no nurturing outlook—only that plant caregivers seem to already be of a nurturing mind-set.

Plants are another way to connect with students in the classroom, whether by drawing analogies between growing plants and learning each day, or by teaching students to take care of the plants. Given plant-growing responsibilities, students develop life skills otherwise not attained from most curricula, skills such as caring for living things, attentiveness, self-esteem, confidence, and awareness of what's needed for basic life—food, water, shelter, sunlight, and space. Am I making too much of the impact of caring for plants in the classroom? Not at all. Take a chance: get three or more plants for the room and ask three different students to keep those plants thriving. Regardless of academic ability, they'll more than rise to the occasion. They'll bring in and decorate their own watering cans, and they'll protect their plants with a fervor that rivals any farmer and his crops.

As far as which plants work best, I recommend Swedish ivy, wandering Jew, fittonia, aloe, dracaena, Boston fern, spider plant, philodendron, African violet, various cacti, and even a small rubber tree plant if you don't mind having to replant it outside after it grows too big. These tend to be hardy plants that are fairly adaptable to different locations in the room, and they all do well with indirect sunlight, which is usually the best sunlight you'll be able to offer. Don't forget that plants make messes that rival animal messes. Every time you water, for instance, you'll probably have overflows, drips, and soaked areas outside of the planters. Hang or set them appropriately, knowing this will happen. Ferns and some other plants shed dead leaves as well. During months of extreme weather, make sure to take home your plants if there's a long holiday. You can ask students to take them, too.

How many plants are needed? If you're just starting out, try three plants. If you're nervous about remembering to water, start with a cactus. If all goes well, boost the population of plants up to eight or so to really make a difference in the room. Double-check with students about their allergies. Some plants may trigger them.

Lighting

Lighting can make or break a lesson. If students see a glare on the television monitor and can't see the video you're showing, you're wasting their time, and behavior issues aren't far behind. If someone can't see the chalkboard with the day's assignments because the lights are off, you can't blame them for being off task. It can be subtler than this, however.

Sunlight has a full spectrum of colors, each of a different wavelength. We need that full spectrum as living creatures on Earth's surface. In many classrooms, however, there are no windows, and the room is lit with tubes of fluorescent light. Most fluorescent lights do not have the full spectrum of colors that sunlight has. They're missing the wavelength for red. This is a big deal to teachers and students because the absence of red causes animals (including humans) to produce the chemical that induces sleepiness. Peak Learning Systems educator and speaker Spencer Rogers says this comes from living in the outdoors. When the sun sets in the evening, non-nocturnal animals (diurnal) go through a physiological change in their bodies, preparing them for rest and sleep. When the sun's full spectrum returns in the morning, the chemicals for sleepiness cease production and we awaken.

The strategy for teachers, then, is to teach in classrooms with windows, and whatever we do, get those blinds open if they are closed. Even sunlight bouncing off brick walls and trees outside our room is better than no sunlight at all. If this is impossible, but the budget is there, teachers can purchase full-spectrum fluorescent light bulbs (tubes). They're expensive, however; ten dollars per tube at last check. It might take a small money grant to replace all the tubes in your ceiling fixtures.

Some students and teachers also complain about the general glare and/or flicker from fluorescent bulbs. This is a valid point. Though they burn cooler and are much more energy efficient than incandescent bulbs, they can cause problems for some people. A good compromise is to have desk and floor lamps around the room if possible, even though they are more of a safety issue than fluorescent bulbs. Talk with your administrator about having at least one "softer light" (incandescent) lamp in the room. To be honest, I prefer such a lamp on my desk for grading papers and doing lesson plans over the classroom fluorescent lights in the ceiling.

Handouts and Overheads

In most modern classrooms, there is not much excuse for faded or unreadable handouts. We have the technology to make clear prints, whether it be through photocopy machines, computers and their printers, or mimeograph machines. In a good middle school classroom, it's standard operating procedure not to skimp, not to take shortcuts, not to think, "They're only kids, they won't mind if it's messy or faded."

Teachers' handouts and overheads are one of the clearest daily indicators of their professionalism. Misspelled words, cluttered layouts, faded ink, messy corrections, poor grammar, and insensitive word choices don't just lower students' and parents' high opinions of teachers; those opinions plummet. It's very difficult to recover from such a nosedive. The message is obvious: This handout and my child's interaction with it weren't important enough to warrant careful attention to spelling, layout, grammar, ink, proofreading, and appropriate phrasing. When I look at my own children's teachers across the conference table at report card time, it's hard to concentrate on other matters if these same teachers have been lazy and unprofessional in the handouts given to my children. The negative feeling affects all subsequent interactions.

Be professional and respect your students. Write legibly or use a word processor. Proofread your handouts and overheads. Better yet, have someone else look them over. You can't do this all the time, but make sure you do it with as many as you can. Try following your own directions on those sheets—do they work? Have someone else give it a shot, and revise as necessary. Check the layout, too—is it too busy? Do your eyes naturally flow from one component to another as you'd like students' eyes to do? Is there enough space to write responses or should students answer on a separate sheet of paper? Remember, most students in middle school have larger-than-normal adult handwriting. Some are still mastering cursive. They'll need a lot of space in which to respond.

Keep to one or two fonts per page. More than two different fonts tend to be overkill, and they can be confusing. Watch where you write information, too. If you place a critical piece of information on a one-inch line written diagonally across the lower right-hand corner, you can't blame the student when he says he didn't see that direction until after the project was done. Write important information in bold, large letters and put a box or circle around them. Rather than cramming everything on one page, use both sides of the paper and include a large note at the bottom of the front page that directs students to the back side. Leave plenty of room on the page for students to write notations as needed.

Cartoons go a long way toward helping students remember the handout's content and to creating a good feeling about the assignment. They also draw attention to specific information on the page, such as when an excited cartoon face has its eyeballs focused on a specific line of text with "Wow, check this out!" written in the dialogue bubble above its head. Political cartoons and subject-specific cartoons can even communicate content under study. Start collecting cartoons from books, magazines, and newspapers to use on handouts and overheads, or buy yourself an inexpensive book on cartooning so that you can make your own.

Consider different-colored handouts as well so they can be quickly isolated from a notebook stuffed with a grading period's worth of Daily Oral Language exercises or lab write-ups from September. One caution about colored paper, however: Some companies use dyes that are not ecologically safe. If that's the case in your school, use white paper and ask students to mark along the right edge of it with a particular color of marker. Or you can color the side of the paper while it's still in its pile waiting for distribution.

Overheads have less material on them than handouts. It's often best to follow some of the rules for PowerPoint presentations such as no more than six or seven lines of text, bullet your points with single-word or phrase identifiers, and use color to call attention—red having the greatest impact. If everything is red, however, it's too distracting; the effectiveness is lost. If you attach cardboard frames to your transparencies, you can record lecture notes, answers to math problems, and other information you want to remember on the cardboard margins so you won't forget it. The frames also increase the transparency's longevity.

A great trick with overheads and chalkboards: Use a pen with permanent ink to write your math problems or language sentences on the clear transparency. Or use a computer and printer, if you like. There are colorful markers in office supply stores that will mark on chalkboards, but the ink comes off only with water. Use a marker with nonpermanent ink on the transparency, and regular chalk on the chalkboard, to work the problems or analyze the sentences. At the end of each period, wipe off the nonpermanent ink, or erase the chalk with a chalkboard eraser. This leaves the sentence or math problem in its original state, so you don't have to rewrite it for every class period.

What Do I Do with the One Computer in My Classroom?

Finances don't always match our technology desires. That's not a brick wall; we can think creatively until they do. Some schools today have computers for every child, some for every three children, and some have one computer for every classroom. There are some classrooms that do not have a computer at all. Most of us over thirty-five did very well without a computer in our childhood classrooms, so it isn't the end of good teaching and learning if we don't have one. A computer is one of many instructional tools at our disposal. In computerless classrooms, we find other ways to teach or to access the technology.

Many classrooms have at least one computer for students and teachers to use. Managing its productive use can be tricky. Ask your colleagues how they schedule the various tasks they and their students perform with the computer. You'll find some new and intelligent uses that will work in your room as well as practices that are impossible to implement with your style and your curriculum. Those suggestions may give you an idea for something else, however, so it's worth asking the question.

As for you, the teacher, the classroom computer can be your prime pipeline of communication with other staff and with parents if you have an e-mail program. You can check and respond to e-mail several times a day, even about things that were not planned as of that morning but now loom large and are happening that very afternoon—and oh, by the way, you're doing the first part of the presentation to the faculty today. Yes, it sometimes happens like that. Computer-facilitated information exchange speeds things along.

Be professional about this, however. Your greatest priority when students are in your room is to attend to those students, not to the e-mail waiting in your mailbox. While it's fun to check to see if you have mail, be mature about it. Don't give in to curiosity by constantly hovering around your machine and disregarding students and their very short time with you. If students are working quietly on something, your time is better spent monitoring their progress, checking for their misconceptions, or modeling the learning by doing the task along with them. You could also read a professional book so they see you reading for information, too. Reading and composing e-mail messages can be so absorbing and, occasionally, emotionally draining that it's hard to get back to the students and the day's lessons. Try to read and respond to e-mail when you don't have students in the room. If you do this, there's also less chance that students will read a half-composed private message on the computer monitor while you dash away for a moment to answer a student's question.

Teachers also use the computer to store grades and attendance records, compose newsletters to parents, and keep the thousands of instructional handouts they need during the course of the year: worksheets, graphs, sample paragraphs, tests, quizzes, project directions, student samples, PowerPoint and other presentation software applications, classroom signs, matrices, graphic organizers, student rosters, and forms. There are a number of excellent software packages that can do many of these things for you. Check with your technology coordinator and your department chair to see which software you have site licenses for. Ask to be trained in the software program. If you are storing grades electronically, make sure to print a hard copy of your grades every other week or after every session of adding grades to the database. Servers have a way of crashing, computers a way of deleting or freezing, and printers a way of jamming just when you've added the last of several hundred grades and right before you press the "save file" button. It most commonly occurs around report card time.

Warning: Do not, do not, do not download or install any software on your classroom computer without the permission of your technology coordinator or school principal. Many teachers have made that mistake and regretted it. They have been fined by software companies for not having a site license, or they have unknowingly downloaded or installed something that corrupted the already stored data and software, and all their hard work and that of their students is lost. You can't be too careful. My school is so concerned about viruses that we do not allow any 3½ -inch disks to be inserted into the disk drives unless we see the store's plastic wrapping around the disk coming off for the very first time, indicating its virgin use. Weekly, if not daily, we back up important files to a separate zip drive, our server, or to a set of 3½ -inch disks.

Be sure to have a locked place in the room or a nearby storage room in which to keep all backup disks and computer peripherals such as manuals, modems, mice, microphones, digital cameras, and software disks. Things tend to "wander" with so many folks using the room and computer. One strategy that works well is to provide each student with his own 3½ -inch disk (or CD, if you have a CD burner) on which to store work during the year. If you have a school server, give each student his or her own account on the server. Having an account on the server is particularly appealing because students can work on a file in one class and download and work on it in another class or anywhere in the school. They may record lab results, for example, in science class, but write up the lab in English class, or do research in the library and organize it in history class. An added benefit: schools with servers usually have someone who backs them up regularly in order to protect the data.

Students use the classroom computer as well. They can compose and store anything they write, work with tutorials, edit videos for projects, design presentations, design and establish their own Web sites, conduct research on the Internet, take notes during a lecture or while reading, see mathematical principles graphically portrayed, gather data, compose music, and create artistic masterpieces. My list is limited, given today's technological advances and our students' quick-learning "cyber-smarts." The computer can be liberating if managed well. The problems are finding time and monitoring students' efforts.

Posting a rotation schedule for who has access to the computer at specific times of the day doesn't work well in most middle school classrooms. Such assigned rotations mean that students either have to miss whatever else is going on in the room or miss their computer access at the allotted times. A student's particular sequence of learning may not be at a point where she can use the computer purposefully. In this situation, computer time is only that: computer time. It doesn't advance the student's understanding of anything. Classroom technology should advance a student's mastery of a topic or skill beyond what can be achieved without the technology. If it doesn't, the technology should be abandoned. Our time with students is too short and our curriculum too lengthy to be wasted in efforts of dubious return. It's the same issue when a teacher uses a lot of bells and whistles with a PowerPoint presentation that could've been more efficiently presented on the chalkboard.

A better suggestion is to negotiate computer time with students who need to use the computer, and post that schedule on a nearby wipeboard. For example, three students who are ready to write their final script for a dramatic portrayal of Galileo on trial in the Renaissance need to access their rough draft file this morning, and someone else may need to get a citation from a Web site before finishing his report. In these cases, the computer is a useful tool. A forced rotation schedule wouldn't be helpful. An adaptable rotation schedule, where a person or group can pass on their assigned times if they don't need the computer, may be the best bet. Sometimes all we can do is offer to let students use the computer during teacher-advisory periods, after or before school, during lunch, or during our planning periods, if students have permission from their other teachers.

To make things go smoothly, bookmark the Web sites on which students can find the information they need. This will eliminate the time spent searching and evaluating information for use. It will also be one more way to prevent student access to inappropriate sites.

Positioning the computer strategically in the room is important. If students use the computer, it has to be set up in a position that affords the teacher a clear view of what's on the monitor. Your awareness of what students are creating and accessing protects both you and the student. The problem with this is that the rest of the class can see the monitor, too, and it can be distracting. If you use the same computer as the students, there are times when you don't want students to be able to see what you're doing. You may be working on notes to parents, an upcoming test, grading student work, or responding to an emergency e-mail from the front office. So how do you set up the computer so the screen is in full view but can be made private?

One way is to connect the computer to the classroom television, if you have one. The computer sits with its back to the classroom so students can't see what you're doing when you are working on it, and the television is turned off when you are working with sensitive material. When students work on the computer, they turn on the television so we can see what they're doing wherever we are in the room. If that television is located to the side or back of the room, it won't be as distracting to classmates. We can also put the computers to the side or the back of the classroom with the screen side of the monitors facing the class. As students work on the computers, we can see what they're doing from anywhere in the room. In my own classroom, however, my students sit in groups. There is no real back to the room other than the fact that there is a wall opposite the front chalkboard. Wherever I put the computer, someone will see the screen unless I purposefully turn it around with its back to the room, leaving only four feet between the computer cart and the wall—enough space for a chair or two. The computer is in an area that I frequent during the course of every lesson, so if students are distracted by a classmate's computer work, I can turn off the television yet still check up on the student's work in a timely manner. In some years, I've made sure computers were on carts with wheels so that I could pivot them as needed.

One of the best strategies is to let students know your concerns and ask them to help you figure out the best practice for the classroom. It's a great opportunity for problem solving and discussions of Internet-access policies and personal ethics. There are also many professional resources available that have practical guidelines for computer use in the classroom. The Association for Supervision and Curriculum Development (ASCD), the National Middle School Association (NMSA), and Incentive Publications are among the best places to find books devoted to technology uses in the classroom.

Education technology expert Caroline McCullen says that some middle school teachers can be overwhelmed by how to use technology intelligently in their lessons. She reminds these folks to work in small chunks, starting with those pieces with which we are most comfortable. If the computer is attached to the television, she says, teachers can display Web pages and maps, go to art museums to see paintings and sculpture, go to science museums for pictures of artifacts and online exhibits, and take students to locations where novels and historical events occur. It's virtual, but vivid. The television projection of the computer's screen isn't just for conveying content, though. It can also demonstrate a technique or inspire students to try something. Once students have seen the technique or inspiration, they move back to their seats and respond to it.

Using the television in this manner changes the way instruction is conducted, McCullen says. Students may gather around the television in a large group or in small groups, for instance, rather than sitting in seating arrangements across the room. The trick, she says, is to develop routines for moving students around the room quickly. Once we have a system, we can teach a chunk of the lesson from the Internet with students rotating through the experience. Student groups can rotate onto the computer, too, performing assigned tasks while other students work on other tasks. McCullen recommends training a group of interested students to be "technoids" who are skilled at solving computer problems and to whom classmates can turn when trouble occurs. Technoids are told that they have to make up any work they miss while assisting others, of course, but their deadlines may be extended at our discretion. Some classes rotate the tech-noid position, she says, in order to give everyone equal opportunity and responsibility.

McCullen recommends that teachers post their computer rotation systems so everyone knows whose turn it is to use the computer(s) in the room. She advocates that students work only as singles or in pairs because more than that really can't work effectively at the screen. With the posted chart, students can regulate their use of the computer and remove that burden from the teacher, who is trying to teach a mini-lesson on the side. Students accept this as fair and are willing to wait their turn, McCullen says. She's also seen laminated passes work. A student uses the pass while at the computer, then, when finished, places it on the desk of the next person on the list. Again, there is no need to interact with the teacher with such a system. Some teachers post a chart in which students mark off or move a card to a new slot to indicate when they are done with their computer task. This enables the teacher to look from across the room and see at a glance how things are progressing and who still needs to use the computer.

If we take our classes to a large computer lab, things can get a little hairy. In one lab we had twenty-eight machines and thirty-five students processing, beeping, and burping while I ran around trying to direct them, solve problems, and answer questions. It was a whirlwind and my bones ached trying to ride it. One trick that worked, however, was to place the bottoms of two different-colored plastic cups against each other and tape them together, forming an hourglass shape. It's best if one of the cups is red. I placed one of these end-to-end cup sculptures at every computer station with the nonred color on top. The nonred color indicated that all was well—the student didn't need my assistance. When students ran into a problem and needed my help, they inverted the taped cups so the red one was on top. I was able to look down the length of the room and instantly see where the problems were. Students didn't wave their arms or call to me, which can get on our nerves after a while. It kept things calm. I still use this system today, if necessary. If you do it, remember to invert the cup after you go to a computer station and offer assistance.

One other bit of advice for the computer lab: If you want students' focus turned away from the computer, direct their knees. Computers, keyboards, mice, and the often-close quarters of a lab can be distracting. If you need students' attention, ask them to turn their knees toward you and to take their hands off the mice or keyboard. If they move their knees toward you, their bodies have to twist in order to face the computer. It's uncomfortable, so their upper bodies follow along—and face you.

By the way, in many of today's computer labs, there is one machine that is linked to all the other ones, and it is from that machine that we can "lock" the screens of all the other machines in the room. We can also send messages to the whole class or just to individual students while they work, and we can monitor what's on their screens as well. It's worth checking to see if your school has such a setup.

A final computer concern while we're on the subject: plagiarism. Copying and pasting from the Internet has become a huge issue in today's classrooms. Manipulating information and displaying it effectively for a specific audience is a useful skill, and students who do it well have a marketable talent. It's important for them to know, however, when it's plagiarism and when it's not, as well as to develop the mental acuity to use the Internet beyond just find-copy-paste-print tasks. McCullen recommends that students be taught the proper ways to ask research questions and to make sure those questions are not simple factual ones. She says that students should be asked to do something with the information gained from the Internet, not just find and report it. Also, middle school teachers need to teach students how to evaluate Web site information for accuracy and bias. The Web site www.ncsu.edu/midlink.com has a terrific tool for evaluating Web sites.

This is what technology is for—doing things we couldn't otherwise do. Imagine how technology will change our middle schools during the second half of your teaching career. Imagine the powerful learning. What a great time to be a middle school teacher!

Sharing Classrooms

Sometimes budgets and space are tight; in order to accommodate the student population, all classrooms have to be used every period of the day. As a consequence, some teachers have no rooms of their own. They move from classroom to classroom, using whichever room is free according to the regular classroom teachers' planning periods. This is an unfortunate, but fairly common, practice, and often it occurs to new teachers. Though I didn't have to move my supplies around on a cart from room to room, I did have to share a classroom during my first year. Sharing classrooms can be a positive and successful experience, provided teachers keep a few basic courtesies in mind.

First and foremost, the "host" teacher and "guest" teacher must talk regularly. Don't let things fester. For example, the host teacher covered some of your students' posted work in order to put up an instructional bulletin board. You see the value of the bulletin board, but wish she had asked you about alternative posting sites for your students' work. On another day, your host teacher starts preparing for a major class activity for the following period while you're currently in the middle of a quiet, focused lesson—and your students are watching her instead of doing the lesson. Or you have five stacks of papers you've collected during the day and your colleague doesn't like to have stacks of papers around the room. Don't give resentment a chance to breathe. Be clear about expectations and establish a relationship in which you and your host teacher can talk openly without feeling threatened by each other should situations for which you have not yet accounted occur.

Make sure both teachers have space for displaying student work, space for instructional bulletin boards, and space for supplies, both personal and professional. If your host teacher is sensitive, she will realize that you are in a tight bind space-wise, and she will offer you some of her space—a small sacrifice on her part compared with what you're dealing with in this first year. Don't be afraid to suggest it if space isn't offered, however. Folks may be lost in other concerns and not realize your need.

Whatever you do, spend extra moments every class period cleaning up after yourself and have students do the same. Leaving the room in good shape is right up there with rewinding the videotape for the next person and putting down the toilet seat. It's basic courtesy.

When the host teacher remains in the room while you teach, be thankful, not threatened. That second adult is a second pair of eyes if something goes awry, and you have someone who can watch the class for a few moments if you have an emergency phone call or need for the bathroom. Just having another adult in the room keeps students in line, too. Classes are better behaved. In addition, if your school employs any kind of peer observation program as part of its professional development program, you have a natural setup for using it.

Chad Cooper, a sixth-grade humanities teacher at Palm Middle School in Lemon Grove, California, has had extensive experience with being the "floating" teacher. He offers a number of great suggestions.

Remain positive. You have an opportunity that many teachers don't. You get the opportunity to have another educator in the room with you. This will make you more comfortable when being observed . . . I am extremely comfortable with other adults in the room with me. It makes observations and having visitors less stressful.

If the teacher is willing, use informal collaborative techniques. Last year I taught social studies and language arts in Rebekah Pogue's room. Rebekah is a fabulous math teacher. When fractions or decimals would come up in sixth-grade language arts or social studies, I would take a big opportunity to point to the fact that we were doing math in SS or LA class. Mrs. Pogue would loudly applaud. The same application works with different grades sharing rooms within the same subject.

Share supplies for students (scissors, crayons, colored pencils, compasses, etc.), but remember, it is important for each teacher to have personal teaching supplies. What about things that are in the middle? Talk with each other about classroom libraries, school-bought teacher supplies, desk space, and so on.

There needs to be sharing among nonconsumable supplies bought by the school (like scissors or pencils). If you share teacher supplies, make sure to keep things stocked. It is too easy to get in the habit of depending on the other teacher for supplies. Share big things like stereos and overheads.

You need to build rapport with your roommate. The last thing either of you should do is gossip about each other or each other's students.

Address concerns with each other. Always try to consider the other teacher's viewpoint. Administrators need to spend their time dealing with kids and our school's vision, not mediating petty teacher disputes. Try to realize that you are both in a building owned by the taxpayers, and you're both there trying to do good things for kids.

Consider doing cross-curricular bulletin boards with the other teacher. Kids need ownership in the room, even if they are in there for only one hour a day. In the middle school, students travel, too, so they really don't realize that you're there for only one period a day.

Teachers also need space on the board. Again, just because you are there for just one period a day doesn't mean that your kids can learn on one-sixteenth of the writing space in the room.

Have everything ready in each room for the next day's lesson. Bargain with your principal to get more supply money, for the many things you may need in triplicate or whatnot. This is one area where sharing a room has really helped me out. I am now very efficient and organized. I hope to keep these same habits of being ready for my students when I get my own room.

Being a traveling teacher is an extra duty; politely address this with your administrator. See if you can use this reasoning to skip an extra hall duty. You will spend an extra twenty to thirty minutes daily dealing with your constant reorganization as you move from room to room.

Establish your one prep area. It is easiest to have a home area to drop off papers and such. Maybe you can get a desk in the back of the media center or the back of another room. Otherwise you are apt to misplace many things.

Establish a homeroom where you can be found fifteen minutes before and fifteen minutes after school. Reluctant learners are just as reluctant to look for extra help after school if they have to track you down. This goes for parents, too, and it alleviates the pressure of having an all-call every time the front office is looking for you.

Talk with your room sharer about room maintenance and configuration. "CC" her with work orders or technology issues. Also, furniture rearranging can be a shocking surprise if one doesn't give proper notice.

Leave yourself plenty of time to pack up. I trained my kids to play a "fact or fib" game during the last two minutes of class as I was frantically cleaning up. This also led me to build empathy for the kids who get no time to be organized. I cannot pack up effectively after the bell rings, and neither can my students. This is one thing I hope I remember when I get my own room. Make use of table captains to patrol their personal areas while you patrol your own personal area.

Final Thoughts

The physical classroom is both test of and testimony to an accomplished middle school teacher. The first priority of the physical classroom is to facilitate instruction. The ways we shape, structure, and supply our classrooms enable or thwart our students' achievements. Those classroom structures are a vivid confirmation of what we consider important. As we evolve during our first and second years of teaching, we develop a personal style to go along with the substance of our curriculum and practice. We experiment a lot in those first years, designing an educational feng shui for what makes students and ourselves most inclined and able to pursue great thoughts and tasks while together in that room. The two greatest factors in this endeavor are our creativity and our flexibility as we adjust components for each situation we encounter. In both, we remain receptive to the input of students and colleagues but focused on our mission: developmentally appropriate instruction for young adolescents. Dirt floor, linoleum, or carpet; hut, forty-year-old schoolhouse, urban high-rise, portable classroom, or modular pods; crumbling ceiling or new ceiling; chalkboards, wipeboards, or Smartboards; desks or not enough desks, money or no money, state-of-the-art technology or no technology—it doesn't matter. As professional middle school educators, we can maximize learning with the physical space and structures we design. When we sculpt the learning environment for purposeful learning, our students soar.

5

Grade Books, Tardies, Absences, and Other Record Keeping

There is a story of an applicant for admission to a famous graduate school, who, when asked by the Dean of Admissions whether he had graduated in the upper half of his college class—replied with great pride: "Sir, I belong to that section of the class which makes the upper half of the class possible."

—Julius Cohen

A nearby school burned to the ground a few years ago. Though no one was hurt, everyone was devastated by the loss. One group of teachers was particularly troubled. They had left their grade books inside the building. Report cards were due at the end of the following week. How could they reconstruct the matrix of grades and notations from the current quarter in time? While this doesn't happen to most teachers, the fear that it could makes us protect our grade books like they were the Holy Grail. Indeed, even if they have no papers to grade, several of my colleagues take their grade books home every night.

Grades are the almighty treasure, right? Until now, most of your experiences with grades have been on the receiving end. Today you start giving them. Such power, you wield! Why, grades can . . .

Wait a minute. Teachers don't give grades—students earn them. A big difference. Please see yourself as one who helps students achieve success, offering helpful feedback in the form of grades along the way as part of the job. While on one level you are the gatekeeper with the grades you record in the grade book, on another level your decisions reflect the student's mastery as it relates to society's expectations. You speak for the community when you grade a student's assignment, and you maintain standards that assure a healthy future for both student and community. If you accept the big picture, then, you will provide frequent and varied assessments with accompanying feedback rather than develop a grading neurosis by grading everything and worrying over each half a percentage point.

Grades are a big part of our culture, and professional middle school educators pay them due attention. There are, however, ways to hold on to our first priority—learning—while maintaining order and sanity with our grade-keeping practices.

Some teachers record grades on an electronic grade book on their computer in addition to recording grades in a standard grade book. If your computer occasionally crashes or if you like to have a portable grade book for grading while traveling in addition to a centralized grade book for quick calculations and completion patterns, dual recording is a good move. Though we don't want it to be this way, feeding the always hungry grade book is a large part of how we spend our time as teachers.

We have to be careful, though. Some of us fall into the trap of equating a lot of grades in the grade book with a lot of learning, which is not always the case. There have been many grading periods in my own classroom in which students' mastery was indicated by only three letter grades in the seventh week of a nine-week quarter. The products students created were complex demonstrations of tremendous competence in a wide variety of areas, but it all boiled down to a few grades. This is okay; it does not indicate a lapse in rigor. I've also had some less-than-proud grading periods in which I had a ton of grades by the middle of the quarter but felt like we were just spinning our wheels, rarely investigating anything in depth. While the number of grades you use can vary, most middle school teachers say they need at least six different grades in order to have enough material for a valid statement of mastery (a grade) at the end of each grading period.

Setting Up the Grade Book

There are as many ways to structure a grade book as there are teachers in the world, but here are some models that hold up year after year, with good reason.

Figure 5.1 Grade Book Sample in Which the Teacher Groups Assignments by Weight or Category

	Writings (3X)			Tests (2X)		Homework (1X)			
	Essay on Energy and Matter	Dual Nature of Light Lab Explanation	Summary of Video	Test on Periodic Table of Elements	Test on Alkalinity	Vocabulary Practice	Page 23 Questions	Average	Grade
Ballard, Bob									
Carson, Rachel									
Ride, Sally									
Sagan, Carl									

Model 1: Group Assignments by Weight or Category

In modeling assignments by weight or category, there is a section for tests, one for projects, one for quizzes, one for writings, one for homework, and sections for whatever other data we want to include. When determining a grade, we average each section, multiply by its weight (indicated in Figure 5.1 by a number followed by an X), and average it with the other sections. Our professional opinion as to whether or not a student has mastered the material should be more important than a numerical average. An average is just a starting point of evaluation. If you have clear and consistent evidence that a student has mastered more or mastered less than the numerical average indicates, change the grade accordingly. You are the expert, so be clinical and decisive.

Model 2: Sequence Assignments by Date

Model 2 categorizes assignments by date. This model is for teachers who want a bird's-eye view of a student's learning progression (see Figure 5.2). It's very effective for assignments that build on earlier work, thereby providing evidence of growth. It's also a helpful format when judging patterns of achievement against other factors in a student's life such as a slide in grades because parents were out of town for two weeks. (Hint: One great way to see at a glance how students are doing in each assignment category, such as tests, quizzes, projects, writings, or homework, is to color-code the columns with different-colored highlighters, one color for each category.)

Figure 5.2 Grade Book Sample in Which the Teacher Lists Assignments by Date

	Essay on Energy and Matter 9/25	Vocabulary Practice 9/27	Test on Periodic Table of Elements 10/5	Page 23 Questions 10/6	Test on Alkalinity 10/14	Dual Nature of Light Lab Explanation 10/20	Summary of Video 10/22	Average	Grade
Ballard, Bob									
Carson, Rachel									
Ride, Sally									
Sagan, Carl									

Model 3: Sequence by Learning Objectives, Standards, or Benchmarks

Model 3 is great if your focus is on standards of learning objectives, or benchmarks from your state or district (see Figure 5.3). Place the standards or objectives at the top of a section of columns, then list the assignments underneath that column. In a heartbeat, you can tell how students are progressing with any particular standard. One problem with this model is that many assignments are complex and indicate mastery of more than one standard, objective, or benchmark. That's okay—just put the assignment in more than one place in your grade book. When using your professional expertise to decide on a grade, be sure that the grade is an evaluation of the particular skill or content knowledge indicated by the column head, not the skill or content knowledge indicated in another column.

Note: The gray squares reflect the average of the four assignments for each particular standard, objective, or benchmark. To average the final grade for the quarter, find the average of the scores in the gray boxes.

Other Grade Book Hints

The following are more suggestions for setting up a convenient and efficient grade book.

- If you have enough pages, write student names on every other line. That way you can go back and change grades without too much of a

Figure 5.3 Grade Book Sample in Which the Teacher Groups Assignments by Objectives, Standards, or Benchmarks

Standard	Analysis		Synthesis		Prediction			
	Test on Alkalinity	Page 23 Questions	Vocabulary Quiz	Summary of Metals Video	Test on Alkalinity	Inert Gases Behavior Activity		
	Essay on Energy and Matter	Dual Nature of Light Lab Explanation	Test on Periodic Table of Elements	Comic Strip of Covalent vs. Ionic Bonds	Heisenberg Uncertainty Principle Lab	Dual Nature of Light Lab Explanation	Average	Grade
Ballard, Bob								
Carson, Rachel								
Ride, Sally								
Sagan, Carl								

mess. Invariably students will redo tests and assignments or make up missed work that will require changing a grade.

- For students who join your class in the middle of the year, just add their names to the bottom of your roster in your grade book. It's not worth rewriting all those names and grades just for the sake of alphabetization. Of course if you're maintaining an electronic grade book, you can use the "sort" function to insert the names in their proper alphabetic position. Today's schools see a higher transiency rate than in past years; students come and go a lot during the course of the year. Prepare for such situations by finding an easy way to insert and delete student names and their corresponding grades, whether you use electronic or manual grade books.

- Write a note at the bottom of the first page of every class record (or staple a note to the inside cover) that explains how grades were determined. If something happens to you and you are not able to finish report cards, or if it's in between sessions or during summer vacation and a parent questions a grade, an administrator can take a quick look at your grading logic before looking at the grades, then make an intelligent response to the parent. Otherwise, you'll probably get a call from the administrator asking you to stop by the office or send in an explanation.

I write this explanation in my grade book at the end of each quarter rather than the beginning because things always change during the course of the quarter and I'd rather write the note only once.

- Photocopy your grade book once or twice a quarter and keep a copy at home. The original can get lost, stolen, or damaged. Should this happen, how grateful you'll be to have a hard-copy backup at home! If you use an electronic grade book on the computer, print hard copies every few weeks (or after every new assignment, if needed). First-year middle school teacher Joanne Payling describes an added benefit: "As a teacher, I tell my students to keep their work until they see a grade printout (approximately every two to three weeks) showing that their work is recorded, and recorded correctly. I make mistakes, and that way they can prove to me that I made the mistake. I am thrilled to correct them and raise the grade."
- If it's not convenient to use your grade book at the moment, use those sticky Post-it notes. Write your scores or grades on them, then stick the notes inside the cover of your grade book or on the corresponding class pages for careful recording later.
- Roxann Rose encourages teachers to match the marks they record in their grade books and on students' papers as closely as they can to the symbols used on their report cards. Such consistency makes it easier for teachers to grade and for parents and students to understand.

Percentages, Points, or 4.0?

The decision to use percentages (94–100 percent = A), points (370–400 points = A), or the standards-based 4.0 scales (4.0 = a description of the standard of excellence for the assignment) is really about what you want to emphasize—grades or learning. If you want Mario to explain to Mom and Dad that he would've achieved an A if he had answered three more problems correctly, use percentages or points. If you want him to state that he would've achieved an A if he had been able to make clear the connection between the economy and the South's secession from the Union, then use the 4.0 scale with its associated descriptors. Whatever the teacher emphasizes, the students will emphasize, too. If you speak in terms such as "This artwork needed to use lines and texture to affect mood, Sarah," or "Your analysis did not account for the effects of gravity as indicated in the rubric, Soraya," students will focus that way. Anything we can do to get them off the grade-myopic train, the better. With the 4.0 scale, the focus is on learning and achieving excellence, not on how many problems Katie did correctly.

By the way, statistical analysis proves that smaller scales yield higher interrater reliability. This means that a B+ in my math class is likely to be a B+ in the math teacher's class at the school across the district from me if we both use the same 4.0 scale with the same descriptors for each level. Such consistency is valuable. Smaller scales decrease subjective grade inflation or deflation.

Remember, the standards-based grading/reporting formats such as the 4.0 scale are very flexible. You don't have to use the 4.0-point scale at all. For example, you can use a 5-point scale to give a bit more flexibility and accuracy in grading, or you can decrease the scale's length to create more interrater reliability. In some cases, you may want to just use more traditional grades, A, B, C, D, and F, instead of 4, 3, 2, 1, and 0. The problem with this is the general public already has an opinion of what constitutes an A, B, C, D, or F, and those opinions may not match your descriptors for the assessment. For instance, is a 2.0 on your scale what an average student should be able to do—the image of a C grade in the public's eye? In some regions, a C indicates failure; only an A or a B will do. Maybe your description for what constitutes a score of 2.0 is the grade-level standard for excellence and the 3.0 and 4.0 scores are left for students who exceed those expectations. Using a numeric scale focused on levels of performance or achievement provides more information to students and teachers, and is easier to use than the traditional letter grades, even though it sometimes seems logical to use the letters instead. Remember assessment's true function as a teaching tool. The 4.0 scale with descriptors keeps the focus on informing and guiding instruction, not labeling products or students. Our first goal is instruction.

Achievement Versus Work Habits—Accounting for Effort?

It's really hard to be an evaluator when a student works tirelessly on a project every day for three weeks, but the project earns only a D+ on the grading rubric. Everyone's disappointed—the student, his parents, and us teachers. When it's time to grade the project, we pause momentarily to consider the outstanding effort that went into its creation. Our resolve crumbles; we fudge the grade and write C. There's not one among us who hasn't done this at least once. In the long run, however, we hurt the child by changing the grade. We never should have caved. It wasn't until my seventh year of teaching that I had enough confidence in the negative effects of incorporating work habits into final grades to stop doing it. I hope it won't take you that long to see how it subverts your goals and disadvantages your students.

Grades indicate the extent of mastery of content and skill. That's it, nothing more. Tony understands how to divide fractions very well, acceptably well, poorly, or not at all. When doing the final assessment of his mastery, we don't consider the effort it took to complete nine pages from the textbook, the hours it took to create the associated Web project, the time he spent helping peers, or the after-school work he did. The bottom line is what he can do here and now with fraction division. The grade is an undiluted report of his competence. As a parent, this is the kind of feedback I want for my own children. How can we as parents and teachers make any kind of instructional decisions for the next step in our students' development if grades aren't a pure indicator of what a child knows and is able to do? We can't. Fudging a grade for effort sends a message to the student that if he works hard but doesn't happen to achieve, he'll still meet his goals in life. What a misrepresentation this would be! When he reports for work and puts effort into everything he does but produces nothing, he'll be fired. We don't pay a plumber who comes to our home and works really hard but never fixes the sink. In fact, we don't even hire him.

Accounting for work habits is important, however, so how do we reconcile that importance with the need to have pure achievement grades? One way is to report them separately. For each subject, have a grade for achievement and one for work habits like completing homework, meeting deadlines, maintaining a learning log, heading papers correctly, and working cooperatively with others. This leads to some interesting reporting possibilities. While most of the time there is a direct correlation between a disciplined work ethic and high grades, sometimes there isn't. When a student gets an A in English achievement and a D for effort, it suggests that the course work is too simple and an alternative advanced program may be needed. This discrepancy can also occur if a student gets great grades on tests and projects but never does homework. If I weighed effort (i.e., homework completion) heavily, the final grade would be an inaccurate indicator of his content mastery, a C perhaps. If the homework did not further his understanding or help him learn, it was a waste of time for him and shouldn't have been assigned. To hold him accountable for useless homework is punitive, not instructional, and our goal is instruction. On the other hand, if a student earns a D, yet has an A for effort, something is amiss. He's working very hard but not understanding the material. This is a red flag for further diagnosis and alternative instruction. Either way, separating work habits from achievement is a valuable practice.

If we have to incorporate work habits into an achievement grade, the wisest course is to weight work habit grades with no more than 10 percent of the total grade. This seems to be a good middle ground for parents and teachers wanting to account for both. Any more than 10 percent skews the grades too much to be an accurate indicator of subject mastery.

Recording Specific Mastery of Analyzed Content and Skills

Sometimes there are particular skills or content for each student that we want to assess and record for later analysis. Using an analytic rubric instead of a holistic rubric makes sense in these cases (an example of each is provided in Appendix A). It's also wise to have a folder with multiple matrices for each student. I've set mine up at the beginning of each year and then added blank sheets as necessary. It's a good use of prep time. Figure 5.4 shows one example for an English class based on a matrix I set up when I was teaching the six traits of writing as defined by Vicki Spandel and Richard Stiggins in their book, *Creating Writers* (1997).

It doesn't matter what we teach. The idea is to maintain matrices of scores for assessments of specific content and skills that might otherwise overwhelm our regular grade book. We maintain these assessment matrices alongside our grade books. We can't crowd our grade books with these

Figure 5.4 Matrix for Specific Skills

Writing Piece:	Ideas and Content	Organization	Voice	Conventions	Word Choice	Sentence Fluency	**Score:**
Reading Autobiogr.							
Poem About Transition							
Personal Narrative							
Essay: Challenge to a Generation							
Total:							

Scale:
5 = Surpasses Standard of Excellence
4 = Meets Standard of Excellence
3 = Meets Standard of Excellence with some exceptions
2 = Does not yet meet the full Standard of Excellence, significant exceptions to the Standard
1 = Does not yet meet the Standard of Excellence
0 = Unscorable

marks—we'd run out of room after three assignments. I've kept mine by class in separate manila folders for years.

Students Keeping Records

Here's a time and sanity saver: Have students take responsibility for some of the record keeping in your classroom. They can do it, they'll do it honestly, and it teaches them responsibility and clerical skills. For example, ask them to record their own grades on their privately maintained grade sheet so they never have to ask, "How am I doing in this class?" Every time we hand back a graded paper, we can spend one additional minute allowing students to record the grade on their grade sheets. Students can also mark off papers that are turned in if we have large amounts of compiling and just want to see where everyone is. They can also count assignments, do inventories, record names, set up specialized rosters, sort files, maintain a database of book reviews or reports, grade oral presentations with a rubric (to augment our own evaluation), conduct peer critiques of student work, file papers, complete order forms and equipment requests for our signatures, record their own tardies, record reasons for not doing their homework as well as their parents' phone numbers on official forms that we provide, and maintain classroom calendars, schedules, and duty rosters. We are not helping them grow if we do everything ourselves. Sure, we might have to look over their shoulders and check their work, but it really does speed things up when we let them do some of the record keeping.

Notice that I did not mention grading other students' papers. This is one of several aspects of the job that is so sensitive it should be done only by us. We need to be sensitive to all students, even those who get good grades. Not everyone feels good about his or her grades being known by someone else in the room, let alone a whole class. By no means should we ever ask for grades to be called out across the room, nor should we return papers according to grades—A's first, then B's, and so on, which is another form of broadcasting grades and humiliation. The damage that often comes with such practices can undo months of healthy self-esteem growth, and it can tarnish a student's reputation and subsequent effort and achievement for years. This is not a trivial thing. Those who say it motivates students to try harder are teaching without regard to the developmental nature of the young adolescent—a reckless and unprofessional approach. Even in professional development courses for adults, we find it inexcusable for professors to declare grades publicly. It's a form of harassment and humiliation that has no place in good classrooms.

If you want to tell the whole school something, lean over and tell a few people to keep it a secret. It'll get around soon enough. It's the way humans are, and middle schoolers are humans in the making, not always under solid impulse control. If a classmate grades J. J.'s history test, anyone who wants to know the grade can find out, regardless of J. J.'s right to privacy. Anything recorded in a grade book is a private school-district document, protected by law. Most districts say that this protection does not extend to anything not yet recorded in the grade book. It's simple courtesy, however, to protect a student's privacy in every step of his learning process.

Protecting students' privacy includes making sure a parent sees only his own child's grades in your grade book. If a parent is looking over your shoulder as you record his child's grades in your grade book, ask him to wait a moment and tell him you'll make a copy for him. Meanwhile, cover all other students' grades. Choose courtesy over convenience and keep grades private.

Of course, in addition to protecting your students' right to privacy, grading assignments will help you see the level of mastery your students have attained. The grading and analysis of student mistakes will, we hope, affect instruction the next day. If someone else grades the papers, that intimacy with student abilities is lost, the teacher gets a superficial look at mastery, and the subsequent instruction is not as effective as it could be.

Having said all this, you'd think I never allow others to grade my students' papers. That's not correct. In crunch times and only with assignments that were not heavily weighted, I have resorted to speeding things up by allowing classmates or room parents to grade papers. I usually allow this to occur about once a quarter. I'm not proud of it, but it's one of the things that I will occasionally do in order to have time to love my wife and children, eat meals, and teach 150 students an overloaded curriculum. The goal is to avoid it, but I don't always succeed. It's the same with all record keeping in middle school—sometimes you have to take time for other things, returning papers a week or two later instead of two days later. Give yourself permission to be human. In the long run, you'll be a better teacher for your students. Organization and documentation are very important, but it's critical to be present emotionally, intellectually, and physically with your students.

Tardies and Absences

It's not a perfect world. Stuff happens, minds forget, and students arrive late to class. In the middle school, this occurs often because students are still developing independence and responsibility. We spend a large part of the short two to three years we have with our students teaching them how to manage their learning, not just what to learn.

The best lessons on punctuality, then, are structured but reasonable. First, find out from your teammates or school what is considered to be late to class: Is it coming down the hallway when the bell rings, walking through your classroom door, in the student's seat, or in his seat with assignments and writing instruments set up for learning? Whatever it is, be consistent with your teammates. Consistency will prevent repeated headaches down the road, and anything that reduces our reliance on ibuprofen is a good thing. Be as strict as you feel comfortable being, but back up what you say and document all transgressions. For most middle schoolers, it's normal to have an occasional tardy, even ones that are unexcused. With our tenacity, they'll get it right by the end of the year. When tardies become a pattern, it's time to take action. We can't see the pattern, however, if we haven't kept solid records.

Roxann Rose recommends that teachers not hold the student responsible when he is late for first period. She says it's likely to be the parent's fault when tardies occur on the way to school. Students are not mature enough to take such responsibility. "Be glad he's there," she says. "It's a terrible way to start the day to be yelled at for being late to school. It ruins everything else that day."

One strategy that works well is to have a sign-in notebook. Use a notebook set up in a corner or against a wall near the classroom door. When Travis arrives late, he doesn't have to interrupt you with explanations, excuses, or notes. Instead, he goes directly to the book and records his name, the date, the time, the number of minutes late, and why he was late. Figure 5.5 shows a sample of the one I use in my classroom. You can put four of these forms on a page in order to save paper. At my next free moment in the lesson, I can swing by the notebook and read what Travis wrote, then make an appropriate response. The notebook provides the documentation needed to see patterns. Because I check a student's explanation relatively quickly during the lesson, I've never had a student lie or write something ridiculous in the sign-in book; they take it seriously. Recording the number of minutes late and the reason for tardiness, and signing it forces students to accept the responsibility for their behavior.

Some folks like to have one page for every student and/or a section for every class. Some have students record tardies in the next available space no matter what class they're in so they can be seen chronologically for the whole class or team. Whichever sequence you choose, these make great documents to bring to parent conferences with students who struggle to be on time. Be sure to have consequences established for chronically tardy students.

Figure 5.5 Sample Tardy Record

Tardy Record

Student: _____

Date: _____

Time: _____ A.M./P.M.

Number of Minutes Late: _____

Reason for Tardiness:

Signature: _____

Once you have a system for taking care of the tardies the moment they occur, spend a few more minutes establishing a roster of student names with places to record tardies and absences. This might be a section of columns in your grade book, another grade book converted to attendance recording, or something else. It's prudent to transfer attendance records to one central location for easy reference. Again, we catch patterns of attendance issues that would otherwise go unnoticed and we have documentation in case there is a question about it later. For recording in your attendance record, try using "A" or "Abs" for absent, "T" for tardy (or "ET" for excused tardy and "UT" for unexcused tardy), and "LE" for when students leave early.

Important: Take roll every single period! At any given moment, a school should know exactly where a student is located, and the teacher is the school's officer in this endeavor. It's very embarrassing for a teacher to mark someone present when she is not, or mark someone absent when she is present. More important, however, it's a safety issue. A student may be skipping class or school, become sick in the bathroom, or otherwise be in need of help. If we take roll, then we discover absences and can take action in a timely manner. It's also a demonstration of our commitment to students. Imagine not even realizing someone was absent today—what message does that send? A loud message that the person isn't memorable. Before I get on my soapbox, however, know that almost every day I have at least one student I can't account for; that is, I can't remember whether or not they were in class. It's hard to keep up with all 150 students every single day of the year, but it's important that we try.

Figure 5.6 A Chart for Recording Tardies and Absences by Period

Tardies and Absences	
Period 1	Period 5
Period 2	Period 6
Period 3	Period 7
Period 4	Period 8

Another method for keeping track of tardies and absences is to create a chart on which you record names of absent or tardy students for each class period (see Figure 5.6). At the end of the day or during your planning period, you can compare your list to the list compiled by the attendance person for the whole school. If a name doesn't match, investigate.

By the way, hall passes are another way to keep track of students. Some schools use professionally made hall passes with large cards on plastic trays that students take with them. Students can record their names, the time, date, and destinations on the card, and teachers put their initials on the cards indicating their approval. Adults can check these passes as they encounter students in the hallways. If you don't have such passes, many professionally published assignment notebooks have the same setup in the back pages, and those notebooks can be used as hall passes. Using the notebooks as hall passes helps students remember to bring those notebooks to class.

Another great hall pass idea is to have a unique object with your name and classroom number on it. The object sits at the front of the room and students take the pass when they leave, returning it to the front of the room when they return. Students may leave the room only if the pass is available. This keeps the number of students leaving the room down to one or two, depending on how many of these objects you have. In the past, I've used an old hiking boot, a piece of round wood decorated as a pizza, a large C decorated by a student—the C standing for Crusaders Team—, a piece of rectangular wood decorated as a book, a decorated Frisbee, and a toy fish.

Making Up Missed Work

Despite our best efforts to keep students healthy and present, some will miss school. Student absences may be not only annoying because of all the makeup work that we need to facilitate, but also a real threat to success for the absent student. For some students, absenteeism is a chronic issue that makes an already challenging curriculum into a futile and exhaustive pursuit, similar to humans trying to fly by flapping their arms. There's more reward in giving up.

Some teachers lay the burden of completing makeup work on the shoulders of their absent students. If they really understood the nature of young adolescent learners, however, they would see that many of them are not mature enough to accept such a challenge. Sure, they want to take the steps to complete the makeup work, but the structures and initiative to do so are not yet developed. It's not enough to say to Danny, "You were out for three days. Make up the missed work or you get an F on all of it." Danny might be eager to complete the tasks, but he doesn't know how to begin. As a middle school teacher, this is a life skill we must purposefully teach. To say, "I told you so," when Danny bombs the quarter because of missed work and learning is a weak and punitive response. If we're out for student success, then we need to give them tools to achieve it. Ask your colleagues what they do for absent students. Here are a few suggestions.

Homework buddies Make sure every student has two homework buddies in every class. It's an old-fashioned name, but it's what we've used in a number of middle schools and it works. These buddies are two people the absent student can call to ask about homework on days that are missed. Everyone gets two individuals' names and phone numbers (and/or e-mail addresses) in the first week of school. It's important that students have two homework buddies in every class in case one is absent as well or did not get the homework or the learning for some reason.

Internet posting services There are many high-quality, free Web sites for teachers where they can post assignments, announcements, reviews, electronic flash cards, tests, advice to parents, study strategies, and anything else that might be helpful to students who were present in school, let alone those who are absent. The Web sites www.schoolnotes.com and www.blackboard.com are particularly useful in my district. One of the advantages of providing this service is that students can check the sites twenty-four hours a day, seven days a week, from anywhere in the world. Parents can check the site from work if they have Internet access, so everyone's in the loop. Many parents who do not have access at home or work will go to the public library or community center at least once a week to see how things are going. Since I started using such services several years ago, there's been a dramatic increase in homework completion. An added benefit: When parents know what is going on in our classrooms, they're much more supportive, which is always a good thing.

Copies folder(s) Anytime you give students something such as a work-sheet, project directions, or printed announcements, put copies in a box or place in the classroom where students who are absent can get them when they return. Some teachers have a folder for each day of the week. Because of the paper shuffle and the fact that we're working with humans in the making, I often run five to ten extra copies of every handout and place them in these folders or boxes. They come in handy when someone comes to me in a panic after having lost the directions for the project due the next day.

Class scribe (also known as makeup work expert) Choose one student each week to make a second copy of the daily homework assignments and to be responsible for helping students get caught up with makeup work when they return. These students can explain lessons, obtain supplies, and answer any questions returning students may have about missed lessons. Scribes help those students who were absent "on their watch," which may or may not be the current week. Most likely it will be the previous week. When I've done this, everyone ends up being "on duty" for two weeks out of the entire year.

Review previous learning This is obvious, but we don't always take the time to do it. One way to help those students who've been absent to get back into the flow of things is to incorporate a minireview of the previous days' learning in each new lesson. This helps students who were there, too, as the brain focuses on content with which it is familiar. If that previous background is activated, students are more inclined to pay attention and receive the new learning.

Phone and E-mail Logs

Think about this: In the corporate world, we'd be CEOs or at least among the higher management ranks if we were in charge of 150 or more work-ers. Middle school teachers have a high-stress, high-responsibility job in which a lot depends on thinking clearly. Just as corporate CEOs do, we need to keep logs of all our contacts in order to follow up on promises, pur-

Figure 5.7 Sample Contact Log

Parent(s) Name:	Parent of:	Date:	Phone/E-mail:
Summary:			

sue goals, and document the progression of a problem and its response. In today's world, many of these contacts come from phone calls and e-mails.

In my two decades of teaching, I never developed the consistency that it warranted, but I tried to maintain a contact log of every phone call or e-mail conversation made between a student's parent and myself. In each entry I would list the name of the parent, the phone number or e-mail address, the student, date, time, and a short summary of the call (see Figure 5.7). You can easily fit four of these logs on one sheet of paper. Over the years, it has been an invaluable resource at parent conferences, planning sessions, and for student assessments and instruction. Some teachers carry their logs with them wherever they go in the building and take them home at night. I don't seem able to remember to bring it everywhere I go, so I carry a small notepad, record the conversation or e-mail, then stick the note in my log for later transfer.

Palm Pilots, PDAs, and Other Handhelds

In some classrooms, the former chalk and slate have become a Palm Pilot and its stylus. In the last few years, more students are bringing such devices to school. While a few might be using them as toys, most students are using them as serious time- and work-management tools. The most common use is as an electronic assignment notebook tracking assignments, deadlines, and reminders. If these devices are becoming popular in your community, it might be wise to provide docking ports for handhelds to hook up to your classroom computer to download material from your machine to the handheld device or vice versa.

The technology for handhelds is evolving at an amazing rate. Very soon, if not already, many students will submit homework from a handheld and they will expect feedback the same way. The great part is that there are now ways to download directions for assignments and individual grade reports to handhelds, and they can be used to gather data in the field; graph results; play back video clips with narrative analysis; access encyclopedias, reference materials, and the Internet; and assist learning-disabled students as they take notes. This is one more case in which technology really seems to have a positive impact on student success.

Veteran middle school teacher Mendy Gannon uses her Palm Pilot in other ways. In a recent posting on the middleweb.com listserver, she writes,

> My Palm has become my portable memory. Our team keeps our contact info on the students in our address book and we use the note function to keep track of phone calls. I keep all my locker numbers and combinations on a spreadsheet so that it's handy when they ask me. The team is working out a way to store discipline info (we have a "step" program) consistently in a shared document. Teacher's PET from www.coffeepotsoftware.com is indispensable to me—it's wonderful to have my grades with me all the time, especially when I run into a parent while out and about, or when I export grade reports to Excel for printing. I sprang for WordSmith (www.bluenomad.com), as it has the feel of Microsoft Word—complete with basic formatting (italics, bold, underline, bullets) and use my Palm for word processing frequently (I also have a keyboard). Can't imagine doing without it.

Check out the new world lexicon and applications eighth-grade social studies teacher Carolyn Beitzel uses to describe her use of her PDA:

> I use my PDA every day for attendance, grades, discipline, and parent contact. I purchased a program from adlsoftware.homestead.com called Suite for Teachers for $30. It has six different programs, all to manage your daily teacher life. It interfaces with a software (included) called TBR reports, which prints out discipline reports for you. I also have Documents to Go, which allows me to hotsync Word and Excel documents from my PC to the PDA. I use Excel for grading and Word for lesson planning, notes, etc. If you purchase print software you can also print directly from the PDA to an infrared printer without cables. My school also has a site license for a grading program that this year I am going to put on my PDA, and that way I can use the Macs at school as well. Don't forget to get a keyboard as well. This makes getting the information into the PDA much easier than using the language shortcut or the touchkeyboard

on the PDA. I have a Handspring Visor, which is compatible with any Palm software. It has been great for me. When I get that call from the principal about an issue, all I have to do is look it up on my PDA and I am set to go. I can document EVERYTHING, which is a plus, since my brain is usually on overload and I can't remember a thing!

Record keeping is initially a daunting task, enough to make some of us run for the hills. As we move through our first year, however, it gets easier. We become comfortable with the systems we've established, though they may need revisiting at the start of every year we teach. We discover how valuable accurate and frequent record keeping can be. With well-maintained records we can make the timely and instructionally sound decisions that help our students to achieve.

6

Grouping

There's an old (business) school stunt, in which a professor presents his students with a jar full of jelly beans and asks them to guess how many there are. Their answers are always wildly inaccurate, but the average of those guesses—the class's collective guess—is invariably within three percent of the correct number.

A couple of years ago, Norman Johnson, a physicist at Los Alamos National Laboratory, sought to quantify this phenomenon in an experiment of his own. Using a computer simulation, Johnson built a maze that could be navigated via many paths—some shorter, some longer. He had a group of individuals wander through the maze one by one, trying to find their way out in the least number of steps. The first time through, it took the average person 34.3 steps to get out. The second time through, it took the average person only 12.8 steps.

Johnson then took all the choices each person had made at every turn in the maze and went with the majority vote, to arrive at what he called the group's "collective solution." That path was just nine steps long. In subsequent trials, Johnson found that the bigger and more diverse the group, the smarter the collective solution was.

—Quoted from the New Yorker *magazine, October 9, 2000,*
posted on the middleweb.com listserver

Every new teacher's nightmare: You're working with a quiet group of students at the side of the classroom while a small group of students on the far side of the room is supposed to be working on a group task. Unbeknownst to you, however, they are terrorizing a classmate, editing your grade book, stealing office passes from your desk, and accessing inappropriate Web sites. You look up for a moment only to see your principal standing in the doorway holding a surprise evaluation form while staring first at you then at the misbehaving group then back at you, his face turning red, his brow furrowed.

You wake up in a cold sweat, slow your heartbeat, and talk soothingly to yourself, repeating it was only a dream . . . only a dream.

And it is. This sort of thing just doesn't happen in most middle school classrooms. It's not worth spending energy worrying about it. We can train our students to work in groups successfully, supervising themselves. With such positive effects on instruction, grouping students from time to time is worth doing—and first-year middle school teachers like you can do it well.

Reasons for Grouping

Purposefully grouping students, whether it's with the class as a whole or in small groups for specific instructional experiences, is worth the time spent doing it. Strategic grouping is one of those important elements of good middle school instruction that we often forgo when we're lost in a swarm of urgent standards, assessments, parent phone calls, and paperwork. At such times, grouping students doesn't seem like the meat of our lessons, so we spend more time on that opening hook, worksheet, or assessment and group students by default: that is, however they're currently grouped or not grouped.

In America, we educate everybody, not just the lucky or the privileged. It's one of our hallmarks as a country. To achieve such a noble cause, we have to set up schools in such a way as to facilitate effective instruction for the masses. While mentoring students one-on-one in the apprentice–journeyman–master craftsman tradition is probably the best education approach available, we do not have enough teachers or facilities to provide such instruction for everyone. Instead, we group students into classes and group classes into schools. We get it down to one teacher for every 100 to 170 students, spread among four to six classes or, in elementary schools, one teacher with thirty students, teaching multiple subjects.

Still, we can't teach properly with those numbers. We have to break those twenty to forty students in each class down to smaller groupings in order to meet the unique needs of young adolescents. While teaching the whole class can be highly effective, it's not appropriate 100 percent of the time.

Remember that young adolescents crave positive social interactions with peers and meaningful participation in school. Cognitive scientists claim that the brain is innately social, requiring interactions with others in order to bring meaning to content, which allows information to be stored in long-term memory. Learners cannot be passive recipients and still learn well. Teaching students as a whole group or asking them to learn independently, while sometimes effective, does not provide enough opportunity for meaningful engagement with classmates. Sure, we might think we have more control when students are all in their seats and focused on us, but in reality, we lose their attention and sacrifice their achievement when we don't give them positive social interactions and meaningful, participatory experiences. We provide such experiences when we place students in smaller groups.

Middle schoolers navigate emotions, society, and growing up by interacting with others. In socializing, they belong, and belonging to something means security in a time of their lives when they want to both stand out and be normal. The social give and take helps them form an identity; self-worth is often defined in light of what others think. Because social interactions shape students' personal view of themselves and their studies, we want such experiences to be healthy, and we want students to develop the skills necessary to handle difficult social interactions in positive ways. On a practical note, we might as well harness all the energy our students devote to socializing for something that advances them personally and academically, rather than let it manifest as an irritating group of talkers in the back of the room. Grouping and regrouping students over the course of a unit of study and coaching them in the skills for successful group interaction are among the most useful and developmentally appropriate experiences we can facilitate.

Does this mean we never teach the whole class at a time? No. Time, teacher-student ratios, facilities, and other aspects of being an institution require us to do whole-group instruction most weeks, and good learning does occur in whole-group teaching. In addition, there are some experiences that require a critical mass of twenty to forty students in order to be effective: simulations, demonstrations, lectures, guest speakers, panels, performances, and some instructional games. The issue, then, is to keep a balance of whole-group, small-group, and independent experiences in order to be instructionally sound and developmentally responsive. What tends to happen is that middle school teachers use one approach with which they are comfortable and rarely venture into the other two approaches. Develop teaching dexterity, and prod yourself to use whole-class, small-group, and individual instruction.

Group Membership

Consider students who are at the same point of mastery regarding a topic. If we present them with material beyond what they are developmentally ready to receive, nothing we teach is moving to long-term memory. If we present them with material they've already mastered, we're wasting their time and our time, and we might be alienating them from the subject or school in general. It's disrespectful. If we match instruction to their readiness level, learning occurs. For the sake of effective learning, we sometimes group students according to their readiness level.

If we want a valid indicator of what students understand about a topic, we ask them to demonstrate mastery in a way best suited to them. We don't want them to struggle with the assessment format or with their expression of content. Because of this, we might group students by similar academic strengths when asking them to demonstrate mastery. When students are grouped according to strengths, they can clarify their understanding of the topics with one another in ways best suited to them, such as when making analogies: "Okay, so what you're saying is that the carburetor of a car is like the measure signature for a musical piece. It regulates the rhythmic firing of the pistons, like the measure signature regulates the timing of the notes in music."

Students in like-minded groups respond powerfully to learning, demonstrating a greater mastery than could be achieved working independently. A group of kinesthetic middle schoolers who build an amazing three-dimensional model of a system of government with its checks and balances have learned much more than if they were asked individually to answer comprehension questions about the same system.

Differentiated Instruction Groups

In differentiated instruction practices, there are three general ways to group students. We can group them according to learning profiles, to interests, or to readiness.

Learning profiles refer to students' multiple intelligences, personality types, learning styles, and similar attributes that make their learning unique. That profile might also include attributes not readily identified by surveys and instruments, however, including unique ways of thinking, such as seen in students who are unusually pragmatic, eccentric, or myopic in focus. For a number of years, I had a number of eleven- and twelve-year-old students coming through my classroom who had only recently started going to a formal school; they had been soldiers in Central America before escaping to the United States. This would be something to add to the learner profile I maintained on these students. Some of my students have been gang or wanna-be gang members, and some have come from impoverished homes. Some have parents who were high-level scientists, politicians, engineers, and business leaders in their countries of origin, but here in America they work the nightshift cleaning the office building next door. Some have demonstrated mental illness or are dealing with a close family member's illness or death, and some are living in local homeless or protection shelters. Some have severe test anxiety, some were fetal-alcohol babies. Some have unshared phobias, and some have issues with members of the opposite gender. All these factors are part of students' learner profiles.

How do we become aware of such attributes in our students? Being with students in a variety of situations works well. As the proverb says, "We learn more about a person after one day with them climbing a mountain than we do in one month living with them in a valley." We also need to facilitate regular and nonthreatening forms of communication, such as learning logs, confidential folders, and e-mail. If you're interested in surveys and other instruments that get your foot in the door with students' academic proclivities, see Chapter 2, "What to Do on the First Day and in the First Week."

Interests refer to the common interests among students—hobbies, backgrounds, preferred literature genre, sports, and musical groups. In order for information to move to long-term memory, it has to be meaningful. Students who get to interact with their personal interests find meaning in what they do, resulting not only in increased motivation but long-term retention of information. They make connections and think with more complexity because of the lesson's piquancy. If a group of students is really into basketball, then asking them to draw analogies between basketball and the topic of the lesson becomes enticing and even illuminating, not just one more part of school to endure until the bell rings.

Readiness is used to indicate where students are in their mastery—just beginning or well down the road of understanding. Notice that we use *readiness* and not *ability*. Ability suggests something innate and permanent, while readiness indicates something temporary, capable of changing: "I'm not ready now, but I will be soon." Using *readiness* is a healthier approach when working with students in transition, such as we find in middle schools. Students see their competence as a process and as changeable. There shouldn't be a stigma associated with a beginner's competence level.

When grouping according to readiness, keep track of which objectives students have mastered. For instance, there are five essential skills you want students to master in a given lesson, but some students are ready to pursue only three. Hold those students accountable for only the three and record the remaining two. Then, at some later point, make sure to spiral back with those students to teach them the not-yet-mastered concepts and skills. This is not watering down the curriculum; it's teaching intelligently. You're holding those students accountable for the same five objectives, but not at the same moment in time. You're teaching the material when students are ready to receive it, which means it will be learned—your bottom-line goal. What students take with them is more important than what or when you teach. Teach in a way in which they'll take the knowledge with them.

When we group by readiness, do we always have one group well down the road of mastery, another a few steps behind them, and one just beginning to learn about the topic (as ability groupers might do with high-, medium-, and low-achieving students)? No. We group according to what we've determined from preassessments. We might have four groups who've mastered most of the material and need more complex lessons, and one group just beginning to explore the topic. We might have the reverse in other class periods. I tend to lose my sanity when there are more than five groups, so I try to keep the number of groups to five or less. Sometimes that means only two groups, or maybe one group, with unique approaches for four different students. Most of the time, I start out with two or three groups, keeping open the option to have more or fewer, as warranted during the course of instruction.

Remember that group membership is dynamic, not static. As we work with groups and individuals, we monitor their learning progress. If we find that one group has outgrown the place where one member is comfortable, or that one group member has moved beyond where the rest of the group is comfortable, we remove that student, telling him we know he's frustrated and we are going to place him in another group in which he'll find success. Rather than feeling stigmatized, students most often express relief accompanied by an eagerness to do well in the new setting. Remember, middle schoolers crave competence. Moving them enables them to achieve. If we have a classroom atmosphere that embraces differences among learners, it's even easier to do. Students see that we are out for their success, not to be punitive or ridiculing. Young adolescents are making such quick, erratic, and big cognitive leaps, we can't be successful as teachers without permeable group membranes.

Contextual Learning

One last important reason to group and regroup young adolescents: Learning is contextual. We associate learned information with the physical environment in which we learn it. College campuses understand this concept. They allow students to study for tests in the evenings in the rooms in which they'll be taking their exams the next day. If university sophomore Alicia reviews the

Krebs cycle while looking at the exit sign of that room, the information will be triggered by that sign when she looks at it the next day while taking her biology test. In our middle school classroom, if Jeff learns about exponents while staring at our wall of math cartoons, he will associate exponents with math cartoons. Whenever he sees those cartoons, he'll be reminded of exponents. When you move him to another portion of the room, Jeff has one less access point to the information. Now he's staring at the fire extinguisher and he's with another set of classmates. He can't access the information as easily. If you move Jeff around a bit during the course of instruction, however, and he experiences the same content in different contexts, his brain develops its own dexterity with the topic, learning how to call upon its own resources to retrieve the information instead of relying on external stimuli.

Some teachers move students to new seats with new classmates every two weeks. While this is a nice goal, I don't always make it. Rearranging students' seats once a month is about all I can handle. Maybe you can do better. Even within one class period, however, we can ask students at the north and east sides of our desk clusters to exchange seats for twenty minutes with their counterparts at other desk clusters. Or maybe, "Students with verbal-linguistic proclivities move over by the window, and those with interpersonal proclivities move their seats to the front of the room." These groups last from five to thirty minutes or more, then students move back to their home positions. Interacting with content in a variety of contexts and with varying classmates is an effective strategy. It's nice if the facility supports such practices by not bolting the desks to the floor or making tables so heavy they can't be moved, but if this is the situation in your classroom, don't let it stop you from moving the students themselves.

Homogeneous Versus Heterogeneous

Homogeneous grouping is not a dirty word in well-designed middle school classrooms. It's completely supportive of the middle school concept.

Wait a minute, you say, aren't middle schools supposed to avoid tracking students through subjects? Aren't they all about heterogeneous grouping? Am I committing "middle school concept" sacrilege?

Not at all. Sure, we don't want to group kids according to labels and keep them isolated from one another day after day, week after week. *Turning Points 2000* (Davis and Jackson 2000), *Great Transitions*, and a host of other evidentiary reports make convincing arguments against such homogeneity in middle school classrooms. The homogeneous grouping that I'm talking about refers to the mini-lessons and amoebalike groups that we purposely form in the course of instruction to help students with specific learning.

When we grade essays, for example, we might find that nine students don't understand the idea of presenting a main idea followed by adequate supporting details. While the rest of the class works on another activity, we pull those nine students to the back of the room and do a fifteen-minute minilesson with them. We might meet with this same group four or five more times in the next seven days. This kind of temporary homogeneous grouping is developmentally responsive to young adolescents. Temporary groups can last anywhere from two minutes to two weeks or more.

Heterogeneous classes are the best way to go for the many reasons cited in the reports mentioned above. The one subject in middle schools that seems to still be in question, however, is mathematics. Current research does not show the same significant gains in student achievement in heterogeneous grouping in mathematics classes as it does with other subjects.

Be careful with assumptions, however. The lack of clear positive gain does not mean heterogeneous grouping in mathematics is detrimental. I've seen highly effective instruction in both homogeneous and heterogeneous math classes. The teachers in the heterogeneous classes employ the best practices of differentiated instruction like compacting the curriculum, using open-ended activities, flexible grouping, respectful tasks, scaffolding, and tiered lessons. Their students perform well. If both ways of grouping kids work equally well, I'd still go with the heterogeneous grouping, given the positive impact on affective elements of students' growth. It's closer to the real world and there's opportunity for modeling of successful learning and coping strategies from all students in the room.

How Do We Keep Student Groups on Task When We're Not Directing Them?

In our world economy, teaching students how to work in groups is among the greater gifts we teach. Young adolescents don't come to us fully equipped for group success. Some middle school students need a great deal of guidance. The quick answer to the question above is that we don't. In great middle school classes, the teacher doesn't supervise every group every minute. She teaches students to do it themselves. Let's take a look at several effective experiences that teach students how to conduct themselves in a group.

Fish Bowl Activities

In a Fish Bowl activity, a small group of students gathers in the center or front of the room where everyone can see them. They perform a task

(Socratic Seminar, debate, novel study, project design, dramatic presentation, experiment, study session, peer critique) while their classmates observe individuals' behaviors to see what helps and what hinders group success. Usually this analysis is done against an already identified list of successful behaviors, often in rubric form. These behaviors may have been brainstormed with the class earlier in the day, or they may have been given to them as is.

The students in the small demonstration group may be portraying roles given to them by the teacher. These roles are ones that the teacher wanted to highlight for some reason, either to emulate or to avoid. They include the incessant talker, the whiner, the diplomat, the quiet one, the daydreamer, the manager, the "yes man," the courteous group member, and any other role likely to occur.

Once the demonstration is over, the observers tell the "fish" what they noted about their behaviors in the group. The teacher facilitates the conversation, focusing on what to do and what not to do in order to be successful.

The next step is to divide the class into two pairs of groups (a total of four groups). The class is divided in half and each half is divided into two groups: A and B. The pairs identify one of its groups as Group A and the other as Group B. Group A then performs a task together and unscripted for ten to twelve minutes while Group B observes, once again recording individual group member responses on a rubric of exemplary behaviors. The demonstration group members are trying to portray successful behaviors. At this point, it's helpful to assign one observer student to watch one specific demonstration student during the task. Then the groups switch places, Group B doing a task while Group A observes and completes the rubric. After all four groups have an opportunity to perform the task and observe each other, the observation notes are shared.

Videotapes

Videotape a group performing a task, then lead students through a non-emotionally distorting discussion of what worked well and what didn't. You can also videotape one group while working with another, then watch the tape privately later to monitor the group's success. Small groups that have a camera recording their behavior tend to stay on task.

Cooperative Learning Strategies for Groups

For great ideas on how to set up groups for instruction, consult books on cooperative learning. I recommend books by Spencer Kagan, Robert

Slavin, or Johnson and Johnson. The basic foundation of the approach is the successful grouping of students. They'll offer ideas such as making sure that each group member has a role in the successful completion of the group's task. Cooperative learning activities also help students understand what it means to be successful and unsuccessful group members, then motivate them to participate successfully. In the larger world, making positive contributions to one's group and dealing with conflicts in a healthy manner are just as important as learning how copper wires wrap around a nail and attach to a battery to magnetize that nail. Cooperative learning tasks are preferable to group tasks that can be executed by one or two eager students while the others sit, watch, then later take equal credit for the effort. Some cooperative learning programs also advocate assigning a role, such as time-keeper, reporter, or facilitator, to each group member.

Small Beginnings

If your six- to eight-person groups aren't working, try a structured interview between two students, in which each student takes a turn asking the other a question and recording the response on a sheet you collect. When the partners have the give-and-take of conversation down, try giving them a topic that doesn't have scripted questions but rather has a menu of questions from which they can choose. In another session, ask them to design their own questions before the next conference. When they've mastered this, combine the partners into foursomes with that menu of questions. You may still want students to record what each other says at this level as both a way to reflect and a way to hold them accountable to each other and to the process. Also consider keeping the first small-group task short, from five to seven minutes, then working your way up to twenty-five or more minutes.

T-List or T-Chart

Draw a line down the center of a large writing surface that all students can see. A short way from the top of this vertical line, draw a perpendicular, horizontal line across the first line, making a large *T* out of the two lines. Above the horizontal line on the left side, draw an eyeball and above the horizontal line on the right side, draw an ear. On each side, list the positive attributes you are seeking in small-group work. Under the eye, have students list what could be seen if the group was successful. Under the ear, ask students what could be heard if the small group was successful. Once created, reference the T-list (or T-chart) before, during, and after the small-group experience, reflecting on what was achieved and what still needs improvement. See Chapter 3, "Discipline," for an example and further discussion of T-charts.

Literature

Find and read aloud (or have students read aloud) stories or poems about groups working well together. It's safe to hear how others do it while comparing it to your own efforts in a group. Young adolescents respond very well to stories as illuminators, and they personalize the messages easily. You'll find significant results in the very next group session, whatever the task.

Final Thoughts

Grouping for instruction can be done intelligently to great effect or haphazardly to great detriment. Seek the advice of colleagues and take it slowly. Experiment in your own practice with groups of two and their analysis at first. Realize that students need to experience content individually, in small groups, and as part of the whole class. With experience, you'll grow those famous teacher's eyes in the back of your head that will sense when groups on the far side of the room need your attention. It pays to move around frequently, however, in order to ensure every group's success. Carry around a small notepad to record the things students say and do that promote successful group work, then share your affirmations with the class. Make sure every group has a clearly defined task as well as a physical product to present to you once they are done.

Loneliness is a problem for many young adolescents these days. Belonging is crucial to everything they do, including academics. The need to belong will transcend cognition and positive forms of relating to others if not compassionately facilitated. Prepare them for the world by exposing them to varied groups over time and giving them the skills necessary to navigate those waters.

7

Teaming

I used to assume that the trust just evolved over time and that once you had it, it would remain. Now I think that you must continually nourish the relationships to keep the energy and spirit flowing in any team. If I had to say what the prerequisites were for a healthy team, I think I'd say mutual respect and honesty. If those elements are present, I think you can work through all the stress and daily wear and tear. A sense of humor that allows you to laugh together and at yourselves is very helpful too.

—*Deborah Bambino, middle school educator and author*

A large laminated calendar of the current month hangs next to the team's meeting table during their planning period. Science teacher Jan Blake holds the black felt-tipped pen as she pauses while recording big assignments and tests on the calendar. She turns to Steve Cantor, the team's history teacher.

"We have a huge animal taxonomy project due on Thursday," she says. "I can move it to Friday if your political cartoon project is so big that having my project on top of it would make for an ugly Wednesday night for the students."

Steve nods. "It might. If you're okay with it, let's split them up, my project due on Thursday, yours on Friday."

"Just to let you know," Gail Warren interjects, "I'm giving a small-slope, y-intercept quiz on Friday. They should be able to do it and get your project done, Jan."

"Thanks, Gail," Jan responds and records the quiz and taxonomy project on Friday's square. "Anything else?"

When no one says anything, Jan moves to the next item on the meeting's agenda. She looks to Scott Greenwood, the team's English teacher.

"Scott, do you have the bibliography forms you'd like all of us to use when we assign research projects?"

"Yes," Scott replies and distributes two handouts to each team member. "Here's a copy for each of you. I also threw in the editor's proofreading marks that we use for editing rough drafts. All students on our team use these marks. They are the ones that professional newspaper editors use. Please ask students to use them in your classes, and if you can, use them yourself when responding to student writing in your classes."

"Consistency, right?" Steve says.

"Exactly."

Sharon Lowell, the team's Learning Disabilities specialist, leans forward. "This reminds me, did anyone ever teach our students to edit in waves rather than looking for everything all at once?"

"You mean reading through a draft looking for just one thing, like comma problems, then reading it again but this time looking for something else, like spelling?" Gail asks.

"Yes. It seems to work better for students with disabilities in reading and writing," Sharon replies.

"I don't think we did officially," Scott says, "at least not in my class."

"We've reviewed editing in waves in my math class," Gail says. "It works well for most of my students, not just those with disabilities."

The five of them nod in agreement.

"Then let's do it. Let's make wave editing a technique in all of our classes," Steve concludes.

"Agreed," Jan responds. "If anyone needs assistance in how to use it effectively in their subject area, can they come to you, Scott?"

"Sure. Sharon and Gail teach it as well. They'd be another source," Scott replies.

"Good point. Thank you to all three of you for helping us with it," Jan says. "Our final item: Jenny Richards. Her mom is coming in tomorrow for a follow-up meeting to see how she's doing after our conference a month ago. As you recall, we had identified four modifications to lessons that we promised to use with Jenny in order to get her back on track. Let's hear what's worked and what hasn't worked so far. Gail, how are things with Jenny in math class?"

Rationale

Imagine the positive health of a child when teachers coordinate projects and tests so the world doesn't crash around them. Imagine the powerful retention and connections that are achieved when every team member is teaching the same techniques and messages. Imagine the sense of camaraderie when every voice is accepted as important to the group's success. Imagine the clarity of thinking and subsequent sound decisions that are achieved when students are considered by many adults in multiple contexts. Now imagine what is lost by never getting together in the first place.

I'll admit my bias right away: Teaming is the way to go. With teaming, we share the wisdom and the work, and the focus is on the students, not just our subjects. It makes teaching and learning a lot more enjoyable and effective. Students feel like they belong to this large endeavor called school, and that they are known well by the adults in their lives. Our collective wisdom as a team enables us to plan for at-risk students, as well as to coordinate assignments, tests, special events, and discipline. We improve the quality and frequency of communication with home, and we increase the number of scheduling options, should we need to move a student or group of students from one period to another.

One of the greatest aspects of teaming is the ability to use everyone's talents. Each of us is just one person with just one set of life experiences and skills. Together, however, we have two, three, even five times the amount of strategies to use and knowledge to share. The connections and new discoveries generated by such exchanges amount to more than the sum of us individually. When we have a pool of three or four other colleagues, we are better equipped to meet the needs of young adolescents and the curriculum. The creativity and subsequent effectiveness that come from teaming are amazing.

In traditional junior high schools, all science classes are located near each other. So are math, English, and history classes. Students move in cattle drives from farm to farm in a sense, gathering nutrition from whatever each farmer grows. No farmer talks to another farmer in order to make a cohesive response to the needs of the cattle, and each farmer thinks his crops are the most important part of the cattle's journey.

Even though we're tempted to equate their ceaseless gum-chewing with bovine cud mastication, our students are not cows. The cattle drive among disassociated farms doesn't work with growing humans. Such departmentalization makes it difficult for students to find connections personally and academically, or to find relevancy in their studies. It leads to a middle school "mad cow disease" in which students are disenfranchised wanderers, rarely learning how to think for themselves or how to care for others. Instead of cattle, let's consider students as farmhands working with the animals and crops, farmhands who have been apprenticed to us to learn all they can about our subjects in the short time we have with them. They work with us as we deliver instruction and, just as on a farm, the work is coordinated, everyone doing his or her part. Young adolescents in fragile transitions need a familial atmosphere in which they are known well by a small cadre of teachers committed to their success. They need teaming.

Teaming isn't easy. We can't close the classroom door and hold court in our private little kingdoms. We have to open our practices to the influence of our peers, and that can be threatening and frustrating in some cases, empowering and inspiring in others. In the hands of mature, creative, student-focused educators, teaming works. If colleagues lack positive communication skills, are inflexible, or are subject-focused, teaming can be a nightmare. If this is the case, time is better spent building unity among staff members than forcing unwilling colleagues into teaming situations.

Most of us trained in the middle school concept already have a sense of what constitutes a good team. We also realize its life and greatest usefulness is more in the journey than the arrival. Middle school educator Brenda Dyck paraphrases educator and author Margaret Wheatley when she says, "Life is not neat, logical, or elegant. . . . It's mess upon mess until something workable emerges. It takes a lot of repeated mess to get it right." It's true when working with students or with our colleagues.

No one year of teaming will be the same as any other year. People and situations change. There will never come a time when you feel as if you have the perfect team, so don't get stuck in a mind-set that there is only one way to be a successful team. Start and maintain a healthy approach instead—you and your colleagues are always progressing, not stagnating. Whatever we encounter in our first year of teaching becomes comfortable and we often latch onto it as the way all teaming should be. Avoid digging such ruts.

Being a Positive Contributor at Team Meetings

"I'm a first-year teacher. They've probably thought of that idea already."
"What could I possibly know about this? I'm only a first-year teacher."
"I better know my place in the hierarchy of the team. I don't want to rock the boat with new ideas."

Remember, when you received your teaching degree, you were judged to be competent at what you do. You have something to contribute, and your voice needs to be heard. Your approach is the fresh energy and perspective the rest of us need to hear every year. Don't be intimidated by the experience of those sitting around the table with you. You can offer ideas in such a manner as to be respectful of their experience: "That sounds good. Would it work even better if we focused only on those students in the lower quartile?" or "I'm not sure I follow what you're saying. Can you tell me at what point you consider students as tardy to class—in the door, in their seats, or in their seats with homework out for checking?"

Accept the fact that open disagreement is healthy, not something to avoid. Just do your part to make sure everyone is heard—the quiet team members and you. In order for others to hear your ideas, remove all put-downs and sarcasm, and commit to the idea that everyone is on the side of student achievement and teacher collegiality. This means you'll have to suppress hidden agendas and the urge to preach or politicize. You'll want to come across as open to discussing ideas, not close-minded. Don't see compromise as a sacrifice, but rather as a coming together that couldn't be achieved by either side alone. Speak with honesty, but remain nonaccusatory and emotionally neutral. You don't want to raise your teammates' defenses; you want to keep the conversation going. A little light humor from time to time is welcome, too.

Some team members will have a different philosophy than yours. Learn all you can from them. Listen to them for two reasons: first, to see if there is something their experience and wisdom can teach you; and second, to understand them and to be able to make better decisions when interacting with them. They are your colleagues, and colleagues differ from us. There is no sense in claiming all is lost or demeaning a team member in front of students or other colleagues when we disagree with them.

Instead, talk with a teammate who frustrates you. Share your concerns openly. Chances are he or she will appreciate the opening to talk with you, too. If the differences are insurmountable, ask if there might be a compromise of some sort, or a "he does his thing, I do my thing" relationship for this first year, then ask to be reassigned to another team the following year if it's just not going to work between you two. That's drastic, but you have enough to deal with in this first year. Don't hesitate to go to your team leader or administrator with your concerns and ask him or her to mediate a conversation between you two.

Sometimes the concern is just about someone who is late to team meetings or who in some other way breaks the professional protocols of good teaming. Describe your concern to your team leader and let him or her approach the individual, if you don't feel comfortable doing so, which is very understandable. If the leader is the one with whom you have the issue, ask that it be placed on the agenda for the next team meeting. Express your concerns in a clear but nonthreatening manner, using an I-message if possible:

> I feel frustrated when I work very hard to get here on time, putting aside things I really want to get accomplished, and then arrive only to find that others do not have the same respect for starting meetings on time. I know some emergencies happen, but we haven't

been able to start on time for most of the past two weeks. I could use the time we spend waiting for others to finish their tasks and arrive for my own work; and then we have to rush through the agenda because our time is short. Is there any way we could renew our commitment to getting here on time?

Successful team members arrive at team meetings on time. Do whatever it takes to make sure this happens. In the few minutes before the meeting, don't try to download that intricate map of Indonesia on a slow modem. Don't make that supposedly quick call to a student's parent, and don't go down the hall to photocopy tomorrow's test. Arrive at the meeting early instead. You can grab something to drink, take a professional book or journal to read, or maybe bring a few papers to grade, but be on time.

As a professional middle school teacher, you have a responsibility to make meaningful contributions to team meetings. It doesn't matter whether you're a first- or thirty-first-year teacher. What you contribute may or may not be feasible, but at least you're making a sincere effort to help. Give yourself license to misunderstand what others mean, to make mistakes, to share ideas already tried and discarded, or to not have considered all the variables involved. When the feedback from colleagues comes, take it as such and improve the next time; don't crumble. Chalk it up to a big learning curve and thank your teammates for caring enough to correct you.

It's important to get what you want on the team's agenda for those meetings, too. You can do this by requesting that items be placed on the agenda via e-mail, personal note, or in person with the team leader. If you're nervous about rocking the boat, you can come across as asking for assistance when really you're raising the concern for others: "I'm having trouble finding time to stand in the hallways between classes in order to keep the peace in the locker bay. Does anybody have any ideas?" Their responses to you will open their minds to your intended topic. Sometimes you can invite a resource person or an administrator to join the meeting. Clear this with the team leader ahead of time, of course—you don't want to step on his or her toes. A visitor keeps the team focused on the agenda items and his or her presence leads to the discussion of the topic you wanted to address.

You can also volunteer to be a team leader for the year if no one else wants to do it. Sure, you'll make mistakes, but you'll also learn a lot and get items on the agenda that you find important. While I don't recommend this for everyone's first year, I know a number of folks who've handled it well.

Once the meeting begins, make every effort to show that you are 100 percent present for your colleagues. Remove papers to be graded, journals, and any other distractions from your view—off the table, if possible. This is not the place for them once the meeting starts. Face your colleagues when speaking and listening to them. Record notes, if that helps clarify your thinking or retain information. Nod, ask questions, and offer body language that lets others know you are listening to them. Remember Stephen Covey's advice: Seek first to understand, then to be understood. That's hard to do when we're forming in our minds what we're going to say to a person who hasn't yet finished his point, but we can try.

Keep to the topics on the agenda. We're all guilty of wanting to vent, of getting excited about something interesting, or of not being in the mood to conduct business, but successful and mature team members are disciplined and move carefully through the meeting's agenda. We don't want to be known as the one who always gets the team off track. When we stick to the topics, we finish earlier, too, and there's time for everything else we want to do.

Whatever you do, keep team business inside the team. Confidentiality is critical to trust and professional conduct. Be known as someone who can be trusted. Integrity is paramount—keep your agreements. If you agree to obtain the field-trip forms for the next meeting, do whatever it takes to make sure that happens. Don't forget to celebrate achievements, too. Humans need to know and be praised for the milestones they achieve. Celebrations affirm everyone's hard work while providing perspective and motivation for continuing. One last bit of advice on being a successful team member: If no one else is smoking cigarettes, don't smoke yourself. The others will be tolerating you (maybe), not embracing you.

Subject Integration

While this book focuses only on those aspects of middle school teaching that enable instruction, and not on instruction itself, subject integration is an integral component of teaming. Any discussion of teaming isn't complete without it. For elaborated studies of subject integration, readers are directed to the list of recommended resources in Appendix B.

There are a few principles we can describe here, however. First, a clarification: Interdisciplinary instruction, or subject integration, refers to approaches that incorporate content and skills from more than one subject area. For example, a science teacher might ask students to use math skills to analyze and graph fish populations off California's northern coast, or a history teacher might teach students how to determine whether an author is presenting his interpretation rather than fact when describing a historical event.

Thematic instruction occurs when different disciplines focus on a common theme as uniquely expressed in each discipline. For example, a team might choose the theme Diversity. Within that theme they identify several principles that will serve as common instructional threads for the next quarter or semester. For Diversity, those principles might include

- Diversity creates conflict.
- In diversity there is strength.
- Diversity generates tolerance and intolerance.
- Diversity is essential to growth.

Given these thematic principles, each of the math, science, history, physical education, and English teachers on the team look for ways to promote diversity through their curriculum. Though not required, some of the teachers may rearrange the sequence of particular units of study in order to make stronger connections. Possible topics of study that would promote these diversity principles include the following:

- Math—fractals, fractions, structural engineering, patterns, multiple approaches to solving problems, identifying and isolating variables, number theory, differently based number systems, attributes of 3-dimensional solids
- Science—biodiversity, ecosystems, energy transfer cycles, periodic table of elements, atomic structures of molecules of multiple elements, bonds, geography's relation to the flora and fauna it supports, dual nature of light, taxonomy, adaptations, mutualism/parasitism/commensalism
- History—multicultural communities, United Nations, civil rights, world wars, imperialism, Native Americans and other indigenous peoples, the Industrial Revolution, immigration, the Constitution, civics, Socratic Seminars, simulations, diplomacy, politics
- Physical Education—the food pyramid and a balanced diet, exercising and cross-training, multiple systems of the body working together for a healthy body, accepting others, progressing at one's own speed and comfort, diseases
- English or Language Arts—point of view, literary interpretation, multicultural literature, effect of setting and time on author's perspective, character development, types of conflict, resolution of conflict, antagonist and protagonist, historical and science fiction, literature with diversity themes, peer-critiquing classmates' papers, literature circles

We can't rely on the lucky coincidence of occasional crossovers among disciplines. Our students will think and achieve at higher levels when we gather together to purposefully orchestrate such vivid connections. Content is revealed, reinforced, clarified, and extended in ways that are impossible to achieve without subject integration through teaming. What might we have accomplished had we experienced teaming as young adolescents ourselves? What enlightenment eluded those of us who attended nonteaming junior high schools?

Teaming approximates the real world. Life is not set up in compartments operating separately from one another. Almost any job our students will one day have will require multiple skills applied simultaneously, not forty-five minutes of one thing, followed by forty-five minutes of something else, then forty-five minutes of something different, and another forty-five minutes of a fourth skill. Skills aren't used in isolation. We read in math, history, English, art, science, physical education, and music classes just as we read while working as dental hygienists, photographers, carpenters, plumbers, and executives. If we're going to prepare young adolescents to be contributing citizens, we can't paint the picture that reading is done only in reading class, math only in math class. They have to be "hardwired" to think in connected ways. Interdisciplinary and thematic instruction by middle school teams open the doors to mental dexterity.

Using subject integration and teaming, we can teach and assess a skill in one or more classes with one or more tasks that the team teachers can grade together. The English teacher can help grade the science lab conclusions and count the grades in his class under "writing conclusions," and the science teacher can count them in her class as well. In one assignment, students get evaluated on mastery in two classes. This cuts down on the paperwork for both students and teachers, especially if the teachers share the stack of 150 labs to assess after agreeing on a rubric.

In your first year of teaching, try to do one successful integration with one other teacher in the first semester. Working with more than one teacher may be overwhelming as you try to master curriculum and discover your professional self. If that first two-subject integration or thematic unit goes well, try another the second semester, or even try one with three disciplines. Don't push yourself to do thematic or interdisciplinary instruction all the time.

Keep the focus on the curriculum in many of your team meetings, even if it means assigning specific days to curriculum planning. On these days, no meetings with parents are allowed, and team members understand the need to table discussions about students. You may need to divide the time among two days, if critical conferences or events impose on that curriculum planning time. Make sure that curriculum is referenced in the agenda items, and that the team scribe or summarizer records the curriculum discussion. This enables teams to take stock of their curriculum planning and helps everyone in their busy worlds stay focused on what's truly important. Again, inviting curriculum specialists to the team meeting from time to time will help keep the focus. It is also helpful if those of you just starting off with a two-subject integration can meet outside of the team meeting time to do any planning and footwork that doesn't require the team meeting to accomplish. Team meetings can also be shortened to allow more time during your planning periods to work on curriculum integration. Don't waste a full team meeting on things that can be accomplished by a smaller subset of the team.

As you teach during this first or second year, you'll come across posters and stationery promoting the idea of teaming: "There's no 'I' in 'Team'"; "T.E.A.M. = Together Everyone Achieves More"; and others. These are nice sentiments, but they are frames of reference at best. Teaming is complex, requiring daily hard work and deep commitment on everyone's part. Be watchful, too: we tend to be gung ho about teaming in the fall, but in the long stretches of February and March, our dedication to its ideals pales next to standardized testing worries, field trips, and the curriculum coverage panic that occurs as the end of the school year looms ever larger.

Hold on to teaming as the way to get you through these tougher times. You'll be more effective as a teacher, and you'll enjoy your job and your students, too. Yes, you're a farmer planting seeds that will take root, though you may not always see the grown crop. Trust that it's there. Those aren't cattle being herded your way, they're farmhands. They're willing to till the soil with you, to irrigate the earth, to watch how one skill enables another, and to see what they're made of. Working together, you and the other members of your teaching team enable students to build their own farms and become honorable citizens of our community.

8

Dealing with Homework

One thing that spurred students in the middle school where I taught was offering options to regular assignments. One of the seventh-grade teams discovered this accidentally. They were offering optional assignments to gifted and high-achieving students—both in the classroom and as homework—in an effort to get these kids engaged and interested. The kinds of assignments they offered were not only more challenging, they were also more creative and more fun! Some involved Web work. Some elicited student opinions and ideas. They got the ideas from reading material on how to engage gifted students in the regular classroom and by inviting the gifted teacher to meet with them and share ideas.

What the teachers discovered was that *all* students preferred these kinds of assignments and that when classroom expectations went up, so did student cooperation and performance! The social studies teacher met me in the hall one day and told me that 93 percent of all his students (he had 150 students) had turned in their homework that day, and had opted for the "challenging" assignment. Grinning, he remarked, "And now I've got to grade it!"

—*Anne, a middle school educator*

I t's ten minutes before the end of a hot and humid Wednesday in your classroom, and both you and your students already have more than enough personal and school-related commitments to fill the time between the end of school and bedtime that night. You announce the evening's homework.

"Okay, listen up. Tonight you need to finish defining your twenty vocabulary words and wrap up your project that was assigned three weeks ago. The final version is due tomorrow. Make sure someone looks it over before you start the final version. Don't forget that we have a quiz tomorrow as well. To prepare you for that, I'd like you to do pages 78–84 in the workbook. It's a good review for what we learned today as well as earlier in the week. Do these carefully; I'll be checking your work."

If you had X-ray eyes, you could see every heart sink. On top of that, you're operating on traditional-good-homework-practices autopilot and can't see the truckload of uninspired papers to grade that is coming your way. It's part of your job as a teacher to assign homework and grade it, right? You weren't doing anything with your weekend anyway. The faint moan inside your own head may not be as audible as your students', but it's there, and the spark of dread that inspired it will soon transform into glowing resentment that will burn through your passion for teaching, leaving nothing but gray dust to blow whichever way the next breeze carries it.

It doesn't have to be this way. Homework can be one of the most renewing and exciting aspects of teaching middle school, but we have to be smart about its structure, assignment, and assessment.

Homework policies and practices press people's buttons; opinions run strong. Every year some parents comment that I don't give enough homework and others say that I give too much homework. Teachers and schools are considered rigorous if they give a lot of homework, almost regardless of the type of homework that is given or the quality of the classroom instruction. Those who teach well but are light on homework are considered weak or not challenging enough. Many middle school students pass or fail purely on whether or not they did their homework, not necessarily on whether or not they mastered concepts. With so much riding on homework, a clear examination of its purposes, management, and motivation is warranted.

Purposes of Homework

One of the big reasons we assign homework is for practice. Mastery takes practice and homework is the way students practice. Homework helps students reinforce clarified concepts. We assign homework to enable students to apply or extend the day's learning outside of the classroom, one of the best ways to move information from working memory to long-term memory. Homework is also done as preparation for a lesson; for example, when students read a chapter before a class discussion or when we give them anticipation guides ahead of a learning experience. Homework provides one more way for students to interact substantively with information.

If homework is assigned to students before the concepts are clarified, however, then it does more harm than good. Learning acquired from practicing incorrectly is very hard to overcome. The brain loves to confabulate. It seeks wholeness, and when it has only a partial understanding of something, it draws facts and perspectives from other areas of the mind as well as pieces of fabricated information and inserts them into the "holes" of learning to make concepts appear whole. Even worse, the brain will convince itself that this was the original learning all along. Enter the teacher, who has to discern what solid understanding the students have, convince them that their confabulations (i.e., their misconceptions) are wrong, and teach them the right learning. What a tough situation! It takes far more time and energy to figure this out and reteach content than it does to teach content fully from the beginning, then have students practice it correctly. If students don't have close to 100 percent mastery of the day's learning, it's best to assign no homework that evening, or at least to adjust the nature of the assignment. Don't worry about not appearing rigorous by having daily homework assignments. Focus on successful student learning, not appearances. Homework given to keep students busy regardless of whether it clarifies, reinforces, or prepares students for learning is irresponsible; middle school teachers should discard the practice.

Homework That Students Will Do: Managing the Workload

If ever we wonder whether or not students follow a religious faith, we need only listen to the chorus of prayer lifted to the heavens whenever there's a major assignment due and the weather forecasters are calling for two to six inches of snow. Will it be enough to close school? Please, please, please, say the students, let there not be school tomorrow—I promise to spend hours on this project. This is one of the few times that homework assignments become an adrenaline rush, although not necessarily for the right reasons.

There are many ways to make homework manageable. First, don't overdo it for the sake of rigor. If the students get the practice or reinforcement by doing ten examples instead of thirty, give them ten. Everyone procrastinates when the workload is heavy, even teachers facing a pile of papers. If the pile is thin, we tackle the task more readily because success doesn't seem so far away.

Another way to shorten homework is to cut the amount that has to be written. Accept the idea behind Pascal's quote, "I have made this letter longer than usual, because I lack the time to make it short." It's true. It's harder to write a 125-word essay than it is to write a 400-word essay. In the shorter essay, every word counts, and nothing can be wasted. In the longer essay, students can toss out a number of key words and hope that some of them will be what the teacher was looking for as he graded. Most middle school students can demonstrate a clear understanding of something in one good page of writing. We don't need the four-page paper to have evidence of mastery.

This is good for the teacher, too, who is more likely to assess a pile of one-page essays than a pile of four-page papers. Just for comparison, on my team this year this would mean the difference between reading and assessing 150 pieces of paper versus reading and assessing 600 sheets—well over a ream of paper—and this is only one assignment! Pity the teacher who gives more than one assignment!

Getting papers back in a timely manner means the students get feedback faster, too. Frequent feedback is a proven motivator. Young adolescents will put more thought into assignments if they are likely to get them returned in a day or three—as opposed to assignments they know they won't see again for weeks. And teachers are looking for these deeper and more complex responses to learning. Homework for which the teacher or classmates gives specific feedback to the student in a timely manner results in greater impact on learning (Marzano 2001). Homework without feedback or with delayed feedback results in almost no learning. Homework assignments are not well designed unless they include how the completed assignments will receive feedback in a timely manner. In sum, shorter writing assignments are a win-win situation for both students and teachers.

Motivating Homework

Homework that is engaging is likely to be done. Break up routine homework with not-so-routine homework. Unique homework includes assignments that require students to interview family members or friends; incorporate artwork, music, drama, or media; and interact with content and skills in meaningful ways. Allowing students to respond via their proclivities, as described in Howard Gardner's *Multiple Intelligences* (1993), is a sure way to get students engaged.

We can also ask students to use each other and themselves in their assignments in positive ways. For example, putting in classmate Manny Aguilar as the one who has to determine the volume and capacity of a U-shaped swimming pool in order to fill it with chocolate pudding for a science experiment (or a party!) in those student-generated word problems is a lot more fun than using somebody students can't visualize. How about preparing pretend business letters for business CEOs using classmates' names? interviewing each other as experts to demonstrate primary resources? creating historical diaries from historical participants based on classmates? How about a poetic ode to classmate Jeremy's pentagonal prism describing its features (edges, vertices, faces)?

Beverly Maddox, a middle school teacher in Little Rock, Arkansas, states further, "In classes that require little homework, few kids fail. Expectations for learning seem to be low, however, and test scores (both SAT-9 and criterion referenced) show poor student performance . . . We need to examine the kind of homework that gets done and the kind that doesn't as well as the reasons we give homework. If we assign homework that kids find interesting and relevant, they will be more likely to do it."

Another way to make homework motivating is to increase its complexity. Students are likely to do more thought-provoking homework. I know this sounds counterintuitive, but it works. Every time I increase the complexity of assignments, more students complete them. Instead of routine assignments that require students only to go through the motions of doing homework, try some of these:

- Design a flag that incorporates the suffragists' goals in its symbols and pattern.
- How does this painting express the theme of passage?
- Identify the mistake in the student's solution and what the student still needs to learn.
- Rank these items in order of importance to Herbert Hoover . . .
- Write a constitution for your underwater city that reflects the politics of ancient Rome.
- Sculpt (literally and symbolically) the meaning of each vocabulary term.
- Create twelve intelligent questions for which the answer is "chromosome."
- Create a television PSA that persuades young adolescents to make good decisions regarding snacks after school.
- Create a six-panel comic strip portraying the event.

Answering basic recall questions can make students feel like they are accomplishing a lot, but the assignments lose their luster quickly. The act of reading material and plucking answers from the text becomes drudgery. Prime the pump with assignments calling for higher thinking levels: comprehension, application, analysis, synthesis, and evaluation.

According to Frank Williams, there are eight levels of creative thought; the first four are cognitive, the last four are affective. All eight levels provide great stimuli for homework assignments. Here are some examples from Imogene Forte and Sandra Schurr's book, *Integrating Instruction in Science* (1996):

Fluency—Think of the characteristics that distinguish a living thing from a nonliving thing. List as many of these characteristics as you can.

Flexibility—Devise a classification system for living things based on characteristics of living things that manifest differently in different kinds of organisms.

Originality—Write a description of life as if you had to explain it to a nonliving thing.

Elaboration—Explain how biologists rely on the methods and discoveries of scientists in other fields to do their work.

Risk Taking—Tell how you feel about the possible benefits and the potential dangers of modern advances in genetic engineering.

Complexity—Discuss the issues involved in the work of a scientist whose discoveries improve some lives, but whose work is based on experiments that harm other living things.

Curiosity—What questions would you like to ask a biologist in order to learn about a typical day in the life of a scientist?

Imagination—Write a brief imaginative account of Marcello Malpighi's first view of the movement of blood through capillaries with a microscope. (46)

Another way to engage students is through their reading material. Journalistic writing is a lot more engaging than encyclopedic writing. Such writing is a lot more fun to grade, too. Have students read articles from *Discover, National Geographic, Cobblestone, Calliope,* and similar magazines about the content you are trying to teach. Journalistic writing differs from encyclopedic writing in terms of voice and the reader's engagement. The journalistic approach begs to be read; it begs to be read aloud, in fact. Asking students to write journalistically about a topic while incorporating an understanding of concepts is not only motivating, but rigorous and effective learning. Take a look at these two versions of writing about bioluminescence:

Journalistic Version: The autumn night on the Pacific beach was raw and wet, our bones chilled to their marrow, but the show before us warmed places deeper than our skeletons. We were mythological creatures of the forest, spraying green stars from our fingertips, lighting the world with the mere pressure of our feet against the ground. And so it seemed with one flick of a finger we could send neon-green lightning bolts down the length of the incoming ocean waves' rising troughs. Mother Nature's show put us over the edge—we giggled in the dancing light. All around us were tiny dinoflagellates and plankton that lit the darkness each time they were disturbed. Though they lit only for a fraction of a moment, there were billions of them mixed into the sand so wherever we stood, the pressure of our weight made the sand glow bright green for several inches beyond the edges of our feet. When we ran, we left a trail of glowing footprints. We kicked the sand, and green lasers shot fan-shaped light trails more than three yards away. We scooped sand in our hands and let it fall in between our fingers, watching tiny Tinker Bells take flight in the cold November air. On that shore we walked in a fantasy world all the more fantastic for it being real.

Encyclopedic Version: Bioluminescence results from a chemical reaction within an organism. The chemical that produces the light is luciferin, but the chemical that starts the illumination is luciferase. New luciferin is brought into the organism through diet or internal processing. In some organisms, however, all the chemicals necessary to create light are already present and they light up when particular ions are added. In the sea, single-cell dinoflagellates light up because of forces that reshape their surface. When the cells contort, light is emitted when protons from acidic vacuoles are put in contact with other cell components that contain the chemicals necessary for bioluminescence. Most dinoflagellates flash their light for 0.1 seconds while the luminescence found in jellyfish can last for more than a minute.

Once students read the journalistic version, they are hungry and primed for the encyclopedic version. Better yet, everything they read in the encyclopedic version now makes sense and has meaning. Their eyes don't glaze over as they read; the knowledge is compelling.

Assignments in which students have to manipulate accurate information in a specific format for a particular audience is also engaging. Writing a rap song is one example. The word play and rhythm serve as mnemonics for retaining the information when it is performed. The most effective learning, however, occurs in the song's creation. In the process of creating a rap song, students must identify the critical attributes of the concept they are exploring and try to teach it to others. As they say the phrases over and over, they memorize the facts and the information moves to their long-term memory. When students follow a beat, they can remember long passages that would rival Homer's *Iliad*. Regardless of your own comfort with the medium, take a chance and ask students to write raps, poems, lyrics, and stories that accurately express the content they have to master. With these assignments, working with a partner or in a group works well, students have fun, and they learn the material—three good reasons to incorporate them into your homework repertoire.

Creating Motivating Homework Assignments

There are several guiding principles for creating highly motivating homework assignments. Choose the ones most appropriate for students' learning goals and your curriculum:

1. Give students a clear picture of the final product. This doesn't mean everything is structured for them, or that there aren't multiple pathways to the same high quality. There's room for student personalities to be expressed. Students clearly know what is expected, however. A clear picture sets purpose for doing the assignment. Priming the brain to focus on particular aspects of the learning experience helps the brain process the information for long-term retention. Setting purpose for homework assignments has an impact on learning and the assignment's completion rate (Marzano, Pickering, and Pollock 2001; Cooper 2001).

2. Incorporate a cause into the assignment. Students are motivated when they feel they are righting a wrong. They are very sensitive to justice and injustice. As a group, they are also very nurturing of those less fortunate than them. Find a community or personal cause for which students can fight fairly and incorporate your content and skills in that good fight—students will be all over the assignment.

3. Give students a real audience. There's an audience for the students' work and it isn't always us, the teachers. For example, when students work on something that uses a lot of technology such as a PowerPoint presentation or a Web site, it's not the technology that's motivating—it's the fact that there will be an audience other than the teacher. Somebody will see this, they realize. What will they think of it? they ask themselves. When writing news articles, the audience could be a local newspaper editor. Foreign language proficiency assessments could be done with native speakers from the local market, bank, or immigration office. Science class literary magazines could be sent to museums and the local observatories for comment. Real audiences motivate middle schoolers.

4. Incorporate people whom students admire in their assignments. Students are motivated when asked to share what they know and feel about these folks. We are a society of heroes, and young adolescents are interested in talking about and becoming them.

5. Allow choices, as appropriate. Allow students to do the even-numbered or odd-numbered problems, or allow them to choose from three prompts, not just one. Let them choose the word that best describes the political or scientific process. Let them identify their own diet and its effects on young adolescent bodies. Let them choose to work with partners or individually. How about allowing them to choose from several multiple-intelligence-based tasks? If they are working in ways that are comfortable, they are more likely to do the work. By making the choice, they have upped their ownership of the task.

6. Incorporate cultural products into the assignment. If students have to use magazines, television shows, foods, sports equipment, and other products they already use, they are likely to do the work. The brain loves to do tasks in contexts with which it is familiar.

7. Allow students to collaborate in determining how homework will be assessed. If they help design the criteria for success, such as when they create the rubric for an assignment, they "own" the assignment. It comes off as something done by them, not to them. They also internalize the expectations—another way for them to have clear expectations. For example, with some assignments we can post well-done versions from previous years (or ones we've created for this purpose) and ask students to analyze the essential characteristics that make these assignments exemplary. Then we can ask them to create the rubric to assess their attempts at the same assignment. Besides a sense of ownership, students who analyze well-done assignments will compare those works with their own and internalize the criteria for success, referencing the criteria while doing the assignment, not just when it's finished. This is a scholarly and effective approach.

8. Avoid "fluff" assignments. For example, assigning students to create a life-sized "dummy" of a person found in a novel (or in history, in science, in math, etc.) doesn't further understanding. It's a lot of coloring, cutting, wadding paper, and stapling (or stuffing old clothing with newspaper) for very little return. Make sure there is a clear connection to curriculum, not just something that would look cool when displayed in the classroom. Students will figure out how empty these assignments are very quickly. They'll see homework as serving little or no purpose other than to give them something to do, which sinks motivation like a rock.

9. Spruce up your prompts. Don't ask students to repeatedly answer questions or summarize. Try some of these openers instead: Decide between, argue against, Why did _____ argue for, compare, contrast, plan, classify, retell _____ from the point of view of _____, organize, build, interview, predict, categorize, simplify, deduce, formulate, blend, suppose, invent, imagine, devise, compose, combine, rank, recommend, defend, choose.

10. Have everyone turn in a paper. In her book, *Homework: A New Direction* (1992), Neila Connors reminds teachers to have all students turn in a paper, regardless of whether they did the assignment. If a student doesn't have his homework, he writes on the paper the name of the assignment and why he didn't do it. I started doing this over a decade ago and had students add their parents' telephone number so I could call parents during the day and share what the student said about his homework. Sometimes I've asked students to call and explain to their parents what happened. Parents don't want to be bothered at work. Calling parents usually results in a terrific homework completion record for students—at least for a few weeks. When students know they have to fill out one of these forms and parents will be contacted, they do whatever they can to finish the homework. An added dividend is that classmates don't get as many opportunities to see who didn't do their homework—a student's reputation to avoid.

11. Do not give homework passes. I used to do this; then I realized how much it minimized the importance of homework. It's like saying, "Oh, well, the homework really wasn't that important to your learning. You'll learn just as well without it." Homework should be so productive for students that missing it is like missing the lesson itself. If you're looking for ways to reward students, try a "Homework Deadline Extension Certificate" instead. I use these every quarter. Students really compete for them. On the day an assignment is due, students can submit the certificate instead of their homework and they are automatically allowed to turn in the assignment one, two, or three days late, according to your comfort level, for full credit. If we reward those who've earned these certificates by extending the deadline but not voiding the need to complete the assignment, we haven't diminished the assignment's importance. Of course, students learn to be judicious in their use—if the assignment was to study for tomorrow's test, it won't help them very well on the test to use their deadline extension certificate.

12. Integrate homework with other subjects so that one assignment can count in two classes. Such assignments are usually complex enough to warrant the dual grade and it's a way to work smarter, not harder, for both students and teachers. Teachers can split the pile of papers to grade, then share the grades with each other, and students don't have homework piling up in multiple classes. There are times when every teacher on the team assigns a half-hour assignment, and so do the elective or encore class teachers. This could mean three to four hours of homework for the student, which is inappropriate for young adolescents. And what about students who struggle with learning disabilities? And those catching up from being absent due to the flu? This happens more often than we realize. Because I don't always know about other assignments in other classes, I invite parents to send in a quick note explaining the situation and asking for an extension. The extensions are granted as long as it doesn't become chronic. Sleep, exercise, personal down time, and time for families are way too important to trample in the name of a paragraph comparing two poems that would take the student beyond two hours of homework.

13. Do not give homework on weekends or holidays. I say this as both a teacher and a parent. There will be plenty of long-term projects that will keep students focused over the weekend and some holidays, but the basic premise should be to avoid all weekend homework. This might push things a little on Monday through Thursday, but that's okay. The weekends are for our students to be kids, members of families, and daydreamers. They need the break just as much, if not more, than we do. This means, of course, that there should never be a test or a quiz on a Monday or the first day back from a holiday; otherwise they would spend that weekend or holiday studying for the test or quiz. Projects should not be due on a Monday, either. Let's keep Sunday nights anxiety free. There's already a built-in dread for some students (and some teachers) that the weekend is over and the next day we report early for new stress. It's more effective for students to have a relaxed Sunday evening, looking forward to school (well, at least a little) and enjoying their families than it is to stress them out further. They'll be more productive during the week for having healthier lives at home.

Consider your true goal with homework: learning that moves into long-term memory, right? I've found that the high-pressure homework marathon that occurs on Sunday nights or the last night of a school holiday results in minimal, if any, content going into long-term memory. Cramming is the stuff of partial memories to be parroted for a quiz that week, then lost to an information black hole, never to be seen again. If we are really about teaching so that students learn and not about appearing rigorous and assigning tasks to show that we have taught, then we'll carefully consider all other options before assigning weekend or holiday homework.

14. Occasionally, let students identify what would be most effective. Sometimes the really creative assignments are the ones that students design themselves. After teaching a lesson, ask your students what it would take to practice the material so well it became clearly understood. Many of the choices will be rigorous and very appropriate.

Methods of Assessing Middle School Homework

How does all this play out as we manage homework in the classroom? How do we assess homework effectively? How do we handle the paperwork? How do we make homework truly a learning experience instead of busywork? Here are some ideas:

For big projects with multiple weeks of student responses, such as a science learning log or a reader's response journal, skim every page students have written, but have students select one entry for a letter grade by placing a star on the intended page. The entry should demonstrate outstanding thinking, science protocol, plot analysis, personal response, or whatever you're emphasizing with the unit. If you're worried about having a large enough sample, grade two or three entries.

When checking a list of problems, sentences, or answers to questions, have students work in groups of four or five to confirm answers with one another. If someone gets the wrong answer and doesn't understand why, the rest of the group explains. If the student or group is stuck in understanding how an answer was achieved, they identify that one problem/sentence/question to the teacher when she calls the groups back to the whole class. The teacher reviews only identified problems. While groups are meeting to review homework, the teacher circulates from group to group, recording evidence of successful collaborations (to be shared later with the whole group), answering questions, correcting misconceptions, facilitating student conversations, and identifying areas to reteach. The great thing about this method is the conversation, not just the assessment the teacher does. Students who "talk math" (or English, history, science, art, PE, technology, drama, or music) learn those subjects. The peer connection works, too. It's humbling, but we've all had times when we can't get through to a student, then a classmate says practically the same thing and the frustrated student experiences an epiphany.

Don't grade everything. Some assignments can be marked with a check or a zero for having done it. Spot-check problems two, nine, and seventeen because they represent different concepts you were worried about students understanding.

Keep the student's effort in doing the homework from diluting the grade that indicates mastery of content. That is, separate work habits from the letter grade if you can. Even though I know that good work habits usually yield high achievement, as a parent I don't want my son's grade to be based on anything but mastery of content and skills. If the grade's validity reflects good effort but not mastery, then my son isn't held accountable for learning, I don't have a valid judgment of his learning, and he doesn't have the required knowledge.

In the real world, we do not pay a carpet layer for the job until the job is done, regardless of how many hours or days it took, or how hot it was. The degree of his effort is not relevant, just that the job is done well (the standard of excellence was achieved). High-tech-industry workers may work all night long preparing a proposal for a client, but their efforts are irrelevant to the client who accepts and reviews all proposals equally that cross her desk by 10:00 A.M. the next morning.

Revising and Redoing Homework

Good classrooms often model the senior craftsman or mentor approach. Students attempt the achievement (performance task) of the master crafts-man, then are given advice on how to improve. They revise and try again, and again they are given advice on how to improve. The process is repeated until mastery is attained. The teacher is an expert and a coach. Students are not penalized for multiple attempts, revisions, or for not understanding the first time around. The focus is on achieving the standard of excellence. The feedback to the student is clear: If they don't achieve, they are not given master craftsman status (an A), nor can they set up a practice. They have not yet met the rigorous criteria (standards) for mastery. We can see the revision of important homework tasks in the same way—students do it until they get it right.

Consider the reflections of middle school educator Nancy Long:

We have experimented with dozens of rubric styles over the last few years, and my favorite still is the one that lists all of the content cri-teria and all of the quality criteria on the left side and has two columns on the right side: YES and NOT YET. Check marks are used in the appropriate column to show which criteria have been met and which still need work. I try to schedule deadlines for assign-ments far enough ahead of the end of the grading period so there is time for everyone to get the papers back and do over what was not right before I must assign a grade "in concrete." . . . I am SO thank-ful that in most things in our adult lives, we can mess up and still get another chance to get it right without too large a penalty!

Another successful educator, Bill Ivey, says this about redoing home-work assignments:

It is exactly what we want our children to do. We have an English teacher, Jane Denitz Smith, who, by taking her sixth-grade class carefully through draft after draft, helped them create poetry that was more powerful than many of the poetry contest winners at my high school, where the poetry program is considered to be quite strong. The principle here can apply to any subject and any learning.

Punishing Students Who Don't Do Homework

Recent claims in the media say that students can pass a course while turning in no homework. Certainly if one of my students never does any homework, yet gets straight A's on all tests and projects, then homework serves no purpose for that student. Homework's objective is to be instructional, not punitive. It would be wrong to fail a student for not doing homework when he had mastered all I had to teach. It would, however, indicate that I must not be doing my job very well. If my course is too easy for the student, then I need to make it more challenging for him or pursue placing him in a more advanced course.

Some argue against assessing homework in light of out-of-school pressures affecting a student's ability to do school work. We need to remember that our first task is to teach so that students will learn. Punishing a kid who cannot complete an assignment due to something beyond his control is abusive. We can't just shrug our shoulders and say that a child has to do the homework and if he doesn't, that's just tough, regardless of the child's situation. We can work with families to find a satisfactory way in which to complete the work. I had a student who worked approximately four hours after school every day of the week in order to support his family. Yes, I could have told him and his family that it is illegal to work at his age. Yes, I could have told him and the family that school is his job and it should come first. But food, medicine, and shelter were more basic needs. Completing a worksheet on objective pronouns pales in comparison. If the student masters the material, then why should I fail him for not doing homework in the midst of such struggles? We should do the most effective thing for students, not the easiest thing for teachers. Many of our students live in harsh realities. Our compassion and alternative structuring of homework assignments will prepare those students for adult success far better than the punishment for not doing a set of twenty math problems ever will.

Homework Technology

Online posting services are one of the most amazing phenomena to hit middle schools in the past few years. Depending on the service, teachers can post daily, weekly, and monthly homework. They can post tests and quizzes, project directions, maps, student work, vocabulary lists, photos of students, chalkboard notes, photos of demonstrations, learning aides, chat rooms on school-related topics, announcements and calendars, reminders, encouraging words, affirmations of student achievement, great quotes, research findings, puzzles and brainteasers, syllabi, places to find books, book lists, recommended Web sites, electronic flash cards on information to be memorized, cartoons, health recommendations, and much more.

I've been using www.schoolnotes.com for several years now. It's better than the homework hot line phone-based systems I've used. Almost all of my students have access to the Internet after school hours, whether at home, at the local library, at the local recreation center, or through parents at work. The advantages of online postings increase each year. Parents can download the latest information from my class, even that day's assignments, from their computers at home or at work. Most employers allow this kind of Internet use. Parents know what their child knows. There is no "he said, she said" in the student/teacher/parent triad. Expectations are understood on all sides. The student realizes quickly that he can't get away with anything less than full accountability for the whole homework assignment. If parents need help understanding something so that they can assist their child, they can access the information easily, twenty-four hours a day. There's even a button to push that sends an e-mail message to the teacher, asking for clarification. The Web site also includes plenty of suggested Web sites for student research as well as those electronic flash cards.

Students are "triple-teamed" by parents, teachers, and their own ability to access the information. Those who couldn't record the vocabulary terms or assignment off the chalkboard fast enough one day can see them posted on www.schoolnotes.com. This is a godsend for learning-disabled students who need that extra strategy for success and for parents who've grown exasperated with the daily struggle to ascertain what the teacher wants their child to do. Students who are sick or on vacation can see exactly what happened in class that day from anywhere in the world, in any time zone.

The emotional response is wonderful. Parents and students report less strain on parent-child relationships. Everyone's calmer and fewer games are played around finishing homework. Parents whose children can't be trusted to do homework independently can print the daily postings and ask their children to show them a one-to-one correlation between the product in their hands and the posted directions from the teacher. There's little room for misinterpretation or fudging. The online postings also provide another way for teachers to affirm the moments of strong character, academic achievement, and leadership experienced in their middle school classrooms. Students look forward to seeing themselves recognized in such a manner.

Other highly recommended sites include www.blackboard.com, www.myclass.net, www.teacherweb.com, and www.funbrain.com. Keep your eyes open for online posting services advertised in educational magazines and journals. If you find a good one, send me the name of it. There is a great column in NMSA's *Middle Ground* magazine, called "The Electronic Thread," which regularly provides good Web sites and describes their intelligent use in the middle school classroom.

Online posting services aren't the only way to communicate with Mom and Dad. E-mail works well, too. I give my home and school e-mail addresses to my students and their parents. In two minutes, I can alleviate several days' worth of anxiety or struggle. Students learn to conduct themselves with maturity and "netiquette" when conversing with me, and parents don't feel like they're out there alone when dealing with early adolescent angst. It makes the parents and the teacher truly a team, not "us versus them."

Another technology tip comes from reading Scott Purdy's helpful book, *Time Management for Teachers* (1999). He recommends using a cassette recorder to work with students. On an audiocassette, we can record an explanation of concepts using textbook references or notes given in class. Students can take these home and use them with or without parents present to help them make sense of the material. Students with disabilities can also complete their homework assignments by recording them orally on tape, if appropriate. I've used audiocassettes when reviewing students' writings. As I read a student's essay into the microphone, I share my reactions as a reader and teacher, offering suggestions and affirmations. Parents really appreciate this kind of feedback because they can hear it, too, and help their children interpret it as they work with them. Everyone's on the same page; it's almost like we're right there with them as they work on the next draft.

Some middle school teachers and most students perceive homework as a necessary evil, but it doesn't have to be. Let's give it the vitality it deserves and elevate it to its intended purpose: a highly effective instructional tool. We can perpetuate complacency with homework, or we can change our practices to reflect new student needs and new possibilities. It's troubling that many of today's homework assignments and practices parallel those from the turn of the last century. Today's middle schools require innovative and developmentally responsive homework based on what we now know about the human brain and young adolescents. One of the pluses of teaching and using these sanity-saving, creative approaches is that we get to experience the inspiring products our students create.

9 Parents

Every year my parents brought different occupations and talents into the classroom—the year one of my moms was a med tech we learned so much about germs, bacteria, and she was wonderful; the next year one of my dads worked for the Army Corps of Engineering and our soil unit was unbelievable; another year my student was from Palestine and we learned much from his family as they shared; another year one of my parents worked on the road and was willing to transport the huge Learning Trunks back and forth from the Historical Society in another city so we didn't have to pay shipping and handling; and so on. I found when you truly want their participation they respond. This, in turn, made them trust me, see me in action with their children, and built a supportive atmosphere . . . My out-of-town parents also were involved via electronic bulletin boards, posting digital pictures to our class Web site and/or being a sounding board for projects. It was those distant parents who appreciated being included the most, I think, and I can't tell you how wonderful it was for the student who had never had that faraway parent be able to do anything.

— *Marsha Ratzel, middle school educator*

Well-stated, Tricia. Could you say that again so everyone could hear it properly?" I asked. Though I spoke to Tricia, I gave a teacher-stare to the group at the table behind her. Inexplicably they found the satire of a recent presidential debate on *Saturday Night Live* more interesting than today's exploration of liquids' properties.

Tricia cooperated. "It's cohesion. That's what causes the tension in the water's surface," she repeated.

"Can you elaborate on that, Rehan?" I asked one of the boys at the targeted table.

"Uh, yeah," Rehan began, his tablemates grinning. "Cohesion. Well, that's like when you push two little puddles of water together on the wax paper. When they get close to each other, they leap into each other, forming a bigger puddle."

"Good, Rehan. You were listening," I said, then turned to the larger class. "Given the supplies you see on the desks in front of you, what proof could we find that there is strength in the cohesive forces in the water's surface tension?"

No one spoke.

I waited.

Then I waited some more, fingering a paper clip as conspicuously as I could. You could feel the rising discomfort, twenty-eight minds racing to guess where the teacher's going with this, five more minds thinking about lunch.

"If the water's surface tension was strong," I mused aloud, "it wouldn't break easily. It might even be strong enough to hold something heavier than water. Hmm." I let the paper clip drop onto one student's desk, then picked it up, apologizing overdramatically for being so clumsy. They didn't get it. Time for something more overt. I stuck the paper clip in the corner of my mouth and continued speaking.

"If I could just find something that could float on the water's surface tension, I might have evidence of the strong cohesive bonds among water molecules. But what could I use? Hmm." The paper clip dropped on another student's desk and I apologized once again and picked it up.

Suddenly, a visionary pierced the confusion. "Okay, okay, we get it! It's the paper clip, right?" Matthew conceded from another table.

"Amazing deduction, Watson!" I replied. "Class, using the two paper clips in front of you, devise a way to get one paper clip to float on the water's surface."

In moments we had multiple paper clips unfolded into giant L's, each one lowering a second paper clip laid perpendicularly across its horizontal shelf into water-filled beakers. Surface tension held them all.

"Now add a drop of soap from the eyedropper," I instructed. Students added the soap and we listened to the tiny clinks of fifteen metal clips hit their beaker bottoms.

Tricia laughed. "What happened?" she asked.

I waited again. The room was full of conversation.

"So, Mr. Wormeli, why did it do that?"

"Puppies!" someone yelled. Everyone turned.

In all of my years of teaching, that was a first. Where did they get that? Puppies! What do puppies have to do with . . .

Then I saw Mrs. Cooper, Anne Cooper's mother, enter the room with a box rimmed with seven tan puppy heads and fourteen tan paws, little tails batting the box's sides in eager anticipation. Like an all-powerful black hole, the box of puppies sucked the students from their seats and into the vortex of puppy cuteness. There was no stopping it; it was the drop of soap in my cohesive class. It wasn't so bad, though. I was in the vortex, too, getting a good face licking from one with a big white spot on his head.

Parents can be the greatest allies we have in the classroom. They can also be unreasonably demanding, indifferent, or just plain surprising, as Mrs. Cooper was that day with the puppies. The one thing that's for sure is that we must interact with them in order to teach their children well. We can't go through our days and weeks thinking that if we don't initiate contact, parents won't make much of a difference in our success with their students. Wrong. No matter what we do in the classroom, parents have the greater influence on their children's learning. If we're focused on our students' success, then we have to cultivate good parent relations. It helps if we see parents as the great positives they can be. Sometimes we have to show them how to be helpful, and sometimes we have to quiet down and let them teach us. As professionals, we can be open to both opportunities.

Parents and legal guardians set the tone at home—homework is important or it's not, what the teacher says is correct or it's a lie, the school prepares students for advanced studies or that school doesn't teach anything. Since young adolescents are so influenced by the emotional atmosphere around them, it's in our best interest to get Mom, Dad, or Guardian on our side.

Communicating with Parents

Speak in everyday terms. Get rid of the educational jargon. Our first goal is to communicate successfully so that parents hear and understand what we're saying, not to establish expertise. That will come with the wisdom and open communication we promote.

Do not judge or evaluate parents' approaches with their children. It never works, the defensive walls are erected immediately, and to be honest, we haven't walked ten miles in their shoes, so we don't have the big picture.

Be proactive. Call, write, or e-mail home before concerns get to the point where folks are suspicious or resentful. If you are about to move a student from one student group to another because his current group has moved beyond where the student is developmentally ready to be, and you know this student's parents are unusually watchful regarding classroom fairness, call them ahead of time and explain your decision. Make sure to invite their input, too. They might share something with you that will influence your decision, and they're more likely to support your decision for having included them in the loop.

Do we do this with all our parents? No. Most of our students' parents trust us to make sound decisions. Some parents, however, need that extra bit of interaction to keep the trust. This is okay. We don't need to take it personally. In this fast-paced world, we may have moved too fast, and communication may have slipped. We often see the world only from our classroom's point of view; it's hard to see things from the parents' perspective. As a parent myself, even I sometimes question the decisions of my own children's teachers, only to talk with them later and see their logic, thankful they made the decision they did. Once again, ignorance bred suspicion. If we communicate regularly with parents, we head off issues before they see the light of day.

A caution to those of you without children of your own: there are some things you cannot know or feel unless you have your own children. Trust me—I taught for a decade without children of my own. I thought the dynamics I observed in the classroom prepared me to advise parents on how to handle things at home. Up to a point, there was merit in what I suggested, but there was plenty for which I could not account nor could I suggest effective strategies parents could use. Until we've lived through getting homework done in the midst of sports-chores-help-with-siblings-music-church-Scouts-and-dinner (and Mom or Dad have to work late) on a daily basis, for example, we really don't have a sense of what works best at home. If you don't yet have children of your own, ask parents who seem to be having success with their children to share ideas with you that you can pass along to parents who are struggling. Your role is to be wisdom's conduit, not its pure fountain. Add your own ideas from what you read and discuss professionally as well as what you learn once you have children. Admitting the limits of our experience yet still finding ways to be helpful are among the more professional things we do as teachers.

Avoiding conflicts isn't the only reason we communicate with parents. It's a secondary reason at best. Our primary reasons for regular and clear parent communications are

- to inform parents of their child's instruction and assessment so they can make appropriate academic decisions for him or her;
- to inform parents so that they can support their child in his or her studies, i.e., gathering information and resources, interpreting direc-

tions and evaluations, and arranging tutoring, remediation, enrichment, or after-school help;

- to help parents in planning their family's weekly and monthly schedule;
- to make parents aware of how they can participate in the school's program;
- to make parents aware of school policies and practices;
- to inform parents of their responsibilities as established by the community, and to provide information that enables parents to protect their rights and the rights of their children;
- to provide two-way, accessible channels of communication so that parents will be inclined to share all information with us that will assist us in teaching their children, including feedback on teaching practices, the child's academic and medical background (if appropriate), and parents' goals for their child.

Methods of Communication

There are many mechanisms for communicating with parents.

Phone calls Keep a log, if possible. See Chapter 5 on record keeping for a sample record sheet. Let parents know in a nice way that you can't talk long if your time is short. You can start conversations with, "Hi, Mrs. Jacoby. I'm calling several parents this afternoon about . . ." or "Hi, Mrs. Jacoby, I have just a moment before I have to get to a meeting/appointment/student, so I thought I'd catch you to pass along an observation about . . ."

Letters via the postal service Don't forget the elevated value of a handwritten card or note in today's electronic world.

Home visits I highly recommend home visits. We learn more about students in thirty minutes of witnessing their home lives than in a month's worth of e-mails or phone calls. When we go to a student's home, we are on the parents' turf, too—an expression of great respect toward the family. They're inclined to consider your message seriously, and defenses that might distort their interpretation of information are not present. Even if we teach over 150 students, it's not that hard to stop by a student's house or apartment occasionally on the way home from school if the matter is important enough. The dynamics of parent-child relations in the home are very revealing. In addition to the perspective it will provide, home visits diminish the child's ability to play the teacher against the parent or vice versa. There's little inclination to play "he said, she said" games when both sides are so well informed.

E-mail At the beginning of the year, ask all parents who have access to e-mail accounts to send in their e-mail addresses, then make a separate directory just for these individuals in your electronic address book. For many families these days, it's easier to receive information via their e-mail account at work or home. E-mail has another benefit: a hard copy record of your conversation in case you need to document conversations or follow the course of a decision at a later date. Don't delete e-mails from parents or students, if possible. The drawback to e-mail is that you cannot read the person's body language and intonation as they deliver the message. Humans rely on such inputs in order to fully understand what a person is trying to communicate. Without them, we sometimes mix signals and communicate incorrectly—a comment meant to affirm something comes out as a criticism, for example.

Most schools used to have a policy that the administration had to proofread anything that went home to Mom and Dad. In today's high-paced, information-management society, this is too cumbersome for most schools. Have administrators proofread your team's policy statements, equipment and supply requisitions, big project sheets, field-trip notices, official letters to the whole team, discipline referrals, and other important documents, but keep the daily interactions to yourself, unless they are of significant concern to warrant team or administration response.

Watch what you write. Be concise. Double-check that your messages cannot be misinterpreted. That's hard to do, I know. Have someone else on the team or department proofread it, if you're concerned. Dry humor, satire, and sarcasm don't play well on e-mail messages. Avoid them.

Facsimile transmissions Many parents have access to facsimile machines at work or at home. This might be a handy route if someone forgets to send a completed field-trip form on the day of your trip. Just be careful: Many fax machines are located in common areas where anyone can walk by and read the printed messages. Since most of our communication with parents is private, this may not be an appropriate way to send personal information.

Invite parents into the classroom In all my years of teaching, I've never regretted this. Get parents into the room. They're used to being a part of things in primary and elementary school, but secondary levels are a bit more intimidating. Go out of your way to invite them into the classroom any day they want to join you. It doesn't matter what you're doing that day because every day you should be doing things with students that you consider to be the very best instructional practice you can muster. In a way, parents are the consumers for the service we offer. They should be allowed to inspect it any time they want, even without an appointment. If we deny such visits, they are immediately suspicious: "Why can't I visit? What's that teacher hiding?"

When dropping in any time, parents run the risk of watching students take a test or do quiet seat work instead of an amazing lesson on literary devices, but that doesn't matter. They want a clear picture that something good is going on in your room. The more parents you get into your room, the better. They will go out to the local sports games, places of faith, post offices, and grocery stores and give personal testimony to the high-quality lessons and assessments you give. It'll spread faster than any letter you send home. Many of the critics we encounter during the course of our careers are individuals who've never set foot into our classrooms. They speak from hearsay and through the filters of their own children's emotionally charged views of our classes. Remind parents at Back-to-School Night to believe only half of what they hear about you and the class, and you will believe only half of what you hear about them.

When you extend such invitations, inform parents of appropriate protocols for classroom visitation. This includes how to sign in at the front office and get a visitor's badge, how to get to your room, where to sit once they arrive, and the importance of not disrupting the lesson. If it's appropriate, offer them a chance to participate in the lesson. If a parent becomes a disruption with his visits, or if he stays with you during your planning time when you need to attend to other work, explain your concern to him. Parents are intelligent and caring people who are usually understanding; they'll back off. If they don't, turn the matter over to your administration. It's now a security issue.

Portfolios If you can, ask students to maintain portfolios of their work. Once a quarter, send home their portfolios for parent response. It's easiest for parents if you include a list of questions for them to complete after reading the portfolio. Sample questions from varied disciplines include

- What new skills do you notice your child demonstrating?
- Which problem (task, writing, artwork) demonstrates advanced thinking on the part of your child? Explain.
- How are your child's personality and interests expressed in his or her work?
- Which piece seems the most scholarly and why?
- Which component surprised you and why?
- What's your reaction to your child's comments as to why he placed these pieces in the portfolio?
- Is there another side to your child with respect to [insert subject area] that doesn't seem to be represented? If so, what is it?

- After seeing this work, what goal would you like your child to achieve next quarter?

Report cards and interims   Some report cards, interims, or progress reports have a space in which we can provide feedback beyond the standard marks listed in the form's symbol key. We can use these spaces to provide perspective on the grades, explaining how they were derived and how they might be improved if they are low. There might be space enough for a specific list of missing assignments or other individualized notation, affirming growth or making suggestions for improvement.

A word of caution: Time your comments well, especially when low grades are present. For example, we should spend a lot of time making very specific and elaborate comments for the interim reports that are sent home halfway through the grading period. Informed parents can then work with their children to make improvements before the end of the grading period. Suggestions saved for the final report card don't help; parents never knew something was wrong and there's no time to do anything about a pattern of failure. It's the difference between formative and summative evaluations: formative assessment is used to teach and guide, summative is only to document mastery. If we're mostly about teaching, we'll emphasize formative assessments and early communication with parents.

This implies, of course, that we are caught up in our grading so that we can make accurate comments to parents about their child's progression. Keeping up with record keeping is one of the best foundations for successful parent-teacher communications. Talk with mentors and colleagues about how they handle the paperwork if it's getting to be too much.

Newspaper editorials and articles   Get the word out about all the great things your students are doing. Be specific, and point out those higher-level thinking skills they are demonstrating, too. Communities and businesses love hearing about it. It even affects the local economy. Realtors are flooded with folks who want to live in such a school's boundaries; companies advertise your amazing school when recruiting new employees. As an added benefit, students are publicly affirmed for academic successes, not just athletic ones. There should be ten stories of middle school student successes for every one about a student who made a bad decision. Like it or not, we are educating the community as well as our students.

Class Web site   If you have the option, money, and the time, set up a Web site. Parents can click on it anytime and get the scoop on what's going on. You can post student work, homework assignments, electronic vocabulary flash cards, schedules, project directions, special downloadable forms, equipment lists, rubrics, grading practices, volunteer opportunities, elaborations on how to teach certain topics at home, special reminders, and the URL's to dozens of helpful Web sites. Families will bookmark it.

Internet posting services   I've used www.schoolnotes.com and www.blackboard.com primarily. I know there are other great ones out there. These are free sites on which to post the components listed in the Web site description above. These are different, however, in that the Web site is already established. You have a section of it just for you. You don't have to pay any money for the basic levels, and they're easy to maintain—just fifteen to twenty minutes per day to post the day's homework assignments. Everything else is taken care of for you. Parents can even request to be automatically informed every time you update it so they don't have to waste time going to the site to find it hasn't been updated. Parents can access these sites from work and then communicate with their children about its content before they get home.

Quarterly newsletters   Send home a newsletter from your class at the beginning of each quarter. Include topics of study for the quarter, as well as major writings, projects, and tests. You can also provide suggestions for how parents can assist their children with homework, as well as announcements and reminders about upcoming events, and invitations to visit the class. It's particularly effective to include statements of appreciation to specific parents for their volunteer help or donation of classroom supplies, as well as student writing or creations, if available. The appendix has a copy of one of the newsletters I used recently in my practice.

Postcards   Writing a full-length letter or expanded e-mail might be more than you have time to create, so how about a quick postcard? The idea is to get the message home as often as possible, and anything that makes that easier is good. Ask your guidance department to print address labels for the parents of each one of your students. Most current registration software packages can do this. If this is not available, distribute blank, self-adhering labels to students and ask them to record their parents' name and address on them and return them to you. Buy or requisition a large stack of postal service postcards (prepaid is great, but most middle schools will pay for postage for home-school communications). Whenever your team meets or whenever you have time yourself, jot down a few thoughts about a student's work/attitude/progression, place the proper label on it, and drop it in the mail. It's quick, and the positive effects last for months, even years.

Since a postcard's content is visible to anyone who handles the card, postcards should be used only for reminders, encouragement, affirmation, and reporting positive comments. It's inappropriate to use them to send comments about a student's weaknesses or poor behavior.

Back-to-School Night

Back-to-School Night is your chance to sell yourself and your subject. Look forward to it, don't dread it. You are the subject and young adolescent expert. Rise to the occasion.

One of the best things you can do is to prepare a handout with everything on it that parents would find helpful, such as general goals for your course, the grading scale, late-work policies, the daily schedule, getting after-school help, school contact numbers, required student supplies, volunteer opportunities, and important dates. If it's on the handout, you don't have to spend time explaining it in your already limited presentation time.

Just as important as providing a handout is giving parents a taste of your subject and a great lesson. Teach something. Parents want to see that you are a good communicator and that you are passionate about what you teach. They want to know that you offer substantive and compelling lessons and that their children are going to learn a lot in your room. In the past, I've taught parents where to put the comma in a divided quote; about the FOIL method for factoring polynomials; about the Reconstruction era following the Civil War; and about neurons of the giant squid.

If time allows, give a brief background of yourself. Emphasize your interest and experience in the subject you're teaching as well as in other areas: being a local soccer or swimming coach, making the best green chile enchiladas this side of Santa Fe, camping for two weeks in Yosemite with your family last summer, coordinating the school's recycling efforts, and reading undersea adventure thrillers. It's important for parents to know that their children's leaders are active, moral, and contributing members of the community. Additional topics for your presentation might include a summary of the curriculum's big topics with a reference on how to get a detailed copy if desired; a list of ways parents can help their children study at home; and comments about the positive effects of exercise, proper diet, and plentiful sleep on students' academic achievement.

Make sure to talk with your teammates and mentors about their Back-to-School Night presentations. They'll give you ideas on what's appropriate and what's not. The group of you might also coordinate a different team topic in each room: one discusses discipline, one, locker issues, one, field trips, and one, parent volunteers, for example. Make sure that one of your team colleagues or an administrator proofreads your handout. You want to make a good impression. Some parents will let one misspelled word or misplaced punctuation mark threaten their opinion of your strengths—they may not listen to anything else you say. Don't put such worries on their radar scope.

Display student work on the walls. Parents want to know that students are the focus of the room and that they've been productive. Clean your room, too. Replace clutter with organized samples of teaching materials: computer software running on a computer, textbooks open to sample units, sample score sheets or rubrics, sample lessons, calculators, manipulatives, sample novels, and anything else that gives a sense of the year ahead.

Most of the short time you'll have with parents on Back-to-School Night will be spent with you talking and the parents listening. If they ask questions, however, you can handle it well. You are a professional, and as such, you have no problems responding to a parent's inquiry. Sometimes you won't know the answer, and that's fine; no need to panic. Respond maturely: "That's a good question. I don't know the answer to it, but I'd be glad to do some research or ask a colleague and get back to you within a day or so." Experts know when they don't know. You'll come across as a neophyte if you try to answer something without conviction or with only partial accuracy. Conversely, you'll strengthen parent-teacher relations by saying, "I don't know" when you don't know the answer. Trust is vital.

If there is already controversy in the community around, say, the adoption of a new textbook series or the use of calculators on tests, speak with a department colleague or administrator ahead of time about how to respond to parent questions about it. You'll want to give an answer that is consistent with that of your colleagues or the administration. If it's something about which you haven't yet formed an opinion, say so:

> You know, Mr. Baxter, I'm just now exploring the possibilities this new book provides. I don't think I can draw any conclusions until I've taught from it for a semester or more. Please remember, too, that the textbook is not the curriculum. It is only one of many resources at my disposal as a teacher. Rest assured that I will choose what I think is the most challenging and developmentally appropriate route with every student, using more than one source. I'd like to withhold judgment about this textbook until January. In the interim, I invite you to submit written opinions to me or the administration any time you want.

Parents will respect your honesty and that you think for yourself. You've also shown that you look at controversial topics positively and professionally. If you find yourself agreeing with parents that a textbook series or a school district policy is not the best thing for students, you have every right as a member of the community and as a practicing professional to share your thinking. You may want to speak up at school board meetings, write letters to the local newspapers, or send e-mail to express your views to administrators. You're on the front line of teaching, so your opinions should count. The United States legal system fully supports teachers who practice their First Amendment rights as citizens.

Human interactions aren't that easy, however. Be wise, and accept a few facts: First, folks will see you as new and inexperienced. How could you know better than a group of seasoned veterans who investigated all possible textbook series or school district policies before settling on the current one? You didn't do the hard analysis and contemplation.

To be honest, they're right. You probably don't have the big picture as a new teacher, and your best move would be to observe, research, reflect, and explore the first year or two before declaring your opposing opinions. In addition, no matter how hard people try to embrace diverse opinions, they tend to feel negative toward conflict or those who pose conflict. Your viewpoints may ruffle some feathers in the administration or among colleagues. Be prepared to be perceived as negative, and to receive some angry responses to your ideas. Is your skin thick enough as a first-year teacher? Probably not, and you don't want to burn any bridges so early in your journey.

With everything else you have on your plate during the first year, try not to take on something so stomach-knotting as a current education controversy. Give yourself time to build skin. Go with the wisdom of your department colleagues or those who made the decisions, and make a few adaptations in your classroom practice if they're subtle and will get you through the year. Whatever you do, maintain nothing less than complete respect for those who made the current textbook selection or policy decision. Share with parents how difficult their decision was. Trust that steps were taken to elicit response from all stakeholders. Even in conflict, when you affirm the good faith of those on the opposing side, you come out looking good, and later, your suggestions for changes will be received with greater credence.

Back-to-School Night, however, is not the forum for educational debate. Remind parents of that if your presentation is sidetracked by parents' personal agendas: "I know that's an important issue in the community, but it's beyond the purview of tonight's presentation." Invite them to schedule an appointment with you or the administration to discuss the matter further. This works, too, for parents who want to ask questions about their children. Back-to-School Night is not the time to have such conversations. Invite parents to schedule a conference with you or the team (highly recommended) and give them the school's phone number. If you feel comfortable, remind them of this as you begin your presentation so you can head off inquiries.

Handling Difficult Parents

Assume good faith on the part of parents. There's no handbook for raising young adolescents. Many of them are figuring it out for the first time, and it's a little scary. Each week they're worried, proud, confused, heartened, and exasperated, hoping that the human hormone Tilt-a-Whirl before them will morph into a competent adult. You and I have been trained in what to expect during these years, but parents have not. We can cut them some slack when they misperceive something or when their emotions run close to the surface. Sometimes a lot of what we do with parents is to catch them up on the wisdom we've found in our teacher preparation courses and experiences.

National Board Certified teacher Beth Huddleston offers this advice:

> Plan for conferences. Decide on the points you want to emphasize with each parent. Begin with the positive growth you are seeing. I do not care how hard you have to look for it in some children, always find it. No parent likes to hear only about what is going wrong. I know because I am a parent, also. Then talk about areas on which we need to improve. Ask the parents for input; be partners in improvement. Yes, we as educators are the classroom specialists. However, the parents are a wealth of information and can help us achieve our goals.

Despite our good intentions and big-picture perspective and training, at some point in our careers parents will become angry at something we've done. Feelings will get hurt. If it happens during our first or second year, we can't lose our confidence or love for teaching, students, or their parents because of it. Instead, we get advice from experienced colleagues, reflect a bit, and handle it with maturity.

When a parent calls or visits us in anger, there are three things we can do to meet their needs and diffuse their frustration. First, we listen and make sure they know we understood what they shared with us. This means not thinking of our rebuttal to a parent while they're talking. Instead, we keep a running list of everything the parent is saying so that we can summarize it and ask for clarification when they are finished. After we've proven to them that we heard and understood what they shared with us, then we can consider our response to it. The greatest technique we can use in parent-teacher relations is listening.

Second, we show them how well we know their child. If I teach 150 students and I can clearly describe their child's strengths and challenges, it shows how much I respect their child and his family. It also shows my professional attention to his success. In addition, it expresses how much thought went into whatever decision it was that resulted in the parents' furor; it wasn't something we took lightly. Our initial comments to parents might sound like this:

> Here's what I know about Monte: He sometimes needs an extended time period to read passages, but what he reads, he remembers. He prefers to talk things out rather than writing out his ideas. His vocabulary is very large, demonstrating above average verbal skills. In addition, he produces better work when he has clear examples of what's expected. He's just learning how to compare his early drafts of something with the 4.0 Standard of Excellence set for the task. I also know that he's taking care of his younger sister each evening while you and his father work two evening jobs in order to make ends meet. He makes her dinner, reads to her, and gets her to bed, in addition to anything else he has to do with his own work. He's a Baltimore Orioles fan and this is his third school in five years. Given this description of his academic and personal background, I've decided to do the following things with him . . . [then later] Do these expectations match your goals for Monte?

It's always good to have supportive evidence for your claims about students. It's smart to have on hand samples of the student's work, copies of previous communications with parents (such as interim reports), and assessment scores. Making your case in such a clinical manner helps everyone keep the focus on the student's success. It's emotionally safe to discuss strategies honestly.

Third, we show them how much we love their child, as much as a stranger can reasonably be expected to do so. This is an opportunity to express our unwavering belief in the child's potential. Our comments might sound like this:

> I enjoy Monte's presence in class very much. He keeps our conversations lively; we can count on him to think of things in unusual ways. Even though we're not seeing his true abilities in these recent assignments, I've seen enough gold in previous assignments and his classroom contributions to know that he has great insight and we should hang in there. When traditional classroom assignments have not enabled him to express his full mastery of what is being taught, I've given him alternative routes to demonstrate mastery, such as doing the live interview with the manager of Pizza Hut rather than the poster of what makes for good and poor interviews, as the rest of the class did. The bottom line is what he knows and is able to do, and boy, does he know a lot. We just have to find the right pathway. Now, in order for him to find success . . .

If Mom and Dad are convinced that we have their child's best interests in mind as we make decisions, they're willing to consider dropping the defensive walls. One key to this is being proactive—talking with them ahead of time and getting to know them as people beyond just being someone's parents, if possible, and enabling them to know you, too. Just like with the students, if we know someone as a full individual, it's harder to get mad at them.

It's important, too, to call parents right away if we've made a mistake. We apologize and take our lumps for making the mistake, then we implement a plan to make sure the mistake is not repeated, making restitution to the student, if appropriate. If we wait a while before contacting parents, we look like we are trying to hide something from them. This will not endear them to us or to our description of the event in question. Their child will most likely tell his parents about the mistake if he knows about it so we might as well make the first time that parents hear of it from an adult's perspective. Admitting mistakes and apologizing sincerely is hard to do, but it's a sign of strength, not weakness. It will bolster your relationship with the student and his parents, not ruin it. We honor the family and our profession when we admit mistakes and rectify them.

Some middle school teachers choose never to have one-on-one conferences with parents. They always want someone else present to keep things calm and to provide a second observation of the conversation in case it's necessary later. This is sound advice, but it's not always reasonable. There are times when someone else isn't available and the conversation isn't going to be that contentious. It's okay to meet one-on-one with parents. Just make sure that you keep a written record of what was discussed and have the parents sign off as agreeing with the summaries as you've listed them.

If parents become even slightly irrational or abusive toward you, stop the conference immediately. You are not obligated in any way to take verbal or physical abuse. Explain to parents that they are speaking in a manner that will terminate the meeting if it continues. If it continues, inform them that the meeting has ended and it will be rescheduled for a time when an administrator can be present. Then escort them out of the building. If they refuse to go, contact an administrator or security officer to escort them from the building.

Parent Volunteers in the Classroom

I've read extensive research over the years about the direct correlation between parent involvement and student achievement. Middle schools with a lot of parent involvement accomplish amazing things, including higher scores on those all-consuming standardized tests.

Get parents into your room. Somehow we focus a little more, and we're more aware of our actions and our students when parents are in the room. The scrutiny is good for us; it results in effective student learning. It also enables students and parents to talk at home with a common frame of reference. Mom can picture her child in the room with the teacher when he describes what happened in our subject that day. This is in addition to the good testimony about quality instruction that gets spread around the community.

Parents can also add expertise, maturity, perspective, and an extra pair of hands, if you invite them to join the lesson. Finally, we can't underestimate the powerful effect on students of seeing teachers and parents working together in front of the class.

There are many roles for volunteer parents in our middle school classrooms. They include

- record keeping (make sure it's not regarding anything that reveals students' private academic achievement);
- creating, building, and maintaining bulletin boards, centers, in-class libraries, supply centers, Web sites, and areas for posted student work;
- preparation tasks such as photocopying, supply distribution, lab setup, project setup, collation, and other tasks to get things ready for specific lessons;
- restorative tasks such as cleaning/fixing/returning equipment, sorting papers, and repairing books;
- instructional assistance such as copresenting lessons, being an audience "plant" for a demonstration, conducting writing conferences, listening to students read, and working with individual or small groups of students on specific skills;
- specific knowledge or skill resource such as when a parent has first-hand experience with a historical event, a science concept, a type of writing, or math application;
- coordinating or helping with specific events like field trips and class celebrations;
- providing feedback to the teacher, such as tallying the amounts and types of interactions with girls versus boys in order to assess gender equity in our practice.

Concerns About Parental Choices

Letting Children Fly Solo

In this first or second year of your middle school practice, you will probably have a student who does poorly on something, and when his parents are informed of it, they will say that they're taking a hands-off approach this year—letting their child fly solo. He can learn the consequences of his decisions the hard way. After all, he's in middle school now.

Persuade them otherwise.

Young adolescence is the time to actually increase parental involvement, not back off. It's the second most rapid and influential period of development after ages zero to two. Parents wouldn't back off midstride from teaching their child how to walk when he was a toddler; they shouldn't back off from teaching him strong character and academics in his young adolescence. Students need clear structures and role models for handling life. Besides, it's important for middle schoolers to know that being in their presence is time well spent for an adult.

Vacations During School Time

Another concern is about parents who decide to take their family vacations during regular days of instruction, not the appointed school breaks for vacations. For example, a parent might come to us and say, "There's no school that Friday because of the teacher work day, so we thought we would just take Michael out of class the other four days as well so we could have a work week and two weekends at Disney World. You don't mind, do you? We go every year at this time. You get all the best accommodations that way."

Our shoulders tense, our hearts sink, we start a slow burn. "Well, it will be a critical time," we say, "because we're finishing our six-week projects and doing oral presentations that week. I was going to count those grades."

"No problem," the parent replies. "I'll have him stay after school for a few days to make it up."

As much as we'd like to, we can't prohibit parents from doing this, nor can we penalize the student for the decision. We have to find a way to make it work. For the moment, though, we hold on to a corner of our teacher's desk and concentrate on not ripping it off. "Sure, have a good time," we say, and we smile.

Taking vacations in the middle of instruction might be for very legitimate reasons: a death in the family, a chance to do scientific study in Antarctica, or building a Habitat for Humanity house. These are not the vacations that frustrate teachers. There's no debate; these vacations are justified—grieving and emotional support, scientific contributions, and service for others. Students will benefit more from those experiences than anything we can provide in the classroom.

The vacations that frustrate middle school teachers are the recreational ones taken because Aunt Matilda's in town; a parent was going away on business and decided to take the whole family for two weeks; it's a traditional trip for the family; Mom got discount travel or lodging tickets; or it's summer in their home country so they're leaving in December and returning in February. Also frustrating are the times when the child stays home with younger siblings while Mom and Dad are away on vacation. Finally, the most common one: taking mental health days when Mom takes Jennifer shopping. If any one of these happened once every five years, it might be okay.

Here's the rub: Parents send in a note asking teachers to send work for their child to do while on vacation so he can keep up with the class while he's away. As teachers we have two concerns about these requests: First, the child is on vacation; concentration and learning will be understandably less than preferred. Second, sending work along that enables him to keep up with classmates implies that being present in school doesn't really matter. Since we do a lot of direct instruction with students in the room, how do we package those lessons for a student to do independently on a family trip to New Orleans?

Some parents ask if their child can stay after for a few days to catch up when they return. With this one student staying from 3:00 to 4:00 P.M., how do we re-create the Socratic Seminar on Civil Rights? the give-and-take discussion of the novel *Good Night, Mr. Tom*? the finals of the team heart-rate-monitor runs? the presentation showing a fuel can crushing inwardly with no visible pressures being exerted on it because of the vacuum we created inside? In addition, all this time spent in catching up the returning student means we're not working with struggling students, grading papers, preparing lessons, making parent phone calls, serving on professional committees, or sponsoring clubs. All those things that we could've done during that time period are now shifted to our evening times, resulting in working later at night with less time with our own families. Besides crumbling foundations of student learning, vacations outside the times allotted in the school calendar are detrimental to a teacher's professional and personal duties.

Having said all this, we all know that one day, our own family will go to Disney World or do something similar, probably during the school year. The difference will be that it's the only time in our children's school careers that it will happen. School is a student's job, not something to take for granted. Just as we rise and show up every day, so can the student's family make attending school a priority.

So, what do we do about these vacations? First, we can be proactive and send home an encouragement not to choose dates for family vacations other than those listed on the school calendar. Second, we can share concerns diplomatically when they arise, including the fact that there's no way to make up the work because of direct instruction and the child will definitely miss foundations. Third, we can relax, smile, and do the best we can with the short time we have. In the big scheme of things, it probably isn't the end of the world. A lot of curriculum spirals back, so students will encounter it again. If this isn't the case with what you're teaching while the student is away, try to send something along. It's better than nothing. Make a note to contact that student a day after his return and review the missed material.

Whatever we do to strengthen parent relations improves our ability to teach our students. We pursue those relations, not just hope they will happen. Twenty-first-century middle school teachers seek innovative ways for parents to increase their advocate roles. Varied and regular communication is key. Middle schoolers and their teachers need personal contact with parents in multiple situations, including surprise visits with puppies—it's the stuff of humanity. Let's invite parents into our classrooms on a daily basis. It makes for a strong and stable parent-teacher-student triangle, not a hollow teacher-student cylinder about to roll off a desk. We have the technology and innovation to do it. United allies make for powerful achievement.

10

Substitute-Teacher Plans

Make sure that all items, worksheets, etc., are out and ready for the day. I spend many minutes trying to locate attendance forms, etc. Allow flexibility. Sometimes a lesson is perfect for you and your background, but it can be a challenge for someone who has not read the previous material that you have taught during the past few days or weeks. It is very difficult to ask intelligent questions about a topic that you know nothing about!

—*Substitute Teacher, KSWteach, giving advice to regular teachers on Guest-teacher.com*

There's a saying that what a teacher's students do when that teacher isn't present is a testimony to the quality of that teacher. I don't always buy that, however, because things happen for which we can't account, especially in an often-impulsive adolescent world. It's a good rule of thumb, however, to make sure students are as autonomous as possible in the event of our absence.

This means making sure that students are well versed in classroom procedures and taking on responsibility. It means teaching them to adapt to the level of authority in the room—not taking advantage of someone too relaxed and loose, not overreacting to someone overly structured and domineering. Adaptability is an important life skill. Taking the time to teach them how to adapt ahead of when they need to do it is time well spent.

Spend a few moments on several different days teaching students what to do when they run out of paper and need more, when they don't understand something and the teacher's working with someone else at the moment, when they need to go to the bathroom, and when someone's annoying them. Also teach them what to do when the printer gets jammed, when someone calls from the main office, when there's no picture on the TV and the tape is running in the VCR, and when the temperature of the room is too hot or too cold. Help them figure out what to do when they need to sharpen their pencils, can't see the board, spill something on the floor, the guinea pig escapes its cage, their lockers don't work, someone's taken their clothing after dressing out for PE, or the paint in the paint jar has dried up. Don't forget to teach them what to do when they sing off key in chorus, access an inappropriate Web site by accident, check out early for a doctor's appointment, or notice that the plants need water; when Mike's mouth turns purple because he bit into his pen and it leaked; and when someone gets a nosebleed. And this is just the starter list.

Let's assume you've enabled your classes to be as autonomous as possible and the day comes when you are absent due to illness, professional development/service, or a personal day. What is a good substitute teacher plan?

Substitute-Teacher Folder Essentials

There's much more to substitute-teacher plans than simply listing pages to be read in a textbook, so put everything into a folder or notebook. Many schools require these substitute-teacher folders to be housed in the front office. I prefer to keep them on the center of my desk ready to be used as needed because I add or delete materials up to the last minute. What I store in the front office are my emergency plans for when I'm not able to make normal substitute-teacher plans. More about these later.

Good substitute-teacher folders include the following items:

- a daily master schedule of when periods start and stop
- seating charts (or squad charts for PE) for every period of the day
- the actual step-by-step plans for each period of the day, including the special events that might affect the day such as planned fire drills, assemblies, pictures being taken in PE class, a book fair, student government elections, or a parent volunteer helping out during third period
- clear descriptions of classroom protocols such as whether or not the radio is allowed during instruction, how students sign out to use the bathroom, where papers get submitted, and how attendance is taken
- a map of the school with fire escape routes marked, accompanied by rosters for each class so that the teacher can call roll while out on the field or in the parking lot during drills or the real thing

- a sheet that explains your classroom discipline procedures so the substitute teacher is consistent—with referral forms enclosed in case students need to go to the office, to a time-out room, or to the clinic for any reason
- rosters of each period, labeled accordingly, with students' preferred names recorded, even phonetically, to aid familiarity
- names of students and colleagues upon whom the substitute teacher can call if she or he needs help during the day
- a list of students with special concerns (This is tricky because we want to protect children's privacy. If someone has a kidney infection, however, and cannot be denied access to the bathroom, this has to be marked. If someone is prone to seizures, this must be indicated, as well as the appropriate response from the teacher. If someone has a severe allergy, this must be indicated. Ask a colleague whether or not someone's special needs warrant mentioning in the substitute-teacher plan.)
- a place and format for reporting concerns and successes with students
- an invitation to join other teachers in the teacher's lounge for lunch; a description of the adult lunch costs in the cafeteria, where to get coffee or juice, where the bathrooms are, and all the other amenities of the school

The Lessons Themselves

When we're absent from the classroom, we don't want a baby-sitter in our place. We prefer someone who thinks and teaches. Our plans should be written for folks we assume to be intelligent and caring substitute teachers and who need the full picture in order to do a good job. As you can imagine, detailed plans enable teaching, while short, cryptic plans usually result in baby-sitting.

If we think there will be confusion over one element of a lesson, we offer two or three strategies that the substitute teacher may want to employ to mitigate struggles. If students might finish early, we offer further activities that are substantive. If one class has a different background or response to concepts, we explain it thoroughly. If there's a dynamic situation in which two or three students should not be allowed to work together, we state such. We don't want to pass things off with a "Oh well, she'll find out for herself" attitude. We're writing the plans with an eye to the substitute's success, not relying solely on her ingenuity and experience.

Figure 10.1 shows a set of plans that I used recently.

Figure 10.1 Substitute-Teacher Plans

Rick Wormeli   **7th Grade English Teacher**
Crusaders Team, 7C   **Rachel Carson Middle School**

Substitute-Teacher Plans
[Today's Date]

Hello. Thank you for taking over for me today. I'm at a required inservice training at another school. Feel free to let any of the activities run longer or shorter according to the mood and energy in the room. Let me know what was accomplished and what wasn't and I'll pick up from there. Remember, I purposely overplanned so there would be plenty to do. Don't feel bad if you don't get to everything.

There is a list of class procedures and other information about our class following these lesson plans. The substitute folder also contains the daily bell schedule. Please take a moment at the end of your day or during free periods and record any comments you have on student behavior and accomplishments. If you or students need to contact me, my e-mail address is rwormeli@erols.com, or my voicemail number is 555-3680, ext. 1740. Thanks again, Rick.

The Day-at-a-Glance:
1st Period—English 7 [8:00–8:57]
2nd Period—English 7 [9:00–9:47]
3rd Period—English 7 [9:50–10:37]
4th Period—Personal Planning Period [10:40–11:27]
5th Period—Activity Period and Lunch
[11:30–11:44 Activity Period, 11:47–12:17 Lunch] ·
6th Period—English 7 [12:20–1:07] [Cotaught with LD specialist]
7th Period—IPR period [1:10–1:57] [Team-planning, period off for you]
8th Period—English 7 [2:00–2:50]
Dismissal [2:53–2:58]

Specific Plans for today, October 4:
1st Period—English 7 [8:00–8:57]

1. Take the school attendance following the instructions printed on the outside of the attendance folder. Use a number 2 pencil! There are pens and pencils in my desk or on the podium up front. [The attendance folder is in the left pocket of this folder.] This is a good time for students to record the homework from the green Boogie Board (a.k.a., Homework Board) near the flag. Then ask them to look over the menu for the day on the front chalkboard.

2. At approximately 8:03, the administration will come on the P.A. system and ask everyone to join in saying the Pledge of Allegiance. Make sure everyone stands up and is respectful. (They will be.) Once the Pledge is done, everyone should be seated, but remain silent for the Moment of Silence mandated by the Commonwealth of Virginia, then remain silent for the morning announcements that follow.

3. Call roll by using the student rosters I provided in the substitute-teacher folder. Record nothing if they're present, "abs" if they're absent, and "T" if they're tardy. Attach any notes/passes students give you to the attendance sheet.

4. Read "The Fish That Went to School" to the class. It is found on page 12 of the yellow and tan book entitled "Best-Loved Short Stories" found under these plans on my desk. We do read-alouds every day, so they should be good listeners. This one demonstrates strong irony, which is one of our concepts for this week. When it is over, ask students to comment on the irony—what was ironic? Did they predict the surprise twist at the end? If so, when? How did the author set us up to believe one thing, then spring this other outcome on us? Was the story more effective with irony or would it work just as well without it?

5. Ask students to take out their root word list for this week. Working in table groups or by themselves (their choice, or your choice, if you are uncomfortable with the noise), have them place the roots in categories of no less than three items to constitute a category. To determine categories, students look at the definitions and look for connections between them.

Figure 10.1 *(continued)*

Every root word must be in a category. Example categories can be things associated with a laboratory, school things, things found in nature, opposites, things that mean the same thing, things that make a noise, things that are scary, things that heat up. Students make up the categories based on the root words' meanings, not the spelling of the word. This means they CANNOT use categories like short words, rhyming words, words I don't know, words that have a lot of consonants.

Students must do one full categorization of the whole list by the end of class. If they finish early, they are to work on their root word chart, or make a completely new arrangement of the root words in brand-new categories. If you have time, you might want to have a competition as to which table group can come up with the most categories, all of which must be legitimate, not fluff.

6. Taboo Cards: Explain to students that we will be playing Taboo with them next Tuesday and they need to make their own deck of cards for that game. Draw the following example Taboo card on the chalkboard:

Root word above the line ⟶

Words commonly associated with the root word (4 or 5 needed) ⟶

Dura
Long-lasting
Durable
Hard
Battery
Forever

These cards are index cards cut in half and turned vertically. They need to make one card for every root word, which means they need to get at least 20 index cards to do this small project. The back side of each card should have the game title, "Taboo," and the student's name on it. If folks don't finish, it becomes homework, but it's not due until Tuesday. It's okay if desk groups discuss possible commonly associated words for each root word. Learning occurs when they talk about things in a substantive manner.

7. Give students a copy of the handout on "Show, Don't Tell." There is a stack of these handouts on the right side of my desk. Read the handout with them aloud—either students reading or you reading. Explain each item in the boxed strategies list near the top of the handout, and have them study the example in the center of the page. Then, read with them the directions at the bottom of the page and let them complete the three requested descriptions. This is due tomorrow, if folks don't finish.

8. If you have time, have students read the sample Reading Autobiographies on their tables. These are desk copies and are not to be removed from the room. Ask students to record five things the student who wrote the sample reading autobiography did correctly. This is to be done on their own paper and turned in to me via the white paper bins near the side chalkboard.

If students finish early, they can do one or more of the following things:
- Finish their root word chart.
- Write a one-paragraph prediction describing how the movie of *The Outsiders* will be different from the book. We're seeing it Thursday and Friday.
- Work on their *Outsiders* projects.
- Work on their own Reading Autobiography (they have the direction sheet for this in their notebook, a copy of which is in these plans).

Need more to do? Check out the end of these plans for more ideas.

2nd Period—English 7 [9:00–9:47]
[Repeat the same procedures described in 1st Period, starting with item #3.]

3rd Period—English 7 [9:50–10:37]
[Repeat the same procedures described in 1st Period, starting with item #3.]

4th Period—Personal Planning Period [10:40–11:27]
You may relax and mentally "regroup" for the rest of the day.

5th Period—Activity Period and Lunch
[11:30–11:44 Activity Period, 11:47–12:17 Lunch]

Figure 10.1 *(continued)*

Activity Period: We do different activities throughout the week. Wednesdays are usually character education days, but today it will be what we normally do on Tuesdays and Thursdays: silent reading, homework, and tutorials. Make sure everyone has something to read or do. There is no sharing of materials, such as two students to one book. Monitor for appropriate behavior. If a student asks to go to another teacher for help or to go to the library, that's fine, too.

Lunch: Make sure students clear out of the locker area and get to the cafeteria before you eat your lunch. You are invited to eat in our Teacher's Lounge located near the cafeteria (on the hallway walking toward the front office), our workroom directly across the hall from my room, in the classroom, or outdoors, if the weather is nice. Lunches for adults in our cafeteria are about $2.50. We have a refrigerator in our workroom across the hall from me if you want to store your lunch there.

6th Period—English 7 [12:20–1:07]
This is a special class. It's a team–Learning Disabilities class. A small group of these students have been identified as learning disabled and there is an LD specialist in the room with you to make sure they do okay. Elizabeth Murphy is that specialist and she will be your partner in the class. In fact, since she knows the students, let her teach the class while you monitor for proper attention. Elizabeth is really easygoing, however. If you've found something helpful from teaching the same lessons earlier in the day, share those ideas with her and the two of you can decide how best to run things. Elizabeth will be able to discern who needs modification of assignments today, if any.
[Repeat the same procedures described in 1st Period, starting with item #3.]

7th Period—IPR period [1:10–1:57]
This is a time for the team teachers to meet. This is another period for you to rest, read a good book, or get a snack. Make sure things are ready for the last period of the day. Do the lessons outlined in period 1, starting with #3. This is also a good time to reflect on your day, noting particularly helpful or frustrating students. I do parent phone calls for every student mentioned, positive calls or calls requesting assistance from Mom and Dad.

8th Period—English 7 [2:00–2:50]
Repeat the same procedures described in 1st Period, starting with #3 and deleting #7. This class already made their Taboo cards. Just remind these students that they will be playing Taboo tomorrow, not next Tuesday.

Warning: afternoon announcements will come on and students must be quiet to listen to them starting about 2:45.

Dismissal—Please stand in the hallway near the lockers and ensure proper behavior and a speedy exit to the buses.

[2:53–2:58]
Turn in everything at the front office. If you have time, jot down comments on your day and on the students. That's it. Thank you!—Rick Wormeli

Notes and Addenda:
1. Our team teachers are English—me; Science—Mrs. Leonard; Math—Mrs. Cutler; and History—Mrs. Buckheimer. These teachers are all located on the same hallway. Mrs. Buckheimer has the locker key in case anyone has locker troubles.

2. There is a seating chart for each period. Feel free to move folks around if they're distracting others or you, however.

3. Please do not allow anyone to touch the computers while I'm away.

4. Students use the wooden "C" located near the front chalkboard as a hall pass.

5. Students may go to the bathrooms, lockers, etc., one at a time, and NOT DURING THE LAST 10 MINUTES OR THE FIRST 10 MINUTES OF CLASS.

Figure 10.1 (*continued*)

6. Papers are all turned in to the large white bins located on the side chalkboard under the clock.

7. No radio or tapes during the periods. Listen all you want yourself during planning time.

8. Supplies in the supply area are for anyone's use.

9. How's your sense of humor? Keep it nearby.

10. Please note the fire escape route on the wall near the door. Have students move in silence and face away from the building during the drill. You must call roll as well, so take a student roster with you!

11. Other discipline ideas: If a verbal warning and a private conversation do not result in the proper change of behavior, send the student to sit in another class on our team. If it continues, send him or her to the office. Send a referral along as to why the student was sent. Referral forms are in the right pocket of this notebook.

12. If a student gets out of line severely (as in an emergency or physical harm might occur) press the button on the silver box located near the doorway and respond to responses from the front office with, "Please send a D.I.P. form to Room C107." An administrator will come instantly. D.I.P. means "Danger in the Pod."

13. Discipline: First Offense—Warning and explanation
    Second Offense—Isolation within the room
    Third Offense—Send the student to another Team 7C teacher's room.
    Fourth Offense—To the office.
       Note: I justify my actions to the students. Please do not discipline to express anger at a student, or because you were offended. Phrase warnings in terms of choice so he/she takes the responsibility. For example, "Do you want to sit and work quietly or do you want to be removed from the class and sit in the back of Mrs. Buckheimer's class?" A very effective threat: I will invite parents of disruptive students to come sit with them during class for a day or two. Please watch for and verbally appreciate quality behavior. It does wonders!

14. No candy or gum is to be consumed at any time by students. Students may consume healthful snacks during their period with me (you). This includes fruit, vegetables, muffins, pudding, popcorn, small juices, water, sandwiches, pretzels, etc. No peanut products, however, because we have students with deadly allergies to peanuts!

15. Aerosol can sprays are to be confiscated—even for deodorant, hairspray, etc.

16. So are water pistols! (Suspension-level offense)

If there's still extra time (Worthy Fillers!):*
- Conduct a Spelling Bee de Strange:
  Students go to the front of the class and spell the words as normal, but instead of saying vowels, they make an unusual noise with their body or mouth. YOU CHOOSE the noises in advance and write them on the board, e. g., a = achoo, e = "thbpht!" (raspberry noise with your lips and tongue), o = oink, oink!, i = ribbit (like a frog), and u = oo-la-la!. You can put a movement with each one if you wish.
     Choose words from the dictionaries, a vocabulary list, or choose your own words.

- You may also play the game PASSWORD with words associated with English class, or other subjects or school in general. Students also know another game called 1, 2, or 3. It's an easy logic game. Have them teach you if you don't already know it.

- Students may also write a letter to me about their day or this period.

COMMENTS ON THE DAY OR ON STUDENTS: (Anyone particularly helpful or particularly disruptive?) [Use the next sheet of paper.]
* See *Time Management for Teachers* by Scott Purdy for more ideas.

Whew! A lot of detail, eh? Do we write this level of detail every time we leave plans? Yes and no. In today's modern age, we can keep the basic template for every time we're absent, changing only the date and the specific plans as described in first period. Of course, we need to update the addenda at the end of the plans with new protocols and situations, and we'll have to add or delete information from different periods if they are not at the same point in instruction, just as I did for period eight in Figure 10.1. We have to update our student rosters as well. For my first set of plans it might take two hours to write all of this. For each set of plans after that, however, it'll take thirty to forty-five minutes—long enough to design the sequence of the basic lesson. We insert the sequence into the template, then print off all four or five pages for the substitute teacher.

Another thing to consider: Imagine that you're sick with a terrible flu. In order to get your plans to school, you crawl out of bed, steady yourself on your feet, throw on clothes that you wear only on Saturdays to clean the garage, get in your car, race through the cold, wet, predawn streets, only to arrive at school and find the front doors still locked. You pound on the doors, hoping the custodial staff will hear you, then you go around to the back side of the building to check the gymnasium entrance, only to return minutes later after finding it locked. This time you find the front doors unlocked by a passing custodian. Once inside, you head straight for the photocopying machine, praying that no one will be using it this early. Wrong. Tom, the civics teacher, is running his booklet for the month. You sponge the sweat from your face with your sleeve and ask him whether or not you can slip in for a few minutes and make 150 copies of two different worksheets for the substitute teacher you have today. He agrees and steps aside. Finished photocopying, you go to your room and lay out the plans on your desk, gathering any other needed supplies. As you make your way toward the building's front entrance, praying for a third time that you won't faint, vomit, or have an uncontrolled bowel movement, you pass Joe from the art department, who hollers, "Only putting in half a day?" then laughs. You crack a smile, but your face hurts. You collapse into your car, drive home, then tumble into bed, wondering if the four blankets you've gathered over you will be enough to quell the chills. You have two final thoughts before drifting into unconsciousness: You have to call the school by 2:00 P.M. if you're going to be out again tomorrow, and you forgot to mention in the substitute-teacher plans that Mrs. Ortez was doing a presentation to your sixth-period class today on her work as a NASA scientist. You'll try to call later and tell someone.

It doesn't have to be this way. Smart teachers set up systems to take care of these sorts of things before they happen. Here are a few ideas: First, consider e-mailing your plans to a colleague with whom you've worked out such a relationship. He'll get your plans off the Internet and do the photo-copying and preparation if necessary because you do it for him when he needs it. If he lives nearby, it might be better to drive hard copies of the plans to his house.

Second, forfeit the day's plans and use emergency plans. Have on file in the front office emergency substitute-teacher plans that are self-contained—they take only one period and they have all the supplies nec-essary to implement them. This takes some work over the summer or in the first month, but they'll give you great peace of mind. Find activities in your subject area that can be done just by reading some quick directions. Independent and group work are both acceptable. I often photocopy inter-esting pages from workbooks, create small-group projects for them to do, like designing underwater cities that reflect the politics of ancient Rome, and look for content-related videos that I preview, then design a scholarly interaction students can do after viewing it. See Chapter 8, "Dealing with Homework," for examples of assignments that make great substitute-teacher-plan activities.

If you have only one or two periods to teach that day because of a field trip, standardized testing, or something else, call a teammate and see if your students can be divided among your teammates for just those periods. List four or five purposeful things they can do in the back of those teach-ers' rooms that will keep them focused while you're away.

Finally, get married if you're not already. Loving spouses show how much they love you by taking your substitute-teacher plans to school when you're sick. It's worth a solid twenty-minute back rub from you on the first evening you feel better.

Substitute teachers appreciate detailed plans. Like most of us, they get nervous in situations in which they have to operate in the dark. And as we all know, one unprepared teacher can quickly find himself in an awkward situation, as M. S., a substitute teacher, describes.

> I was subbing in an eighth-grade science class that was showing a National Geographic video on predators and prey. This particular segment was about tigers. Because it was a National Geographic video, I thought to myself that there might be a scene where two tigers are mating. "Nah," I thought, and shrugged it off. Indeed, fifteen minutes into the movie, they started going at it. "Ooohh, they're doing it kitty style!" was one of the many comments I heard. Trying to maintain a serious face, I walked over to the VCR and attempted to skip this segment. Naively, instead of pressing the "stop" button, then pressing "fast forward," I pressed just the

fast-forward button. You can only imagine what the kids saw next, only twice as fast!

Anything you can do to make their jobs easier will translate to a good day for your students—a win-win situation. Keep them informed.

Don't hesitate to let administrators know when a substitute teacher does something that concerns you. It's your legal duty, in fact, if it was something that violated school rules or suggested inappropriate behavior for a teacher. Failing to report such a situation can land you in hot water, and worse, it can enable that substitute teacher to continue to work with children. Every two to three years we get a substitute teacher somewhere in our building who makes a serious mistake in judgment or whose temperament is somehow inappropriate, and we have to take steps to make sure he or she does not return to the school or district.

Most substitute teachers are wonderful. They are thoughtful people trying to help our schools and earn some money. Many of them develop enduring relationships with staff members and students, returning to the same schools week after week. If you find someone good, get her phone number and call her well in advance to schedule her to substitute for you if you know when you'll be out. It makes a big difference when the substitute teacher knows your style and students. Cultivate those relationships. Remember these folks during teacher appreciation weeks, at holidays, and during the summer months, if possible. If they're substituting for someone else in the building, stop by and ask if they need anything. Invite them to the faculty ice cream social that afternoon. Treat them with the highest professional respect: Substitute teachers have very difficult jobs and they handle them well. Many are retired teachers or other professionals. Some are wise with many years of living and working with others. They earn our deepest gratitude every day.

11

Our Own Professional Development

Know what's weird? Day by day, nothing seems to change, but pretty soon . . . everything's different.

—Calvin from Calvin and Hobbes

Progress is not inevitable.

—Martin Luther King, Jr.

Wait a minute, *you say. I just graduated from a school of teacher preparation. Why do I need to go to more classes and get more training? Let me just teach for a while.*

Embrace your status as a professional educator. Professionals update themselves every chance they get. Airline pilots must complete a certain number of weeks of schooling each year in order to keep their licenses. Accountants take courses every year to learn the latest tax laws. It's the same with lawyers, engineers, computer programmers, and police officers. Can you imagine a doctor who never updates herself on the latest diseases, symptoms, and treatments? To wave off our own development because we have neither the time nor inclination isn't being professional. Young adolescents in our communities deserve professionals, not mere jobholders. In order to maintain that high standard to which we aspire, we need the stimulation and intellectual nourishment that the best professional development can provide.

Professional Development Possibilities

Mentoring Programs

Some of the best forms of professional development can be found in our own schools. Mentoring programs are among the most effective ways to grow as a teacher. Mentors provide perspective and practicality in ways no teacher preparation institution can. They are physically present in the building, their aid immediate. Mentoring programs have also been proven to retain good teachers. Teachers can go to mentors with questions rising from daily classroom struggles: "How can I explain ionic and covalent bonds when the students can't picture them?" "What am I missing with Jennifer? She doesn't understand what she reads." These questions are discussed easily with mentors but rarely occur anywhere else in a new teacher's life—not in the teacher's lounge, not walking down the hallway, not while standing around the photocopying machine, and not while on cafeteria duty. Sadly, not even in most department meetings.

While teachers are being asked to engage their own students in active learning, problem solving, and inquiry, they rarely experience this kind of learning themselves. Mentors provide such opportunities, but to get the most you can out of the mentoring experience there are a few things to remember.

Avoid taking initial failures personally. Allow your mentor to provide you with his or her seasoned perspective. It's hard to have the big picture or long view of a situation when you've been at it only a few months. Your mentor's perspective helps you see the positives in seemingly negative experiences, and makes it easier to get out of bed in the morning. Eventually, it won't all be about just getting through the day without harming anyone. It'll be about taking risks—and even soaring.

Don't hold back from asking your mentor the big questions about which you wonder: Do I have what it takes? Can all children learn? How do I teach creatively with the statewide standardized testing looming overhead? How do I differentiate instruction? Is it okay to group kids homogeneously? How do I decide what's important in the textbook chapter? Do I let students redo homework and tests? How do I know if a student learned what I wanted him to learn? Can the community hold me accountable if my students fail? How do I grade all these papers? What do I do about Mrs. Cooper and her surprise puppy visits?

As you ask your mentor for guidance, don't be afraid to ask the same question five or six times. Mentors know how much you're juggling—they were once new, too. Your questioning also helps them redefine their own teaching beliefs, which can be energizing.

Meet regularly with your mentor, at least once a week. You might think this time is unnecessary some weeks, but once the conversations start, you probably will find new approaches, solutions to unresolved issues, and emotional support. Regularity creates security. When you can count on a definite meeting time, you won't worry as much.

Take comments or attitudes expressed by cynical staff members to your mentor if you don't know what to make of them. While new teachers need to learn how to think for themselves, you may not have enough experience to understand the context of negative comments or to provide reasoned responses to them. Your mentor can provide these.

Be flexible. If your mentor suggests something, try it before judging whether or not it's right for you. Mentors are there to push you, not just listen.

Thank your mentor once in a while. Spread good comments about him or her. Being a mentor is not easy. This person is putting a lot of time and energy into your success. It's very classy to show your appreciation for his or her commitment to you.

Professional Reading

Be well read. Read everything you can about your subject and about middle school teaching and do it every year of your career. Respond to the text—write in the margins, mark up the paragraphs. Talk with others about what you've read. The brain moves information to the front of our minds when we share orally. We need to interact with what we've read. Some of my colleagues write running summaries and personal responses to what they read as well. Some find and share pertinent articles with one another on a regular basis. The interaction is important. Information is more useful when it is at our mental fingertips ready to use instead of being something we filed in a cabinet or on a bookshelf that we can use only when we physically look for it. Talking about what we've read enables this.

Reflective Learning Logs

When I went through National Board Certification ten years ago, I had to maintain a written record of what I did each day as well as a written commentary of why I did it. I had to connect the dots, showing the correlations between what I did as a teacher and what my students learned. After a few evenings of doing this, something peculiar happened: my instructional decisions became dramatically better.

Because I wrote and reflected on daily practice, I gained a big-picture perspective. I wasn't making decisions on the fly. I weighed pros and cons, brainstormed options, and wrote my way into understanding the dynamics of my instruction at a depth the typical daily flurry of activities did not allow. I saw things with clarity. It changed who I was as a teacher. An added bonus: I was far more relaxed and self-assured in the classroom. I didn't self-doubt; my decisions were sound.

In almost all the subjects I've taught, my students have maintained learning logs in which they recorded information on one page and then made applications of the information or personal responses to that information on the other page. I've often joined them in maintaining a learning log, posting mine for comments on a bulletin board. It was always a highlight of the unit, and I learned more about the topic, let alone about teaching it, by maintaining the log. My students' questions and products were better whenever I used learning logs.

Today I do the same thing professionally by writing regular magazine columns, corresponding by e-mail, and writing summaries of new concepts I want to teach. Becoming a reflective practitioner has made me a better teacher. In such a fast-paced, make-a-decision-now world, it might be one of the greatest skills we can model for our students.

Listservers

Think of a student who seems unteachable. He never does his homework, he doesn't care about learning or his grades, he's annoying to his classmates. His parents are nice, but they work two jobs each and are rarely available to him. He's failing your class, but his tests indicate superior ability in all areas. You've tried every trick you know, and you've sought the advice of at least three colleagues at your school. Nothing seems to work.

Post such a description on a listserver of dedicated middle school professionals and you'll have seventeen responses from around the world within five hours. Have a difficult principal or parent? Wonder about a new math software program? Have a question about differentiating instruction, assessment, or teaching parts of speech? Post concerns or ideas on professional listservers and get some of the best thinking out there. Listservers are one of the most productive uses of a teacher's time.

Make sure to join one that is moderated. One of the best is the listserver at www.middleweb.com. As of this writing, it's hosted by educator, author, and editor John Norton. The listserver's tone is ceaselessly professional and courteous, and the postings are substantive—not just "Yeah, I agree," and not crass. John makes sure of that. He also archives conversation strings so that if you just joined and have a question about something that was discussed in depth a few months ago, you can pull up the entire discourse about that topic at once. I've made changes in what I do in my practice as a result of conversations I've followed on that listserver.

An added benefit: Some of the biggest names in middle school education participate from time to time. In the past, Thomas Dickinson, Cris Tovani, Deb Bambino, Brenda Dyck, Michelle Pedigo, Chris Toy, and John Lounsbury have weighed in on topics. Many universities require students to join for the duration of their middle school coursework. Middle-L is another useful listserver. The National Middle School Association has a bulletin board on its Web site (www.nmsa.org) called Teachers On-line that is recommended as well.

Instructional Roundtables

Post a topic on your faculty's e-mail system or on the bulletin board in the teacher's lounge at the beginning of each month. On the assigned day for each month, gather all those who are interested in discussing the topic in one teacher's classroom and have each person share one idea in response to the topic. For example, how to handle the paper load. Everyone brings a small snack and a dozen copies of their one idea about how to decrease the paper load to share with the group. In one hour, you'd have as many ideas as there are people, and usually more because teachers generally can't limit themselves to one idea. Chairs and desks are put into a circle to facilitate conversation. Other popular topics include motivating the unmotivated, authentic assessment, grading, teaching reading in content areas, integrating disciplines, brain research applied to cognitive science, discipline, teaching differently in extended-length periods, seating arrangements that work, incorporating the one or two computers you have in the classroom, teaching grammar, how to be successful with heterogeneous grouping, homework practices, and how to work with parents successfully.

Faculty Portfolio of Ideas

Help establish a Faculty Portfolio of Ideas. These are plastic crates or boxes located at each photocopying machine that contain a folder for each subject taught in your school. When staff members photocopy materials for use in their classes, invite them to make one additional copy and place it in the appropriate folder in the crate or box. These copies can include tests, projects, vocabulary lists, chapter summaries, classroom policies, graphic organizers, unit plans, field-trip forms, parent letters, behavior contracts, bulletin board ideas, articles, diagrams, and instructional samples. It is accepted that anything in the folders is free for others to use or adapt. Remember, however, to get permission when using lessons from grade levels above your own. You don't want to take away from another teacher's plan for next year. These folders accumulate a wealth of new ideas for beginning teachers, as well as a way for all teachers to gauge their pacing and approach. Elective teachers can see what core subject teachers are doing and vice versa, thereby fostering interdisciplinary connections. Different grade levels get a better sense of what students have experienced or will one day experience. At the end of the year, bind the year's ideas from all photocopying machines into one portfolio and store the portfolio in your school's on-site professional library.

Videotaping and Analysis

Ask your mentor or a colleague to videotape you in the classroom. If he cannot do it, he can help you set it up with a media specialist or an off-duty staff member. Afterward, watch the tape privately, noting things you did well, things to improve, and the effects on student learning. There's no evaluation here. If you feel comfortable, review the tape with your mentor. Let him know your concerns and goals prior to viewing. Feel free to stop the tape, rewind it, play it again, and explore alternative responses and strategies. Viewing tapes of your teaching can be eye-opening. I see things I never knew the students were doing, yet during the lesson I felt I was aware of everything that was going on in the room. Thankfully, the camera isn't subject to human vanities. It doesn't interpret or distort. It's best to analyze your practice against a set of standards or goals.

Workshops and Conferences

Keep your eyes and ears open. Some of the best conferences I ever attended were ones I overhead someone else talking about with a colleague. If someone whose work you've read or heard about is coming to a relatively close location to do a workshop, grab the opportunity. Be careful, though. Most seminars, conferences, and school district professional development academies have narrow windows for registration, and those that require an overnight stay have limited hotel space. Act fast. Decide within a day or two of receiving information as to whether or not you want to go, then take action if you do. Getting forms processed by administrators, finding funding, and making travel arrangements can take time. Whatever you do, don't bury the advertisement in your "To Do" tray. If it's anything like mine, you'll find that flyer for the "How to Motivate Young Adolescents" seminar in October when you clean out the tray in December.

Webcasts and Video-Conferencing

Webcasts and video-conferencing are becoming popular with educators as costs for such experiences decrease and concern over teachers leaving the classroom for days at a time rise. In a Webcast, teachers need a computer that connects to the Internet—that's it; there is no other special equipment or software required. At the appointed time, a national expert on the day's topic comes online and posts his slides on his own computer. The presentation is broadcast in real time around the world or to a specific site, depending on the needs of the participants.

As the presenter highlights information on his screen and moves through his presentation, the same thing happens on the screens of all the participants, wherever they are in the world. Participants can call or e-mail questions into the speaker and he answers in real time. The presenter can also ask questions of the audience, and everyone participating sees the responses immediately in a tally bar to one side of the screen. Handouts are sent ahead of time so everyone has the information at their fingertips.

Because it provides great professional development without having to pay for airfares, lodging, meals, ground transportation, or substitute teachers (most are held during after-school hours), and because it is so interactive, Webcasts are a particularly effective form of professional development. Video-conferencing is similar, but requires video equipment on both ends. This is fine if you have such equipment; otherwise, the Webcast is a better choice. As a new teacher looking for easy ways to get professional development in your first years of service, consider Webcasts and videocasts. The National Middle School Association (NMSA), the Association for Supervision and Curriculum Development (ASCD), and Staff Development for Educators (SDE) offer such experiences on a regular basis.

Final Thoughts

Like most things worth doing, teaching is a journey. We never fully arrive, though we travel quite a distance. Oliver Wendell Holmes once remarked, "The greatest thing in this world is not so much where we are, but in what direction we are moving." How appropriate for middle school teachers. We're not superhuman robots doing everything masterfully at once. We're only able to approximate the goal, keeping our eyes on the goal of mastery. Will Rogers expanded on this: "Even a man on the right track will get run over if he just stands there." Remember that while yearly pursuit of outstanding professional development is the right track for you, it requires constant progression. The best middle school educators don't rely only on occasional school or districtwide professional development. They continually pursue their own professional development as well, thereby improving their teaching effectiveness. As a self-renewing, professional middle school teacher, you will serve your students well.

Relating to Students

I would try to be as honest with them as possible. I couldn't have ever pulled off not smiling or acting like a hardnose. It's just not me. But there were things that I was very hardnosed about—teasing, calling someone stupid, not trying, thinking you couldn't do something. Outside of those types of things, I always taught from the perspective that it was our classroom and together we were going to take on something that was tough—spending a year together tackling new ideas and pushing ourselves to grow and learn new stuff. I emphasized the "hard but not impossible." By this I mean I didn't pull any punches about how they wouldn't be perfect (neither would I) in trying to become junior scientists or mathematicians. But that was the beauty of being a class—to help each other, challenge each other, and push each other.

—Marsha Ratzel, middle school educator

I spent six summers as a staff member at Frost Valley YMCA in New York's Catskill Mountains. There were times during those months when things just clicked with a camper. It was especially meaningful when the camper came to us on a campership, which meant he might be someone from an emotionally abusive home, with little money and even less hope. At the end of several days spent hiking mountains, playing sports, climbing, participating in Project Adventure, singing crazy songs, doing service projects, and assisting a cabinmate who underwent kidney dialysis every other morning, we gathered around a campfire after sunset and let the deeper talk flow—the normally inviolable walls around emotions dissolved. A hardened twelve-year-old boy, who'd been a wisecracking, obnoxious member of our group, sat next to me. The deep blue shades of Lake Cole filled the evening background behind his head while an orange glow from fading embers flickered on his face.

"I've never thanked anyone before," he said, his voice as small as the river stones around us.

"What do you mean?" I asked.

"I mean, really thanked them. You know, someone passes you something and you nod or maybe joke about it, but you're not really aware of what they did for you to have that thing," he replied. "It's just expected. No big deal."

"Yeah."

He was silent a moment before continuing. "And so, I just want to say it to you."

I remained quiet, watching the white moon's crisp reflection on the lake's surface.

"So, thank you," he said.

"That's nice to hear," I responded, "but for what are you thanking me?"

He averted his eyes from mine before speaking. "For putting up with me. I know I'm high maintenance, yet every time, you let me start fresh. I take a lot out of people without putting much back."

I turned back to him. "Wow, that's a lot to accept. You're welcome."

We listened to the bullfrogs across the lake for a few moments, the conversation's pause filled, with both of us wanting to hold the moment.

"I like who I am when I'm here," he said.

I nodded and realized that I did, too.

Yes, I know it sounds like a "special moment" greeting card or a television commercial for a religious group, but it's not; this moment really occurred. Such a connection between teacher and student happens frequently in the outdoors, away from an institutional context, especially after working together toward a goal. The trick is to create similar relationships beyond the wilderness, even in our everyday lives at a middle school.

Of course, I am making the assumption that new teachers will want to connect with their students in ways beyond a student's being just one more paper to grade. If this is not the case with you, you may find that there is not enough personal meaning in your work as a middle school teacher to maintain your commitment to the students and profession for more than one or two years. When students and teachers remember their most formative moments in middle school, they will recall a deep connection with someone at the school. Our relations with one another—student to student, student to teacher, teacher to teacher, teacher to administration—

give purpose to everything else we do. Truly, when we look back, we remember the people more than the subject lessons.

One of the best pieces of advice about relating to students took me a long time to accept. It is this: When we interact with students in a manner designed to get them to like us, we end up alienating them and teaching poorly. If we're not sure how to act in a given situation, we should always choose sound instructional practices over opportunities to be a friend. We're out for the long-term, deeper connection, not the short-term, superficial one that will not stand the test of a full year together. Sound pedagogy develops far more positive teacher-student relations than "Look-how-much-fun-I-can-be" teacher presentations.

Young adolescents find professional, well-prepared teachers endearing. They soon realize that insecure and unprofessional teachers who are dealing with their own issues from adolescence are to be avoided. Middle schoolers crave academic success and positive interactions with competent adults, not folks acting like their peers. They gravitate toward us because we offer a positive and mature model of how to be. Teachers who choose to act and think like the students they teach fail to connect with their students beyond the first few weeks of school. Middle schoolers know early on who is going to lead them to success and who is going to threaten both classroom management and student achievement. Young adolescents want to be close to the people who can offer them something more than themselves.

If we want to connect solidly with our middle school students, then, we must merit their trust. This trust isn't just about keeping things confidential. It's about a student's belief that we will not reject them—that we will never give up on them—no matter what impulsive and irrational decisions they make. They can't rely on their own bodies and emotions to behave always as society expects them to, so they need us to accept them, no matter what. The unspoken sentiment is that we are to save them from themselves. They trust that we will not hold them to the level of maturity they are currently exhibiting, either, but that we will see the butterfly within the chrysalis.

In addition, they must be able to trust that we will follow through with what we promise and that if we make mistakes, we will admit them because we are honest people. They trust us to be calm in the midst of emotional upheaval, wanting us to be both tender and strong, both opinionated and open-minded, often in the course of five minutes' time. They want to know that we have an expanded life perspective and that what we teach is accurate and will be useful to them. In short, they want to trust us as their advocates. How do we cultivate such positive teacher-student relationships in our middle-level practice?

Be a Member of Humanity

First-year middle school teachers and seasoned veterans attest that it's not all curriculum and academics in middle school classrooms. Teachers' and students' humanity are present in every lesson. It's good for them to see a trusted adult handling strong emotions, for instance. We can be brought to tears while reading novels in front of our students, and we can express outrage at social injustice such as that found in Bosnia, or the former apartheid situation in South Africa. We become solemn and deeply moved by the testimony of guest speakers on the Vietnam War or the Holocaust, and we share joy at a student's final success after tenacious effort on a rigorous project. Though it's a risk for middle school teachers to show their human sides, it's almost always one of the best things we can do. Sharing our humanity strengthens relationships with students. They want our honesty; they despise insincerity. Notice I didn't say, "sharing a bit of our softer side." Sharing emotions is not something soft. In fact, it can be one of the toughest and most developmentally responsive actions we take.

Musical composer and conductor Igor Stravinsky was right when he commented, "I have learned throughout my life as a composer chiefly through my mistakes and pursuits of false assumptions, not my exposure to founts of wisdom and knowledge." Students have the right to take the positive risks and make the mistakes that are vital to human development—and boy, our young charges are developing. Middle school is the place to fall down and have someone pick you up, dust you off, and get you on your way again. This is the place and time to learn how to handle struggle. This is a stepping-stone to leadership. Author Herbert Prochnow reminds us, "The fellow who never makes a mistake takes his orders from one who does."

A number of students and teachers, unfortunately, see the academic struggle that comes from taking risks as a weakness, not a virtue. They avoid challenge for fear of appearing weak to others, and they get nowhere. In order to make it okay to struggle academically—to fall down and have to be picked up and cared for by others—we can take on challenges in front of our students and handle the struggle with grace. We can try new strategies, we can teach new material, and we can learn new skills while students watch us, warts and all, make our way through the process. We don't do it once in September and spend the rest of the year showing only our most proficient side, either. We establish a culture—a way of doing things—that expects us to take on challenges each week and fail occasionally, only to learn something from the failure that strengthens us. Young adolescents need clear and frequent models in order to see themselves applying the same healthy responses when they are challenged. And here's the key: The amount of risk someone takes is proportional to the strength of the relationships he has with those around him. Our students will risk to the degree they trust us. Cultivating positive relationships with students, then, directly influences their academic achievement.

At the top of my plan book cover it says, "If I had been a kid in my class today, would I want to come back tomorrow?," a quote from Elsbeth Murphy in her 1990 book, *Chalkdust*. Orchestrating the emotional climate of the room in a purposeful manner is just as vital to learning as the lesson plan, the assessment, or the homework assignment we give. Here are some suggestions for creating emotionally inviting classrooms:

- Give choices in assignments so students feel ownership. Just make sure that all the choices serve your purpose with that assignment.
- Display four times as much student work as teacher work on bulletin boards or posters around the room. It gives a clear message that the students are the focus of the room, not the teacher.
- Give students responsibilities/roles in the learning. They will rise to the occasion every time, developing confidence, peer respect, and problem-solving abilities along the way.
- Negate inappropriate comments or behavior immediately so students see that such transgressions are not allowed. Students who make positive comments know they are safe making such comments in your class.
- Use stories. Young adolescents appreciate the way stories illuminate concepts. The brain finds them easier to process, and students enjoy their time with your subject.
- Give the big picture when you begin a lesson. "As a result of today's lesson, you'll be able to . . ." and "Here's how we're going to accomplish this goal. First, we're going to . . ."
- Provide timely feedback every chance you get. Students will put more complexity, more of themselves, and deeper thought into assignments if they know they will get them back within one to three days—as opposed to assignments returned several weeks later. Shortening assignments so you can get students' responses in a timely manner will help them master concepts more quickly.
- Increase the wait time between asking questions and calling on students, or between listening to students and giving your response. These wait times indicate that you expect everyone to continue to think about the topic. Once you call on someone, all other minds slow down and even cease processing, so they don't build the neural net for memory. Of course, if you have a habit of calling on other students to refute, clarify, or support what classmates say, then they won't be so quick to shut down their dendrite production. An added

benefit: The teacher is not seen as the pivot person for learning. Learning can come from peers. They can even learn some of the material when we're not around, for they have each other!

- Facilitate topics that are meaningful to students. Nothing moves into long-term memory unless it has meaning. When learning is meaningful, students develop positive attitudes toward it. If students don't have prior knowledge of a topic, find a way to create some background experiences before teaching the main lesson. For example, before analyzing a general essay on how poetry reflects the time and society in which it was written, read Dudley Randall's stirring "Ballad of Birmingham, 1963," about four black girls blown up in a Southern church during the Civil Rights movement. Talk with them about how the poem reflects the society at the time. After that, the general article on poetry's ability to reflect society will have meaning and they will remember it.
- Create a Rites of Passage program for your classes. Middle school students are not quite capable of seeing their progress. They need us to do that for them, to show them how much they've grown, to celebrate the milestones; it's very motivating. For attaining each level of mastery, have a response for the student: the whole class doing "the wave" for him or her, a certificate of accomplishment, the student's work posted on the wall, a mention in the school paper, or another check mark on a hard copy record of achievement.
- Catch them doing things right and let them know it. They will associate us with stress if all we do is critique them.
- Applaud positive risk taking. Raise the status of students who do this on a regular basis, even if they fail occasionally in the undertaking.

Good middle school teachers learn to let students physically touch them. The power of touch is strong for young adolescents. It builds relationships and trust. Sometimes they touch us just to see if we're real. They miss the coziness they felt with their elementary teachers and their parents. It's not hard to stand still and say with body language, "Yes, I'm still here for you and I'm not going to stop believing in your ability to learn." In my own practice, students have slapped me on the back for a job well done, shaken my hand, even put their heads on my shoulder as we peer-critiqued an essay during class. Their actions may or may not make me uncomfortable, but as long as they are not too extreme, I accept them because of students' need to feel connected to adults in their lives.

To ignore the emotional side of middle schoolers in the name of rigorous academics is to set perfect conditions for school disasters such as Columbine, Paducah, and Pearl. It's frustrating to hear the loudest voices in editorials and in teacher's lounges referring to "self-esteem" as a four-letter word. These folks forget the last time they felt low about something happening at home and tried to show up in the classroom or at a job and concentrate on doing well. Or the time they were feeling on top of the world and no challenge was too great during the course of the day. Self-esteem naysayers may score points quickly in the debate over the role of self-esteem in academics with their selective memories and invented caricatures, but upon close examination, their comments ring hollow.

Affective growth versus academics wrongly assumes a zero-sum situation. They do not cancel each other out. We can have rich academics and rich affective growth. Share students' well-done work with their peers. Allow occasional democratic voting. Refer one person who is an expert on something to another. Do not hold grudges. Post news articles about students' and colleagues' accomplishments. Make at least one positive phone call or send one positive note home for each student per year, dividing your students among your teammates if you teach more than fifty students.

Know Your Students and Their Culture

It's easy to grow frustrated and suspicious of others about whom we know little; ignorance breeds fear. Over the past four decades a number of successful community integrations have taken place because diverse cultures spent time with one another while working on a project. Today, students in most racially diverse schools have no hang-ups about working with members of other cultures. Spend a few summer days digging trails along a mountain ridge with people from America, Africa, China, and Pakistan, and your nationalities and differences become secondary; you become friends working toward a common cause—the stuff of humanity.

It's the same with our students. When we know them as individuals with lives outside of school, it's easier to stay motivated with them and to believe in their ability to learn. Do what you can to learn all there is to know about your students. There are a number of suggestions in Chapter 2, "What to Do on the First Day and in the First Week." In addition, try these:

- Learn their names within the first week of school, even if you teach 150 or more. You can do this—play name games, practice during class, memorize after school, practice while walking down the hallway. Having your name remembered by a respected adult is a big deal to young adolescents. Every year, I get parents who tell me that their children came home glowing because I had stopped to say "Hi" to them in the hallway and I knew their name. That's a lot of positive emotion going your way and toward your subject area. Students with positive attitudes are inclined to give your class extra personal energy.

- Tour your school's boundary area. See where your students live, shop, play, heal, work, and worship.
- Regularly read the local paper for your school community. Don't forget to read the local sports team sections.
- Talk with students and their parents as often as you can—in the hallways, on field trips, in the classroom, via e-mail, in the grocery store, at football/soccer/baseball/basketball games, and anywhere else your paths cross. Find out what's going on and what's important in their lives. You can do this without being obnoxious. Most families are happy to share their happenings with teachers. Some even share major events with teachers such as bar mitzvahs, bat mitzvahs, confirmation, Scouting honors, weddings, swim meets, and dance recitals.

When the going gets tough with curriculum or student behavior, we won't see students as the cause of all our pain if we've taken the time to get to know them as individuals. They are not the enemy. We can approach the struggle clinically: identify the frustrating factors, investigate causes, make a diagnosis (often in collaboration with others), then establish a program to solve the problem. This is a lot better than losing sanity and wringing a kid's neck. It's easier to treat numbers as cold abstractions, feeling no remorse or joy in what happens to them. It's hard to be callous to living, developing humans whose parents work late at night in order to pay the rent, whose favorite food is Rocky Road ice cream (the same as yours), and who aspire to be firefighters or United Nations negotiators. When we know our students, we commit to their success.

Accept Students as They Are, Not as You Want Them to Be

Middle school students cannot be expected to display adult-level expertise and expression. We can't compare their first attempts at technical writing to that of accomplished technical writers in the field. We can barely do that with accomplished high schoolers. Nor can we get angry over their inability to express themselves coherently. They're closer to being children than they are to being adults. It was relatively recently that they were sleeping with the light on while wearing their favorite superhero pajamas, with stuffed animals lining some of their beds. They laugh when people trip, and their tongues become lead when someone on whom they have a crush walks by. They throw out what they consider to be a witty comment only to have classmates look at them like they just belched yesterday's turkey tetrazzini; their heads hang low, their cheeks turn red, and they look for something to crawl under. To expect them to perform at adult levels is cruel. We're there to do everything possible to ensure their success, not to critique their inadequacies.

In her book, *Survival Tips for New Teachers*, Cheryl Thurston reminds us, "Children are not miniature adults. Love them for what they are, not for what you want them to be" (1997, 22). Since our students often interact with us on semiadult levels, we sometimes forget that they are not adults. When their behavior or emotional reaction is immature, we think there is something wrong with them. In reality, it's we who made the mistake. Yes, we can set high expectations, but we can't think all is lost when a child isn't ready to achieve at that level. We don't have justification to become angry, either. In these situations, just getting through the day isn't enough. Instead we must apply our pedagogy and true commitment to the student. Thurston tells teachers to "not get hung up on the way they dress. A student can have green hair and still learn algebra" (24).

Most middle schoolers haven't lived long enough to fully discriminate feelings from truth or hastily generated perceptions from reality. Their attitude toward a subject is often their attitude toward that subject's teacher. In addition, they cannot yet separate themselves from what others think of them. Michael Neal, a guest speaker at a recent Virginia Middle School Association conference, put the student's perspective like this: "I am not what I think I am. I'm not what you think I am. I'm what I think you think I am." As middle school teachers, our every action, word, and intonation will be watched for the slightest hint of what our students should think of themselves in relation to the subject and to the larger world. Let's make sure, then, that we communicate civility, competence, and virtue at every corner.

Respect Students as Capable Individuals

There are three things you'll never find in a successful teacher-student interaction: purposeful humiliation, embarrassment, and a condescending tone. Sure, some of these will happen by accident, but we never set out to use any of them for instruction or relating to one another, and we strive to remove them from the way we interact with others beyond the classroom as well. They are not compatible with classroom success. They force a hurtful and incorrect hierarchy, elevating the teacher to a higher position only by lowering the student. This is what bullies do, not teachers.

Today's students are amazing people. They can analyze problems and take corrective action, and they can draw pithy analogies we never saw. They can extend compassion to the most unlovable yet deserving of creatures, and they can create Web sites and become their own Internet service providers using advanced programming languages. Some can laugh so hard at lunch that milk comes out of their nose and moments later correct a friend who is confused as to the differences between osmosis and diffusion. They doodle on the bottom of each other's tennis shoes, but later clearly delineate the strengths of our government's checks-and-balances system among its three branches. We might smile and roll our eyes once in a while, but our students are worth every respectful nod we give them.

To cultivate those capabilities, we give our students positions of responsibility even when we aren't sure they can handle them. Just as people don't learn to swim by staring at the water, students don't learn to take responsibility by hearing about how important it is. They have to do it. They can record data, lead whole-class review games, host guest speakers, care for classroom pets and plants, co-present lessons, plan events, assist substitute teachers, contact experts, maintain classroom newspapers and bulletin boards, learn to use new technology, help design assessments, and keep areas and equipment clean and in good running order.

To facilitate these responsibilities, we can create a production office atmosphere in which students have everything needed to produce the kind of work we expect of them. This includes space in which to work collaboratively and individually; and office supplies such as pencils, pens, erasers, scissors, staplers, lined paper, unlined paper, file folders, sticky pads, tape, glue, computers, computer disks, portfolios, hole punches, report covers, markers, crayons, Liquid Paper, calculators, rulers, protractors, compasses, graph paper, thesauri, dictionaries, and reference materials. We're creating the same feeling most of us get when we walk into a Staples or Office Depot store: "Wow, I'm feeling incredibly productive. If I had that thing over there, boy, I could produce some great things!" We feel creative, and better yet, we feel like we can actually accomplish something given all the tools around us. Some teachers tell students that school is their job. If that's the case, then the classroom is their office and they need plentiful tools to do their work.

Another way to respect students is to let them know that they make good company. When we relate to them, we can face them, smile, use their names, listen carefully to what they say, ask them interesting questions about what they say, and do anything else that demonstrates that they are worth knowing and being around. We can use hall duty as an opportunity to engage students in respectful conversation about topics in and out of our subject area. Hall duty also enables us to see other sides of students. We get a reality check on where they are emotionally and with friends. With such advantages, watching the hallways is a duty to embrace, not something to tolerate in between what we really want to do. It might be the more important thing we do with some of our students. I've been a teacher for some students who have never set foot in my classroom. They were on other teams, but happened to pass by my classroom several times during the course of the day. Our daily hallway interactions became the medium for their learning. Every moment with a student is an opportunity for something positive to happen.

Be the Adult

A point made in Chapter 1 is worth repeating here: We're in the classroom for the students, the students are not there for us. Everything we ask them to do during the course of the day should make it easier for them to learn, regardless of its impact on us. For example, if there's not enough time for students to order their completed assignments alphabetically for easier processing because they need important information from us for the next lesson, then we can accept the papers unalphabetized and move to that important information. We'll place the papers alphabetically later, on our own time. It doesn't matter whether students choose to use wide-ruled or college-ruled paper, just as long as they demonstrate good thinking. When I was a middle school student, I hated doing research using note cards. They never worked for me and were a big source of angst. I preferred data retrieval charts or notebook paper with research questions written at the top. In twenty years of teaching research skills, I've never required students to use note cards. Instead, I teach six ways to take notes, then let them choose what works well for them. We can be sensitive to what works best for individual students, not what looks uniform across 150 students. Sometimes student success comes when we are flexible and swallow our own preferences.

Good middle school teachers don't take anything personally. They know they are adults. Students are testing the limitations of society and discovering their place in it. They're going to insult people, hurt feelings, and test patience. Middle schoolers are often tired from their attempts to assimilate physical growth and social expectations, struggle with values, and learn their subjects at school. We cannot take the emotional roller-coaster ride with them. We model serious, contemplative approaches to conflicts that arise, being careful not to put emotion into the mix. The sign of a great teacher is the ability to turn those frustrating moments into moments of growth for students.

As professionals, we must rid our interactions of sarcasm. We need to leave it at the curb. Young adolescents use sarcasm and put-downs to relate to an insecure world. Such verbal dueling is clever to them. Status comes by one-upping others. Whatever happens, the teachers can't go there. We can't give in to our egos. It's easy to put someone down—it takes a lot more courage and cleverness to build someone up. Students kid around sarcastically with us, often with the expectation that we won't stoop to that level of hurtfulness. It shocks and disappoints them when their teachers cross that line, even in playfulness. Students secretly believe that the teacher is a model of virtue and the way the world is supposed to be. If we cross the line and put others down, we've diminished their opinion of us and, more important, their positive opinion of their world. In one ten-second moment of trying to be clever with a put-down, we can erase months of rising self-esteem and motivation in a student. It's very easy to let the phrases slip out without thinking, in passing comments.

As adults, we, not the students, are responsible for the course an interaction takes. We are the authority in the room. If we find our buttons being pushed by students, then we have to know enough to remove ourselves from the interaction: "Look, Michael, I'm too upset right now. Give me ten minutes to calm down a bit so I can think straight. I'll speak with you about this privately at my desk at that point." Of course, the greatest advice here is, never get into an argument with students. This is easy to say and hard to do at first, but it gets easier each time we do it. Chapter 3, "Discipline," has specific strategies on how to do this.

Remember, young adolescents crave limits. As the adult authority, you can strengthen your relationship with students by setting limits. When teachers don't set limits, students feel insecure, and insecurity generates distrust and discontent. Limits can be set in a number of ways:

"You have three minutes to do this."
"Who can find the point when the writer went off-topic and thereby weakened his argument?"
"It is harassment for you to touch her in that manner. Remove your hands from her shoulders."
"If your work area looks as messy as this [pointing to a staged, messy work area], then you've been working too quickly and you won't be able to find what you need. Take two minutes now to organize your materials."

A final caution related to being the adult: Never be alone with a student. This is true whether you are male or female. In the eyes of the legal system, you are 100 percent in control of all interactions, regardless of what students do. Today's communities are particularly sensitive to inappropriate comments or actions in regard to children—even the suggestion thereof, regardless of whether or not they were true. Sincere and professional gestures of concern for a child can still be misunderstood. Each year we read about teachers wrongfully accused by students or parents who misunderstood something the teacher did or said. After months and sometimes years of investigation, including removal from the classroom and rampant rumors that hurt everyone involved, the teacher is cleared of all wrongdoing and reinstated, only to resign later due to lingering community suspicions or exhaustion. It's just not worth it. Go ahead and work with students individually, but do it with the door open to a busy hallway, in the library with the librarian in the room, in the front office, with Mom or Dad present, or with other students or teachers in the room.

There are students that we don't like very much. Something about them rubs us the wrong way. That doesn't stop us from caring for them deeply, however. We're adults. We're strong enough to overcome petty dislikes and see the good inside a not-so-lovable student. We can meet the challenge of our profession's true calling: personal and academic success for every child. Despite the occasional frustrating child, most of the journey will be very enjoyable if we focus on developing positive relations with our students. It's critical to their academic achievement and our own job satisfaction. In later years, if our motivation wanes, we might refocus on creating positive teacher-student relationships as a way to reinvigorate stale practice.

We often hear once-troubled students who graduate and become successful adults cite specific teachers when asked who helped them overcome their challenges. Louanne Johnson, author of *My Posse Don't Do Homework* (1994), made a startling revelation to those of us at a National Middle School Association conference a few years ago. She asked us what we thought was the number one reason why people hired private investigators. Most of us thought it was to investigate unfaithful spouses.

She nodded, but said, "I thought so, too, but that's second. The number one reason people hire private investigators is to find a former teacher in order to thank them for all they did."

We were stunned. Some, myself included, had goose bumps. There's more to this teaching thing than we thought.

Positive relations with students has a direct impact on their achievement. We can cultivate those relationships and teach them deeply about our subjects. We teach young adolescents to be trusted guardians of all that is worth keeping; we are their stewards. And even though they're six to eight years into this education life, everything we offer them opens minds and renews hope. For the world we're about to create together, we're on day one.

A Middle School Student's September Plea

Hey, you up there at the front of the room,
The one I see past spiral notebooks and erasure filings,
under the taunting clock next to the question of the day,
while dreaming of brown-haired Melissa,
or staring at pages on which I'm supposed to read along silently as you read
    aloud.
Here it is:

At the end of our time together,
it doesn't matter what you taught.
I am not here to fill a seat
or give you a place to go each morning.

What matters is what I take with me after being with you.
I am here to master all you have to offer,
not skim smooth and round across flat water.
I'm here to dive deeply,
To belong to something larger than myself,
To marvel at questions I didn't know existed,
And to gulp competence.

Please don't settle for mediocrity,
Don't turn to the next page of the textbook
because it's the next page of the textbook.
Don't limit me to your creativity.
Trust me to find connections you don't see.

Fight those who would use me as the canary in the cage,
judging society's health on whether or not I maintain my perch.
Someone who pushes on the mall Santa's belly
in hopes that one day the wedged pillow might be flesh and Santa real,
shouldn't be society's yardstick.

Just remember what it was like to be me,
When the future was wide open, anything you desired.
Then build it—
with every word you say,
Every lesson you plan,
Every hallway you walk,
Every pencil you loan.

Teach me to be a trusted guardian
of all that is worth keeping.
Be my steward.

Which page are we on again?
   —*Rick Wormeli*

Sample Quarterly Newsletter, Rubrics, and Choices for the Historical Novel Unit

First Quarter (Sample Newsletter)

Crusaders Team, 7C   **Mr. Wormeli**

A. First Quarter Focuses on Tools of Learning:

Content Structures (5 formats)   Summarization
Graphic Organizers   Multiple Intelligences
Assignment Notebooks   Rubrics/Assessment
Memorization Techniques   Editing and Revising
Evaluating Against Criteria   Literary Analysis
Library Orientation   Writing Coaches
Word Morphology (prefixes, roots)   Recognizing Good Writing
Determining Essential Information   Study Skills
Introduction to the Six Writing Traits: Reader's Response
    Ideas, Organization, Voice, Word Choice,
    Sentence Fluency, Conventions

B. Ways to Turn in Homework:

1. Hard copy (paper)
2. Send to your account on the school server
3. E-mail
4. In-class demonstration
5. On video (at teacher discretion)
6. On audiocassette (at teacher discretion)

C. Contact Numbers and Addresses:

Phone: 703-555-3600 (School)
Fax: 703–555-3601 (School)
Voicemail: 703–555-3602, box 1740 (School)
E-mail: rwormeli@erols.com (home)

D. Major Writings:

- 1 Reading Autobiography
- 1 Student Choice Writing
- 1 Expository Writing

- 1 Business Letter
- Selected writings as warranted by our studies

E. Novel Studies at a Glance:

Parents, as new novels become available and/or students' needs change during the year, this list is subject to change. Most will stay the same, however. If you have the time, please read the novels ahead of each quarter in which they are assigned, or read them with your child. Experiencing the same story and author with your child, and then discussing them with your child, is an invaluable experience. You'll gain significant insight into your rapidly growing young adolescent.

Novel Studies for the Crusaders Team

Quarter	Required Books	Additional Required Reading
First	*The Outsiders*	1 personal choice novel—classic
		Selected readings from our textbook and other sources
Second	*No Promises in the Wind*	Selected readings from our textbook and other sources
	A historical fiction book (student choice from list)	
	A nonfiction book related to the historical fiction book	
Third	*Goodnight, Mr. Tom* or *Devil's Arithmetic*	1 personal choice book—science fiction, mystery, suspense, or fantasy
		Selected readings from our textbook and other sources
Fourth	*Call of the Wild*	1 personal choice book—modern drama, realistic fiction
		Selected readings from our textbook and other sources

F. Brain Tips:

We remember best what we experience first in a lesson, and we remember second best what we experience last in a lesson. Make sure, then, to try to get a sense of the big concepts of a lesson within the first ten minutes, and then to summarize and reflect on those concepts during the last ten minutes. You'll move a lot of learning into long-term memory—the best place for it to be.

If something is confusing at first, ASK A QUESTION. You don't want something that is confusing going into your mind to be stored that way. Our ability to recall something accurately for a test is primarily based on how it first entered our minds, not so much how we study it just before we take the test. Make sure information enters your mind accurately and clearly in your first experience with it. Let me know right away if something is not clear to you and I'll try a different approach.

Persuasive Writing Rubric (Analytic)

Name: _____ Date: _____

Period: _____

Score:	Writing Structures and Techniques	Persuasive Structures/Techniques	Mechanics/Usage
4.0 Standard of Excellence	Well organized, logical/clear Demonstrates an unusual ability to use language well (strong word choices, good sentence variety, powerful images) 1/2 or more page (typed), more than one page handwritten Good use of transitions Evidence of conference and revisions	Good opening to get the reader interested Positively stated proposition Successfully used at least six of the persuasive techniques identified in class (stronger points at the beginning and end, emotional appeal, testimonies, using facts/research, using logic more than emotion, respected the reader, anticipated arguments and answered them, used enough information to prove points, used vivid examples, repetition, strong conclusion) Reasons are relevant to the point the writer is making Expresses unusual insight (meaning-ful connections or analogies, clever logic and/or resources, mature thinking)	Used correct spelling Used correct punctuation Used correct grammar Used correct capitalization Used there, their, they're correctly Used to, two, too correctly Pronouns have clear antecedents
Weight:	2x	3x	1x

[Note: Circled items are areas for improvement.]

3 = The student demonstrates *good* understanding and skill. Most of the listed characteristics in the standard of excellence describe the student's work—a few are missing or done improperly.

2 = The writer demonstrates *somewhat* of an understanding and skill. Approximately ¾ of the listed characteristics in the standard of excellence describe the writer's work—¼ of the characteristics are missing or done improperly.

1 = The writer demonstrates *little or no* understanding or skill. Few of the listed characteristics in the standard of excellence describe the writer's work—more than ¼ of the characteristics are missing or done improperly.

0 = Not completed or Unscorable.

Your Grade:

Writing Structures and Techniques _____ X 2 = _____

Persuasive Structures/Techniques _____ X 3 = _____

Mechanics _____ X 1 = _____

Total: _____ ÷ 6 grades = _____

Additional Comments: Final Grade: _____

Scoring Rubric for the Historical Fiction Book Project (Holistic)

4.0 Standard of Excellence

- All material relating to the novel was accurate.
- Demonstrated full understanding of the story and its characters.
- Demonstrated attention to quality and craftsmanship in the product.
- Product is a realistic portrayal of media used (examples: postcards look like postcards, calendar looks like a real calendar, placemats can function as real placemats).
- All writing is free of errors in punctuation, spelling, capitalization, and grammar.
- Had all components listed for the project as described on the other side of this sheet.

3.5, 3.0, 2.5, 2.0, 1.5, 1.0, .5, and 0 are awarded in cases in which students' projects do not fully achieve all criteria described for excellence. Circled items are areas for improvement.

Student: _____

Date: _____

Score: _____ **Grade:** _____

Additional Comments:

Day One and Beyond: Practical Matters for New Middle-Level Teachers by Rick Wormeli. Copyright © 2003. Stenhouse Publishers.

Project Choices for the Historical Fiction Novel Unit

Calendar—Design a full-size calendar like you might see on your kitchen wall. Above each grid of dates on the bottom half of each month, draw a picture or write material related to the book. By the time someone has turned to each month and read the calendar, he should have a good sense of the book's plot and main characters. Ideas for inclusion: illustrations of main characters, illustrations of major conflicts, summaries of chapters, poems, comic strips, descriptions or illustrations of the setting, excerpts from the book, literary critiques from professional publications, personal responses to moments in the story. Do at least three or more of these components in order to be successful.

Postcards—Design ten or more postcards out of posterboard. Turn these into pretend postcards from the story's characters about what's going on in the story at different moments in the story. Place these on a poster in the sequence in which the events take place. After reading your postcards, classmates should have a good sense of the characters and conflicts of the story. Make the postcards as realistic as possible, and make the written messages on them full of accurate details and the probable thinking about those events from the characters who wrote them.

Comic Strip (or Comic Book)—Create a comic strip of not less than six panels that reveals the major characters and the three or four major conflicts in the story. By the time someone is done reading your comic strip, they should know the story's general plot.

Board Game—Create a board game in which players get a good sense of the book's plot and characters by playing the game. Interesting twists and turns in the game should focus on the conflicts in the story. A full description of game requirements will be given to those who choose this project.

Bloom's Taxonomy Cube—Bloom's Taxonomy categorizes ways of thinking that get more and more complex. For instance, asking you about a character's hair color requires you to recall a fact. That's easy. If I ask you to describe what would happen if we inserted a character from another story into the story you're currently reading, you would have to think a lot more intensely. The Bloom's Taxonomy sequence in order from simple thinking to complex thinking is: Knowledge, Comprehension, Application, Analysis, Synthesis, Evaluation. In this project, design a cube in which each side demonstrates one of these thinking abilities. Label each side accordingly. A full description of each type of thinking will be given to you if you choose this project. Make sure that the viewer of your cube will understand your novel's plot and major characters by the time he is done looking at all six sides of your cube.

Multiple Intelligences Poster/Mural—Create a poster or mural in which each intelligence (verbal/linguistic, logical/mathematical, visual/spatial, bodily/kinesthetic, musical, interpersonal, intrapersonal, naturalist) is clearly expressed. For instance, you might do a chart comparing and contrasting two characters for the logical one, a script or poem for the verbal one, a diary entry for the intrapersonal one, an interview with a major character for the interpersonal, a musical score for one scene, and a dramatic artwork for the bodily/kinesthetic. Use the sheet of project possibilities given to you at the beginning of the year for more ideas. Make sure to confirm each component for representation of each intelligence with your teacher before proceeding. Put all eight components into one large display. Also make sure to highlight different conflicts and characters in the story in each component.

Placemats—Design and build four placemats that depict the novel's plot and major characters. Each mat should have its own theme and it should be covered front and back with clear contact paper so it can actually be used as a real placemat.

Radio Play—Submit an audiocassette of a radio play in which three or more important scenes of the novel are accurately portrayed. It should be between five and ten minutes long. By the time it's done, the listener should have a good sense of the novel's plot and characters.

Appendix B

Recommended Resources

Allen, Janet. 1999. *Words, Words, Words: Teaching Vocabulary in Grades 4–12*. Portland, ME: Stenhouse.

———. 2000. *Yellow Brick Roads: Shared and Guided Paths to Independent Reading 4–12*. Portland, ME: Stenhouse.

Argus Posters and More. Available at www.trendenterprises.com. Request a catalog or place an order through 1-800-860-6762.

Armstrong, Thomas. 2000. *Multiple Intelligences in the Classroom*, 2d ed. Alexandria, VA: Association for Supervision and Curriculum Development.

Barth, Roland S. 1990. *Improving Schools from Within*. San Francisco: Jossey-Bass.

Barton, Mary Lee, and Clare Heidema. 2000. *Teaching Reading in Mathematics*. Aurora, CO: Mid-continent Research for Education and Learning.

Beamon, Glenda Ward. 2001. *Teaching with the Adolescent Learner in Mind*. Arlington Heights, IL: Skylight Professional Development.

Billmeyer, Rachel, and Mary Lee Barton. 1998. *Teaching Reading in the Content Areas: If Not Me, Then Who?*, 2d ed. Aurora, CO: Mid-continent Research for Education and Learning.

Beers, Kylene. 2003. *When Kids Can't Read: What Teachers Can Do, A Guide for Teachers 6–12*. Portsmouth, NH: Heinemann.

Beers, Kylene, and Barbara G. Samuels. 1998. *Into Focus: Understanding and Creating Middle School Readers*. Norwood, MA: Christopher-Gordon.

Booth, David. 2001. *Reading and Writing in the Middle Years*. Portland, ME: Stenhouse.

Bransford, John D., Ann L. Brown, and Rodney R. Cocking. 2000. *How People Learn: Brain, Mind, Experience, and School*. Washington, DC: National Academy Press.

Brooks, Jacqueline Grennon, and Martin G. Brooks. 1993. *In Search of Understanding: The Case for Constructivist Classrooms*. Alexandria, VA: Association for Supervision and Curriculum Development.

Buehl, Doug. 2001. *Classroom Strategies for Interactive Learning*, 2d ed. Newark, DE: International Reading Association.

Burke, Jim. 2001. *Illuminating Texts: How to Teach Students to Read the World*. Portsmouth, NH: Heinemann.

Burke, Kay. 2001. *What to Do with the Kid Who: Developing Cooperation, Self-Discipline, and Responsibility in the Classroom.* Arlington Heights, IL: Skylight Professional Development.

Caine, Renate, and Geoffrey Caine. 1997. *Unleashing the Power of Perceptual Change: The Potential of Brain-Based Teaching.* Alexandria, VA: Association for Supervision and Curriculum Development.

Canady, Robert Lynn, and Michael Rettig. 1996. *Teaching in the Block.* Larchmont, NY: Eye on Education.

Connors, Neila. 1992. *Homework: A New Direction.* Westerville, OH: National Middle School Association.

Cooper, Harris. 2001. *The Battle Over Homework*, 2d ed. Thousand Oaks, CA: Corwin Press.

Covey, Steven. 1989. *The Seven Habits of Highly Effective People.* New York: Simon and Schuster.

Crockett, James Underwood. 1978. *Crockett's Indoor Garden.* Boston: Little, Brown.

Davis, Gayle, and Anthony Jackson. 2000. *Turning Points 2000: Educating Adolescents in the 21st Century.* New York: Teachers College Press.

Diamond, Marian, and Janet Hopson. 1998. *Magic Trees of the Mind: How to Nurture Your Child's Intelligence, Creativity, and Healthy Emotions from Birth Through Adolescence.* New York: Dutton.

Fluegelman, Andrew, ed. 1976. *The New Games Book.* New York, NY: Doubleday and Company.

Forsten, Char, Jim Grant, and Betty Hollas. 2001. *Differentiated Instruction: Different Strategies for Different Learners.* Peterborough, NH: Crystal Springs.

Forte, Imogene, and Sandra Schurr. 1996. *Integrating Instruction in Science: Strategies, Activities, Projects, Tools, and Techniques.* Nashville, TN: Incentive Publications. (Books are published for math, history, and English as well.)

Frank, Marjorie. 1995. *If You're Trying to Teach Kids How to Write You've Gotta Have This Book*, rev. ed. Nashville, TN: Incentive.

Frender, Gloria. 1990. *Learning to Learn: Strengthening Study Skills and Brain Power.* Nashville, TN: Incentive.

Gardner, Howard. 1993. *Multiple Intelligences: The Theory in Practice.* New York: Basic Books.

Glynn, Carol. 2001. *Learning on Their Feet: A Sourcebook for Kinesthetic Learning Across the Curriculum.* Shoreham, VT: Discover Writing.

Goleman, Daniel. 1995. *Emotional Intelligence: Why It Can Matter More Than I.Q.* New York: Bantam.

Harrison, Allen F., and Robert M. Bramson. 1984. *The Art of Thinking.* New York: Berkley Books.

Harvey, Stephanie. 1998. *Nonfiction Matters: Reading, Writing, and Research in Grades 3–8.* Portland, ME: Stenhouse.

Harvey, Stephanie, and Anne Goudvis. 2000. *Strategies That Work: Teaching Comprehension to Enhance Understanding.* Portland, ME: Stenhouse.

Henton, Mary. 1996. *Adventure in the Classroom.* Dubuque, IA: Kendall Hunt.

Holubec, Edythe J., David W. Johnson, and Roger T. Johnson. 1994. *Cooperative Learning in the Classroom.* Alexandria, VA: Association for Supervision and Curriculum Development.

Housel, Debra J. 2002. *Nonfiction Strategies Grades Four Through Eight.* Westminster, CA: Teacher Created Materials.

Hyerle, David. 2000. *A Field Guide to Visual Tools*. Alexandria, VA: Association for Supervision and Curriculum Development.

"Interact: A Learning Experience." Simulations. Available from www.teachinteract.com.

Jensen, Eric. 1995. *Super Teaching*. San Diego: The Brain Store.

———. 2000. *Different Brains, Different Learners*. San Diego: The Brain Store.

Kain, Daniel L. 1998. *Camel-Makers: Building Effective Teacher Teams Together*. Westerville, OH: National Middle School Association.

Kemper, Dave, Ruth Nathan, and Patrick Sebranek. 1999. *Write Source 2000*. Boston: Houghton Mifflin

Kriegel, Robert. 1991. *If It Ain't Broke, Break it! And Other Unconventional Wisdom for a Changing Business World*. New York: Warner Books.

Kushel, Gerald. 1994. *Reaching the Peak Performance Zone*. New York: American Management Association.

Lane, Barry. 1993. *After the End: Teaching and Learning Creative Revision*. Shoreham, VT: Discover Writing.

Lavoie, Richard. *How Difficult Can This Be? The F.A.T. City Workshop*. Videocassette. Washington, DC: National Public Broadcasting. Also available from www.Ldonline.

Marzano, Robert J. 1992. *A Different Kind of Classroom: Teaching with Dimensions of Learning*. Alexandria, VA: Association for Supervision and Curriculum Development.

Marzano, Robert, Jay McTighe, and Debra Pickering. 1993. *Assessing Student Outcomes: Performances Using the Dimensions of Learning Model*. Alexandria, VA: Association for Supervision and Curriculum Development.

Marzano, Robert J., Debra J. Pickering, and Jane E. Pollock. 2001. *Classroom Instruction That Works: Research-Based Strategies for Increasing Student Achievement*. Alexandria, VA: Association for Supervision and Curriculum Development.

McTighe, Jay, and Grant Wiggins. 1998. *Understanding by Design*. Alexandria, VA: Association for Supervision and Curriculum Development.

———. 2000. *Understanding by Design Handbook*. Alexandria, VA: Association for Supervision and Curriculum Development.

National Middle School Association. 1995. *Prescriptions for Success in Heterogeneous Classrooms*. Westerville, OH: National Middle School Association.

Newton, Cathy Griggs. 1996. *Risk It! Empowering Young People to Become Positive Risk Takers in the Classroom and Life*. Nashville, TN: Incentive.

Parks, Sandra, and Howard Black. 1992. *Organizing Thinking: Book Two*. Pacific Grove, CA: Critical Thinking.

Popkin, Dr. Michael. 1990. *Active Parenting of Teens*. Marietta, GA: Active Parenting.

Porter, Carol. 2002. *What Do I Teach for 90 Minutes? Creating a Successful Block-Scheduled English Classroom*. Urbana, IL: National Council of Teachers of English.

"A Private Universe." Corporation for Public Broadcasting and the Annenberg Institute. Videocassette. Annenberg/CPB Math and Science Projects, 1-800-965-7373 or www.learner.org.

Purdy, Scott. 1999. *Time Management for Teachers: Essential Tips and Techniques*. Solvang, CA: Write Time Publishing.

Purkey, William W., and John M. Novak. 1984. *Inviting School Success: A Self-Concept Approach to Teaching and Learning*. Belmont, CA: Wadsworth.

Renzulli, Joseph S. 2001. *Enriching Curriculum for All Students*. Arlington Heights, IL: Skylight Professional Development.

Rief, Linda. 1992. *Seeking Diversity: Language Arts with Adolescents*. Portsmouth, NH: Heinemann.

Robb, Laura. 2000. *Teaching Reading in Middle School*. Jefferson City, MO: Scholastic.

———. 2003. *Teaching Reading in Social Studies, Science, and Math*. Jefferson City, MO: Scholastic.

Rogers, Spence, Jim Ludington, and Shari Graham. 1998. *Motivation and Learning: Practical Teaching Tips for Block Schedules, Brain-Based Learning, Multiple Intelligences, Improved Student Motivation, Increased Achievement*. Evergreen, CO: Peak Learning Systems.

Rogers, Spence, and Shari Graham. 1998. *The High Performance Toolbox: Performance Tasks, Assessment Designs, Rubrics, Checklists, and Grading, Parental Support, Quality Student Work Reaching Standards*. Evergreen, CO: Peak Learning Systems.

Rohnke, Karl. 1984. *Silver Bullets*. Dubuque, IA: Kendall Hunt.

———. 1989. *Cowstail and Cobras II*. Dubuque, IA: Kendall Hunt.

———. 1991a. *Bottomless Baggie*. Dubuque, IA: Kendall Hunt.

———. 1991b. *The Bottomless Bag Again*. Dubuque, IA: Kendall Hunt.

Rohnke, Karl, and Steve Butler. 1995. *QuickSilver*. Dubuque, IA: Kendall Hunt.

Rutherford, Paula. 1998. *Instruction for All Students*. Alexandria, VA: Just ASK.

Saphier, Jon, and Robert Gower. 1987. *The Skillful Teacher*. Carlisle, MA: Research for Better Teaching.

Silver, Debbie. 2003. *Drumming to the Beat of a Different Marcher: Finding the Rhythm for Teaching a Differentiated Classroom*. Nashville, TN: Incentive Publications.

Sousa, David A. 2001a. *How the Brain Learns*, 2d ed. Thousand Oaks, CA: Corwin Press.

———. 2001b. *How the Special Needs Brain Learns*. Thousand Oaks, CA: Corwin Press.

———. 2003. *How the Gifted Brain Learns*. Thousand Oaks, CA: Corwin Press.

Spandel, Vicki, and Richard J. Stiggins. 1997. *Creating Writers: Linking Writing Assessment and Instruction*. New York: Longman Publishers.

Stephens, Elaine C., and Jean E. Brown. 2000. *A Handbook of Content Literacy Strategies: 75 Practical Reading and Writing Ideas*. Norwood, MA: Christopher-Gordon.

Sternberg, Robert J., and Elena Grigorenko. 2001. *Teaching for Successful Intelligence: To Increase Student Learning and Achievement*. Arlington Heights, IL: Skylight Professional Development.

Strong, Richard W., Harvey F. Silver, and Matthew J. Perini. 2001. *Teaching What Matters Most: Standards and Strategies for Raising Student Achievement*. Alexandria, VA: Association for Supervision and Curriculum Development.

Strong, Richard W., Harvey F. Silver, Matthew J. Perini, and Gregory M. Tuculescu. 2002. *Reading for Academic Success: Powerful Strategies for Struggling, Average, and Advanced Readers, Grades 7–12*. Thousand Oaks, CA: Corwin Press.

Stronge, James H. 2002. *Qualities of Effective Teachers*. Alexandria, VA: Association for Supervision and Curriculum Development.

Sylwester, Robert. 1995. *A Celebration of Neurons: An Educator's Guide to the Human Brain*. Alexandria, VA: Association for Supervision and Curriculum Development.

Tatum, Dr. Beverly Daniel. 1997. *"Why Are All the Black Kids Sitting Together in the Cafeteria?" and Other Conversations About Race*. Boulder, CO: Perseus Books.

Thompson, Randy, and Dorothy Vanderjagt. 2001. *Wow, What a Team! Essential Components for Successful Teaming*. Nashville, TN: Incentive Publications.

———. 2002. *Fire Up! For Learning: Active Learning Projects and Activities to Motivate and Challenge Students.* Nashville, TN: Incentive Publications.

Tomlinson, Carol Ann. 1995. *How to Differentiate Instruction in Mixed-Ability Classrooms.* Alexandria, VA: Association for Supervision and Curriculum Development.

———. 1999. *The Differentiated Classroom: Responding to the Needs of All Learners.* Alexandria, VA: Association for Supervision and Curriculum Development.

———. 2001. *At Work in the Differentiated Classroom.* Videocassette. Alexandria, VA: Association for Supervision and Curriculum Development.

Tovani, Cris. 2001. *I Read It, but I Don't Get It: Comprehension Strategies for Adolescent Readers.* Portland, ME: Stenhouse.

Vacca, Richard. 1999. *Content Area Reading: Literacy and Learning Across the Curriculum*, 6th ed. New York: Longman Publishers.

Winebrenner, Susan. 1992. *Teaching Gifted Kids in the Regular Classroom: Strategies Every Teacher Can Use to Meet the Needs of the Gifted and Talented.* Minneapolis, MN: Free Spirit.

Wolfe, Patricia. 2001. *Brain Matters: Translating Research into Classroom Practice.* Alexandria, VA: Association for Supervision and Curriculum Development.

Wood, Karen D., and Janis M. Harmon. 2001. *Strategies for Integrating Reading and Writing in Middle and High School Classrooms.* Westerville, OH: National Middle School Association.

Wormeli, Rick. 2001. *Meet Me in the Middle: Becoming an Accomplished Middle-Level Teacher.* Portland, ME: Stenhouse

Zinsser, William. 1988. *Writing to Learn.* New York: Harper and Row.

References

Allen, Janet. 1999. *Words, Words, Words: Teaching Vocabulary in Grades 4-12*. Portland, ME: Stenhouse.

Connors, Neila. 1992. *Homework: A New Direction*. Westerville, OH: National Middle School Association.

Cooper, Harris. 2001. *The Battle Over Homework*, 2d ed. Thousand Oaks, CA: Corwin Press.

Covey, Steven. 1989. *The Seven Habits of Highly Effective People*. New York: Simon and Schuster.

Crockett, James Underwood. 1978. *Crockett's Indoor Garden*. Boston: Little, Brown.

Davis, Gayle, and Anthony Jackson. 2000. *Turning Points 2000: Educating Adolescents in the 21st Century*. New York: Teachers College Press.

Forte, Imogene, and Sandra Schurr. 1996. *Integrating Instruction in Science: Strategies, Activities, Projects, Tools, and Techniques*. Nashville, TN: Incentive Publications.

Frender, Gloria. 1990. *Learning to Learn: Strengthening Study Skills and Brain Power*. Nashville, TN: Incentive Publications.

Gardner, Howard. 1993a. *Frames of Mind: The Theory of Multiple Intelligences*, 10th ed. New York: Basic Books.

———. 1993b. *Multiple Intelligences: The Theory in Practice*. New York: Basic Books.

Goleman, Daniel. 1995. *Emotional Intelligence: Why It Can Matter More Than I.Q.* (The Brain Store, 800-325-4769, www.thebrainstore.com).

Holubec, Edythe J., David W. Johnson, and Roger T. Johnson. 1994. *Cooperative Learning in the Classroom*. Alexandria, VA: Association for Supervision and Curriculum Development.

Johnson, Louanne. 1994. *My Posse Don't Do Homework*. New York: St. Martin's Press.

Kemper, Dave, Ruth Nathan, and Patrick Sebranek. 1999. *Write Source 2000*. Boston: Houghton Mifflin.

Magorian, Michelle. 1986. *Good Night, Mr. Tom*. New York: HarperTrophy.

Marzano, Robert J., Debra J. Pickering, and Jane E. Pollock. 2001. *Classroom Instruction That Works: Research-Based Strategies for Increasing Student Achievement*. Alexandria, VA: Association for Supervision and Curriculum Instruction.

Murphy, Elspeth. 1990. *Chalkdust: Prayer Meditations for a Teacher*. New York: Baker Book House.

National Middle School Association. *Prescriptions for Success in Heterogeneous Classrooms*. 1995. Westerville, OH: National Middle School Association.

Purdy, Scott. 1999. *Time Management for Teachers: Essential Tips and Techniques*. Solvang, CA: Write Time Publishing.

Saphier, Jon, and Robert Gower. 1987. *The Skillful Teacher*. Carlisle, MA: Research for Better Teaching.

Sousa, David A. 2001. *How the Brain Learns*, 2d ed. Thousand Oaks, CA: Corwin Press.

Spandel, Vicki, and Richard J. Stiggins. 1997. *Creating Writers: Linking Writing Assessment and Instruction.* New York: Longman Publishers.

Stronge, James H. 2002. *Qualities of Effective Teachers.* Alexandria, VA: Association for Supervision and Curriculum Development.

Thurston, Cheryl. 1997. *Survival Tips for New Teachers: From Teachers Who Have Been There.* Fort Collins, CO: Cottonwood Press.

Tomlinson, Carol Ann. 1995. *How to Differentiate Instruction in Mixed-Ability Classrooms.* Alexandria, VA: Association for Supervision and Curriculum Development.

Tovani, Cris. 2001. *I Read It, but I Don't Get It: Comprehension Strategies for Adolescent Readers.* Portland, ME: Stenhouse.

www.blackboard.com

www.guest-teacher.com

www.middleweb.com

www.ncsu.edu/midlink.com

www.nmsa.org

www.schoolnotes.com

192

200